YOUR GUIDE TO A NEW LIFE

More related titles

Buy to Let in Spain
How to invest in Spanish property for pleasure and profit

'Any book that shows how to have a sun-kissed retirement and get someone else to pay for your holidays in Spain...has got to be worth getting hold of.' – Living Spain

Knowing the Law in Spain
A guide to Spanish Law for the British property owner, resident or long-term visitor

Going to Live in Spain
A practical guide to enjoying a new lifestyle in the sun

'Tips on how to get the most out of this vibrant country so that you can enjoy your new life to the full.' – Sunday Telegraph

Gone to Spain
You too can realise your dream of a better lifestyle

'The author writes with honesty and directness. It is difficult not to be enthused by this book.' – Living Spain

howtobooks

Please send for a free copy of the latest catalogue:
How To Books
3 Newtec Place, Magdalen Road
Oxford OX4 1RE, United Kingdom
info@howtobooks.co.uk
www.howtobooks.co.uk

YOUR GUIDE TO A NEW LIFE

Harry King

howto books

Acknowledgements

I would like to thank Dr Tony Warnes at Sheffield University for population movement details, Joan King for checking the final manuscript and Les Gould for supplying many of the photographs. Chapter 14 contains an extract from *Blood and Sand* by Karmin Mohammadi on licence from www.travelintelligence.com.

Published by How To Books Ltd,
3 Newtec Place, Magdalen Road,
Oxford, OX4 1RE, United Kingdom
Tel: (01865) 793806 Fax: (01865) 248780
email: info@howtobooks.co.uk
http://www.howtobooks.co.uk

British Library Cataloguing in Publication Data
A catalogue record for this book is available from the British Library.

Produced for How To Books by Deer Park Productions, Tavistock
Typeset by *specialist* publishing services ltd, Milton Keynes/Montgomery
Cover design by Baseline Arts Ltd, Oxford
Printed and bound by Cromwell Press, Trowbridge, Wiltshire

Note: The material contained in this book is set out in good faith for general guidance and no liability can be accepted for loss or expense incurred as a result of relying in particular circumstances on statements made in the book. The laws and regulations are complex and liable to change, and readers should check the current position with the relevant authorities before making personal arrangements.

Contents

Preface

Spain – so many things to do and so many places to see. There is the cordiality of the people, the incomparable scenery, the beaches of fine sand, the days of sunshine, the high mountains, the vast plains, the nightlife, the evenings, the magnificent cuisine, the restaurants …

Too many hours and too many pages are required to describe everything that Spain has to offer. There is only one way to find out; come and see it for yourself. Coming to Spain to work, for a long-term stay or for retirement can be a step into the unknown. But if some simple preparation is undertaken it can be a step into sunshine and happiness.

Apart from those following a career, why do people move to Spain? Well, usually the family has grown up and left home, so for the first time people are free to decide how to spend the rest of their lives. Getting to know another country and its culture is an attractive idea and so is saying goodbye to cold winters. Perhaps more important is a feeling of not wishing to continue for the rest of one's life doing exactly the same thing. A desire to broaden horizons, to see new places, to meet new people, to enjoy new hobbies, to have a challenge. These are the ingredients for a new lifestyle.

Many thousands of British, German and Scandinavian families move for these reasons. Over the years they have holidayed in their thousands in Spain, enjoying the country, the people, the climate and being where they can enjoy a standard of living that is just not possible in any northern European country. It is also close to home. Travelling by air, rail and sea or by using the Channel Tunnel can be quick and it can be cheap. Keeping in touch is easier and visits by friends more likely.

Permanent residence is not just a continuous holiday. It starts with a honeymoon period, going to many parties and making new friends. Of course this does not last. But there is no returning home; there is no office, no salary and no pressure. It is important not to get bored. *Cerveza* drinking and sun worshipping can take its toll. It is possible to keep active by:

- working part time in a non-demanding situation;
- joining one or two social clubs;
- taking part in the many sporting activities available;
- having a full and busy life;
- doing the things you enjoy to keep happy, healthy and feeling young.

Of course there are some problems. Charming people as they are, the Spaniards tend to speak very rapidly in a regional language which seems to be quite different from the Spanish learned at night school back home. They have a different body clock too. They can be noisy. Then there are frustrating delays. People do not rush about. If you need something repaired it often takes longer than it should. But one adjusts and learns to be patient.

Spain has undergone an amazing transformation during the last 35 years since the death of its dictator General Franco and the end of his authoritarian regime. Tourists who visited the country before 1975 remember it as a stagnant society with high unemployment, lagging behind the rest of western Europe. Since then the country has emerged as a prosperous and flourishing nation, on a par with the rest of Europe, attracting thousands of retirees and younger people from northern Europe, who have made a conscious decision to come to Spain, not just for the climate, but for a better life.

Change is always at a price. Today, don't look for on old lady dressed in black carrying twigs on a donkey. She does not exist any more, except in old black and white photographs. Instead of a donkey look for a BMW! Don't try to find unspoilt fishing villages along the Mediterranean for they have long been covered in vast swathes of concrete. Where orange groves existed look for an apartment block! In the aftermath of dictatorship, look for democracy. In a modern, industrial Spain its citizens have taken to democracy like ducks to water. All sorts of decisions, in schools and colleges, in offices and factories, among neighbours and parents, and among workmates are nowadays routinely submitted to a show of hands. The habits that go with democracy have put down equally strong roots and the Spanish, in their enthusiasm for Europe, have perhaps overlooked that to be true to themselves they also need to be different.

Agonising over the term 'difference' is a national pastime. Of course Spain is different from France, Germany, Italy, the UK and all the other countries in Europe. Of course modern Spain is different from old Spain. The fear of appearing different, or better translated, of being 'odd' can be obsessive. It all started with Franco who said 'Spaniards are different', which was one of the ways he justified his dictatorship on the assertion that, unlike other Europeans, they could not be trusted to handle their own destiny.

Back in the 1960s someone in the Ministry of Tourism thought up an advertising campaign for which the slogan was 'Spain is different'. The indignation it caused has still not died away almost 40 years later. It is understandable that it should have touched a raw nerve at the time. Yet the phrase itself is still common currency. Mention that something or other is done in another way in Spain and someone will say defensively, 'What you mean to say is that Spain is different'.

It is true that Spain is different. The climate, a laid back lifestyle and cheaper cost of living. A nation with the most crowded dwellings in the EU, overdevelopment and inept urban planning. People who smoke and drink more than any others in the EU, eat at the most ungodly hours, yet who enjoy a high life expectancy, low birth rate and are privileged to have one of the best health systems in Europe. It is Spain's idiosyncrasies which make it such a fascinating place.

An important choice facing Spain in the coming years will be to decide how much of their culture, identity and way of life they are prepared to sacrifice in the interests of integration with the rest of Europe. Spain is going to have to cope with a social environment which looks set to become increasingly multi-racial as the number of Africans and northern Europeans living and working in Spain grows every year. Spain will have to deal with shock waves from the Madrid train bombings which have spread across the globe questioning Muslim influence in the world.

The aim of this book is to provide an insight into modern Spain. A different Spain! Not one of flamenco and bull fighting but one of football, motor scooters and out-of-town shopping centres.

Enjoy a different culture, be revitalised, embark on a new lifestyle and feel young again.

Harry King, Pedreguer, Spain

1
Modern Spain

Fig. 1. Map of Spain.

REINO DE ESPANA – THE KINGDOM OF SPAIN

Mainland Spain covers an area of 500,000 square kilometres and has a coastline of 2,100 kilometres. Spain includes both the Canary and Balearic Islands, administers two small enclaves in Morocco known as Ceuta and Melilla and three island groups near Africa. The British dependency of Gibraltar is situated at Spain's southern extremity.

1

It is a big country and the second largest in Europe after France. The interior of Spain is a vast plateau called the Meseta bound to the north-east by the Pyrenees, to the south-west by the Sierra Morena and to the south by the best-known Sierra Nevada. The Meseta is a mountainous area through which many rivers have cut deep valleys and gorges. Much of the coastline is steep and rocky but there is a narrow coastal plain bordering the Mediterranean. The highest point is Pico de Tiede on Tenerife at 3,718 metres above sea level.

Spain's population of 40 million is lower than many European countries. With 78 people per square kilometre it has one of the lowest population densities in Europe. Despite being 97% Catholic, Spain has a low birth rate of 1.5 children per family with a life expectancy of 75 years for men and 80 years for women. Most Spaniards are now urban rather than rural dwellers. Over a million British now live in Spain concentrated in the capital, Barcelona, the Costas and the Islands.

The principal cities are Madrid, situated in the geographical centre of mainland Spain, being the seat of central government and an important commercial centre, quickly followed by Barcelona, a commercial and industrial city with a large port. There is an intense rivalry between the two cities, both political and sporting. Valencia, the third largest city facing the Mediterranean, is important for car manufacturing and citrus growing. Seville, the fourth largest city located in the south-west, exports agricultural produce such as olive oil, fruit and wine. Bilbao is a major modern port on the north coast.

Spain's main agricultural products are barley, wheat, sugar beet, vegetables, citrus fruits, wine and olive oil. The largest fishing catches are tuna, sardines, mussels, squid and octopus. Coal and iron ore are mined in Asturias. Manufacturing comprises motor vehicles, machinery, ships and boats, chemicals, steel, textiles and footwear.

Exports consist mainly of cars, machinery, fruit and vegetable produce, iron ore and textiles. Imports consist of fuels and petrol, machinery, electrical equipment, vehicles, chemicals and food products. Spain's major trading partners are France, Germany, Italy, the UK, the USA and Portugal.

The economy is changing from a tradition of agriculture to that of a semi-industrial nation, although it still has the largest fishing fleet in Europe, being widely suspected of flouting EU regulations, quotas and net sizes. Ten per cent of the workforce is engaged in tourism with a further ten per cent in agriculture and one per cent in fishing. There is a huge, duplicated civil service. Unemployment is around eight per cent.

Spain maintains a well-equipped armed service with women accepted into all branches. The government has close defence ties with the United States which has maintained naval and air bases in the country.

BIRTH OF A NATION

On 20 November 1975, General Franco died and the Spanish nation was left with the task of restoring democracy in the depths of a worldwide recession. For 38 years all the important decisions had been taken by one man. Until his dying day, Franco had restricted power to those who had refused to countenance change, or accepted the need for change but were only prepared to introduce it slowly and conditionally. If Spain were to change it was clear that much would depend on the role played by the young man who had succeeded Franco.

Two days after his death in 1975, his heir and protégé was crowned – Juan Carlos I, *El Rey de Espana*. His first duty was to attend Franco's state funeral at the Valley of the Fallen, the vast mausoleum hacked from rock which commemorates the dead of the Spanish Civil War and where many are interred. Juan Carlos was not someone in whom Spaniards had much faith. Ever since the age of 10 the young Prince had been projected by the media as a loyal son of the regime, completing his education with distinction and going on to attend all three military academies. He had rarely been seen except in Franco's shadow, standing behind the old dictator on platforms and podiums at official ceremonies. The overall impression was of a nice enough chap but with not enough intelligence or imagination to question the conventions of his background. Few people can have been misjudged as Juan Carlos, for his rather gauche manner hid a penetrating and receptive mind.

Under the constitutional system devised by Franco, the monarch could only choose his Prime Minister from a list of three names drawn up by the Council of the Realm, a 17-man advisory body consisting almost entirely of Franco diehards. When the King's new choice eventually became known, the reaction was of stunned disbelief. The man he had chosen was Adolfo Suarez, who at 43 was the youngest member of the outgoing government. Everything about Suarez except his youth seemed to be at variance with the spirit of the times. He had spent his entire working life serving the dictator in a variety of posts. Not surprisingly, he filled his first government with men of his own age whom he had met on his way up through the state system. 'What a mistake! What an immense mistake!' declared one of Spain's leading newspapers of the day.

Suarez moved fast. Three months after the swearing-in of his government, he had laid before the *Cortes* (Spanish parliament) a political reform bill which introduced universal suffrage and a two-chamber parliament, consisting of a lower house, or Congress, and an upper house to be called the Senate. To ease its passage it was made clear to members of the *Cortes* that the way they voted would affect such matters as who would sit on which committee and whether a blind eye would be turned to certain untaxed accounts. The entire proceedings were broadcast on radio and television and all the deputies were called upon by name to stand up and say either 'yes' or 'no' to reform. One by one the members of the *Cortes*, generals and admirals, ex-ministers, bankers and local bigwigs stood up and endorsed a measure that would put an end to everything they had spent their lives supporting. Spaniards realised that the long nightmare of Franco had really come to an end.

Further reform measures came thick and fast. The cabinet endorsed a procedure for the legalisation of political parties. The Socialists were legalised first, and then the Communists, the right to strike was recognised and trade unions were legalised. Then the government and opposition parties agreed on how the elections should be conducted and votes counted.

A new constitution was agreed, restoring the identity of ancient kingdoms and regions going back to 1492. The result was a kind of United States of Spain, a tightly regulated country having five levels of government. The top two levels comprised a congress and senate of elected representatives from the provinces, the islands and the regions. Then came 17 autonomous regions, called *comunidades,* with their own parliaments and governments, with the autonomous regions further divided into *provincias* and then into the smaller *municipios.* A new, democratic country was born.

A few years later, after a distinguished term in office, Adolfo Suarez resigned. Only days later Spain faced its greatest challenge, and Juan Carlos his finest hour. In the late afternoon of February 23, 1981, Leopoldo Calvo Sotelo was about to be installed as Spain's new Prime Minister when suddenly the doors to the *Cortes* were flung open to admit Lieutenant Colonel Antonio Tejero and a large force of armed *Guardia Civil.* The entire *Cortes* was placed in custody. In Valencia, General Milans de Bosch declared a state of emergency and ordered tanks onto the streets. Spain was again within a hairs breadth of a military *coup d'etat.*

With all the elected members of Parliament held in the *Cortes,* only one man stood between Spain and a return to military rule. Had Juan Carlos panicked and fled the capital, it would have been all over for Spain's democracy. But *El Rey* was made of sterner stuff. Summoning a television crew to La Zarzuela, his private home, Juan Carlos donned full uniform as Commander-in-Chief of the Spanish forces, and broadcast direct to the nation, ordering all units of the armed forces to take whatever steps were necessary to restore democracy. Spain breathed a great sigh of relief, and within hours the attempted *coup* was over. This, to some an embarrassingly comic interlude, consigned the generals to oblivion.

The 1980s

By the mid 1980s it was clear that things were generally working. The economy was showing good signs as inflation fell, productivity rose and the huge budget deficit became a surplus. Under the socialists democracy was firmly consolidated, the military modernised and partly removed from the shadows. The socialist government launched major development programmes in agriculture and tourism and rebuilt the infrastructure, especially the nation's crumbling road system. With the economy improving steadily, money began pouring into government coffers. It seemed a new golden age had arrived.

The new urbanised Spaniard was delighted to appreciate the temptations of modern consumer society; from cell phones to Seat cars, as if trying to quickly acquire those things denied to them under the old regime. By the late 1980s Spaniards had one of the world's highest disposable incomes and enjoyed longer life expectancies than Americans and Britons. Times had changed.

Socially the sexual revolution of the 1980s was described by Spaniards themselves as 'a binge'. Kerb side vending machines sold condoms, and prostitutes named their offering and price in the classified ad sections of the press. Gays and lesbians surfaced openly for the first time. Abortion rates rocketed – one for every two live births, the highest in the western world. The catholic nation that once led Europe in high birthrates now had just 1.5 children per family. London of the swinging 1960s happened in Madrid around 1985.

Approval was gained for phased entry into the EU in 1986 with full membership by 1992. No other nation seemed so enthusiastic over the idea of a united Europe as Spain. The nation's acceptance of foreign leadership reflected a mistrust of Madrid and Spanish politicians. This romance with Europeanism was a complex affair revealing deeply ingrained national traits – a desire to belong to something other than traditional Spain.

Entry into the EU helped create boom days as foreign money poured into the Spanish economy which again enjoyed the fastest growth rate in Europe. The end of trade barriers and government control was like a breath of fresh air and for several years Madrid's stock market was the most active and profitable in the world.

But there was a down side. Imports flooded into the country and exports dropped, a textbook example of what happens to a protected economy when it enters a free market. By the end of the decade international interests owned all six of Spain's car manufacturers; foreigners soon controlled eight of the top ten chemical companies; and multinationals moved in on a grand scale.

Spain's producers, faced with foreign competition for the first time, suffered. In particular the Basque region was burdened with outdated traditional industry – coal, steel, shipbuilding – that had fallen on hard times. Factories were in dire need of modernisation if they hoped to remain competitive, yet foreign investors were wary of the Basque region and its political problems.

Conversely Barcelona, well placed to serve the huge European market, was reaping great benefits from EU membership. Some Catalans began speaking of a Europe of regions rather than nations and had their own lobby in Brussels. Indeed, all Spain was delighted with the huge amounts of cash available for roads, airports, and other public projects.

Internationally Spain's role in world affairs continued to change. No longer would it sit on its hands and watch. The government allowed former US bases to be used as critical staging areas for the Gulf War of 1990. Spain re-emerged as an important diplomatic force in the Americas through its peacekeeping efforts in Nicaragua, El Salvador and Guatemala. It also played a role in the Balkan conflict. Now a stable Spain could lend a hand as Yugoslavia disintegrated into civil war not unlike its own nightmare decades earlier.

1992

Spain's prestige abroad was at its highest as 1992 began. The nation was obsessed with showing its best face. Large-scale public works transformed highways, airports and a new bullet-train between Seville and Madrid was launched. To commemorate the discovery of America five centuries previously, the city of Seville played host to a colossal international exposition called Expo-92. The same year Barcelona served as the home of a highly successful Olympic Games and used the occasion for extensive urban renewal. Not to be outdone, Madrid presented a non-stop series of events as Cultural Capital of Europe.

It also marked a decade in power for Gonzalez and the socialists, far longer than any previous elected government in Spain. There was good reason to celebrate. During the socialists' tenure Spain shook off decades of isolation from the rest of Europe. The bloody past of Spanish history had been laid to rest. Clerics and generals were gone from the stage. Regionalism gave way to rational autonomy. *ETA* was on the wane.

But at the end of 1992 the world economic crisis was having serious effects on the Spanish economy. There were signs that the long national fiesta was over. The Madrid stock market declined 30% in a year. Economists warned the nation was living beyond its means and could no longer consume far more than it produced.

1992 to 2000

Regional autonomy had greatly swollen the ranks of Spanish bureaucracy. In the 10 years to 1992, the number of civil servants working in the 17 regional governments increased dramatically. Catalonia was a virtual state within a state with tens of thousands of public employees. Part of the endemic labour problem stemmed from society's attitudes to work. It seemed too many Spaniards dreamed of having a safe, paper-shuffling job in a government office. This affinity for secure, cushy office jobs reflected the deep-seated attitude of Spaniards.

Spain needed desperately to create wealth, yet unemployment remained high with huge segments of the population standing idle. Instead of the free soup of 40 years ago, many were now receiving regular welfare cheques. The government itself was going broke with a vast cradle-to-grave social system modelled on its wealthier neighbours. In 1994, when public spending peaked at close to 50% of the GDP, about 12 million people were employed and 9.3 million received social benefits.

Facing the problem head on, the government focused on the key weakness: the high cost of labour. Over the years Franco, Socialist governments and the unions had priced Spain out of the labour market. The Socialists decided to dismantle their own creation, the Workers' Statute of 1984, before it was too late.

Yet Spain needed a more fundamental change. Tinkering at the edges was just playing with the problem. The leader of the opposition party was Jose Maria Aznar. Small of stature and mild mannered he had played no role in the post Franco transition. He was the first national figure to come of age in the new Spain. Slowly gaining supporters, his popularity soared after he survived an *ETA* car bomb attack. Aznar was sworn in as the fourth premier of Spain. 20 years after Franco's death, conservatives and not Socialists were finally accepted as a legitimate political force.

The new prime minister promised an austere programme of spending cuts and financial reforms and two years of sacrifice to meet strict EC guidelines for joining the monetary union. Aznar's agenda included major reductions in the civil service and mass privatisation of state-run companies. The nation was ready for Aznar's honest, business-like style. It was time for a pause and fortunately Spain's economy bounced back and remained vibrant throughout the decade. With these strides Spain formed part of the core group to launch the euro, in 1999.

Modern Spain

We move on to the new millennium. Up to 2004 three Prime Ministers have held power since the restoration of democracy – Suarez, Gonzalez and Aznar. Looking back we can see Suarez managed the transition of the country during the formative years of democracy. Gonzalez steered the country to obtain membership of the EU in 1986, thus ensuring Spain's economic growth which has benefited greatly from the EU programme of special economic aid to poorer countries. Aznar tackled the budget deficit, provoking some discontent with resultant strikes, but maintaining the country's strong economic ties with Europe.

Then the Madrid train bombings occurred in 2004. The country was rocked. Eleven bombs wrecked four trains, killing 191 people and injuring hundreds. Spain was back to centre stage in Europe yet again. Grief and shock returned a Socialist government ill-prepared for office. Terrorism suddenly hit Spain as its European neighbours looked on. Zapatero, probably the weakest of all Prime Ministers, dealt with the aftermath of the train bombings, elected by people seeking a pacifist, no war culture.

Although the Madrid attacks were identified beyond all doubt as the work of fundamentalist terrorists, it spurred on the authorities to deal with *ETA*. '*ETA* – how much longer?' was the cry. In late 2004 senior members of *ETA* were arrested in the Basque region of France – their hiding ground since 1975. Have the problems of *ETA* been put to rest?

In 30 years Spain has transformed its political and social structure to that of a conventional Western democracy. A plethora of elections – general, regional, municipal as well as regional referenda – has gone some way to placating the aspirations of the Catalans, if not so much those of the Basques. Her democracy is established and although there may be some rough edges, her economy at least is no worse than many other western nations and better than some. Prominent Spaniards have made the step into EU politics, and Spaniards are active at all levels of the EU administration. Greater visibility and prestige have also accrued from Spain's presidency of the EU and from international peace conferences held in Madrid. These developments, particularly on the political and economic front, are a source of pride for Spaniards. Spain is now a developed European country rather than just a backward, 'sun and cheap wine' vacation spot.

Spain's economy is sound, her society stable. She has, for the first time in her turbulent history, many friends amongst the international community. Her people remain as vibrant, as loyal, and as individual as they ever were. Her national character remains unchanged, moulded by her turbulent history. Spain's democracy is still young, but it is strong, fixed, and under good leadership.

Today's Spain is very, very different to that of the Franco years.

MIGRATION

From Spain

Surprisingly more than 2.5 million Spaniards continue to live outside Spain. They are the sons and daughters who fled in the aftermath of the civil war. During the Second World War, Spain had remained neutral while actively favouring its old supporters, the Axis – Germans and Italians. At the end of the war Spain was in a strange position; not entitled to the rewards of victory nor at risk from the encroaching power of the Soviet Union. There was no incentive to give Spain aid and a very good reason for denying it. In fact the world powers punished Spain for supporting the Axis. In December 1946 the newly-created United Nations passed a resolution recommending a trade boycott. Coming on top of the deprivations brought about by the civil war, which had cut real income per capita to nineteenth-century levels, the boycott was a disaster for the country.

All of Europe suffered deprivation in the post-war era, but Spain, where the late forties are known as the years of hunger, suffered more than most. In the cities, cats and dogs disappeared from the streets, having either starved to death or been eaten. In the countryside, the poorer peasants lived off boiled grass and weeds. But for the loans granted by General Peron, the Argentine dictator, to purchase beef and cereals, it is possible there would have been full-scale famine.

To the villagers in Andalusia – which had been the scene of desperate poverty even before the civil war – the deprivations of the post-war era were the final straw. Individuals, families and, in some cases, entire villages packed up their belongings and headed for the industrial centres of the north. The cost in human misery was considerable. Many Spaniards set off to find work abroad. During the late 1950s and into the 1960s well over a million Spaniards emigrated to Germany, France, Britain and other European countries. A rising standard of living in those countries created jobs which their own nationals were unwilling to fill, but were attractive to people from the poor farming and fishing villages of Spain.

From Morocco

More than a half million Moroccan citizens live in Spain with an additional 100,000 from Algeria and Tunisia. Among the Moroccans, more than 40% are in the country illegally, although this figure changes periodically with amnesties given by the Spanish government. Their presence is obvious due to appearance, language, religion, dress and occupation – they work in agriculture and building, or selling rugs, leather goods and trinkets.

Some migrant workers are very poor; not only Moroccans, but also some Peruvians, Ecuadorians and Dominicans, most of whom speak Spanish, a legacy of Spain conquering the world in the 15th century. They are the main source of cheap labour as many young Spaniards are reluctant to take low-grade employment.

There is a widespread suspicion that the theft and numerous break-ins that plague large parts of Spain are due to the immigrants from Morocco. The crime rate involving property is much higher in the resort areas where foreigners have settled. Well known areas in Madrid, Barcelona and Palma are recognised as Moroccan ghettos and sites for the sale of drugs.

A serious incident of rioting occurred in the town of El Ejido in February 2000, a large agricultural area specialising in the cultivation of hot house, winter grown produce. Enormous demand for agricultural produce had led to the immigration of many thousands of workers from Morocco. The cause of local anger against foreign workers was the killing of a 26-year-old Spanish woman by a mentally disturbed young boy. This was the third case of murder of a Spanish national by a migrant farm worker within a period of only 15 days. Mobs attacked workers, burned down bars and other establishments frequented by foreign workers, some of whom were forced to seek shelter and protection in the local police station. The incident received widespread coverage in the Spanish media.

From northern Europe

Another new migrant group from northern Europe now totals some 1.3 million people … and that's the official figure. Many settle in a twilight world 'non-resident', and of these many own holiday homes. They seek the sun and a lower cost of living. To accommodate this inflow, properties are built at the rate of 100,000 per year and this shows no sign of reducing.

Among northern European migrants to Spain, there are two major groups. There is a large majority who are content to live in a microcosm of their own country. A 'little England' or 'little Germany' based in Spain. And why not? They are among friends and neighbours with whom they can communicate easily, enjoy the same food and replicate life in the 'old country'.

Then there is a minority who feel they must integrate with the Spanish no matter how difficult this may be. They believe ghettos of British or Germans are undesirable. English shops, mini-markets, pubs and Irish bars, Chinese restaurants and English language newspapers bring all the comforts of home, but this group wants to hear the Spanish language, eat Spanish food, drink in Spanish bars and get a flavour of Spanish culture. Again, why not? Remoteness, solitude and self reliance are all excellent values.

How about the Spanish reaction? Tourism and immigration have been important to the economic boom and rising prosperity apparent in areas of Spain along the coast and on the Islands. This can generate a certain amount of envy or resentment by some Spaniards. They may wish to see the old ways remain, or resent the high property prices paid by foreigners forcing locals out of the market or they are simply reluctant to see foreign invaders in their country. Principally they resent foreigners who do not learn Spanish or familiarise themselves with the Spanish way of life. Can they be blamed?

2
INTERNATIONAL AFFAIRS

GIBRALTAR

Gibraltar is at the southern tip of Spain. It belongs to the UK but Spain, with some justification, wants it back. Britain, experienced and pragmatic in these situations says, 'let the people decide'. The people, rather like their brothers and sisters on the Falkland Islands, prefer the regime they know rather than the uncertainty of a new one. And so it goes on. Pressure mounts, as both Spain and the UK are partners in Europe and the semi-European status of Gibraltar needs to be resolved.

Few places in the world of such small size – 5.8 square kilometres in area – have been the subject of international controversy for as long as Gibraltar. Centuries of history have turned 'The Rock' into a symbol of British naval power and a synonym for security. It would be wrong to gloss over the Rock's imperial past, for the minute you arrive on the bizarre airstrip between the Rock and Spain you can see its strategic importance. It is a towering, impregnable fortress on one side of a narrow passage that makes the Mediterranean into an inland sea. It also has a huge harbour.

It is no exaggeration to describe Gibraltar as a link between two continents, two civilisations, two religions, two ways of life and two great seas. It is however as a colossus of British naval history that Gibraltar is best known. Nelson sailed from here in 1805. In the 19th century it was the staging point for a far-flung Empire, and it played an important part in both World Wars, especially as an anti-submarine base. In 1942 the existing tunnels were extended to contain generators, a telephone exchange, food stores, a water desalination plant, a bakery and a hospital.

In perpetuity

The Spanish took possession of Gibraltar following victories over the Moors, and held it until 1704, when it was seized by a joint Anglo-Dutch military force under Admiral Sir George Rooke during the Spanish War of Succession. The peace treaty that settled this war was signed in Utrecht in 1713 and ceded Gibraltar to the United Kingdom 'in perpetuity'. The territory has remained under British control ever since. 2004 was the 300th anniversary of its seizure and the inability to restore it to Spanish sovereignty has been a bitter pill for Spain to swallow.

Second World War

With the fall of France in June 1940 and the entry of Italy on the side of Nazi Germany, Franco was confronted with a dilemma. It seemed a golden opportunity to recover Gibraltar, but Spain was still exhausted from a long civil war, and suffering from both hunger and poverty on an unprecedented scale. On the one hand Franco's friends Germany and Italy had helped him during the Civil War, yet on the other he was in no doubt that Britain would apply a massive blockade preventing ships leaving or entering Spanish waters.

Although sorely tempted, Franco refused Hitler's attempts to force Spain to become an Axis ally but Franco gave permission for a German military team to visit Spain led by Admiral Canaris, and in July 1940 plans were made for a joint German/Spanish assault on Gibraltar. German reconnaissance teams observed Gibraltar's 1,400-foot-high limestone mountain bristling with gun emplacements, guarded by 12,500 soldiers and laced with intricate supply tunnels. But the operation to conquer Gibraltar never got beyond the planning stage.

Franco continued to play both sides against each other in an attempt to stay neutral, while siding with the Axis powers. He sent letters to London and Washington promising to stay out of the war. He answered Hitler's plea for entry into the war with a long list of essential goods that Spain lacked. Despite personal visits from both Hitler and Mussolini, Spain remained neutral, soothing the Germans by allowing Spanish volunteers to fight alongside the Germans in Russia.

Franco then met with the American ambassador who assured him Allied landings in North Africa had no intention of intruding upon Spanish territory. He then gave orders not to allow any German troops to move across Spain to reinforce their troops in North Africa. Franco ended his romance with the Axis, and his dreams of recovering Gibraltar for the moment.

Ironically the growth of a Gibraltarian consciousness was first stimulated during the Second World War. The mixed civilian population was forcibly evacuated to Northern Ireland, Madeira, and Jamaica and deeply resented being sent into temporary exile for the duration of the war. This exile made the Gibraltarians miss their homes and made them all the more determined to return to take an active part in governing themselves in the future.

Closing the border

A low point in Spanish/UK relations was reached in 1954 when Queen Elizabeth II and the Duke of Edinburgh visited Gibraltar on their royal yacht as part of the Coronation Tour. This was waving a red cape in front of a Spanish bull and Franco took it as a personal insult. Mobs chanted and waved Spanish flags, screaming insults and cries that 'Gibraltar is Spanish'. For 13 years, telephone communications between Gibraltar and

Spain were blocked.

A second low point occurred in 1969 when the border between Gibraltar and Spain was closed by the Spanish, imposing considerable economic hardship on the territory. Spain cancelled the work permits of almost 5,000 Spanish workers who were unable to continue working in Gibraltar. Franco even ordered a boycott of ships that had used the port of Gibraltar, and prohibited their entry into Spanish territorial waters. Further pressure limited incoming and outgoing flights through Spanish airspace. The border was reopened in 1985 after having been closed for 15 years.

In 1999 border controls into Gibraltar were tightened again in order to put pressure on the British government over its stance on sovereignty.

None of these actions have endeared Spain to the Gibraltarians. The Spanish however have come to realise that regaining Gibraltar will be by diplomacy and not coercion. Perhaps they will finally treat Gibraltar as a friendly equal.

Change?

Gibraltar's population of 28,000 supports the status of a British territory and has twice given overwhelming support for the continuation of the present arrangement. In both votes 99 percent rejected proposals to full or shared Spanish control. A referendum organised by the Gibraltarians themselves voted overwhelming against the idea of shared British-Spanish sovereignty. The proposal would have given the territory greater autonomy within the European Union as well as the retention of its British naval base and intelligence facilities under the NATO banner.

Ironically this patriotism is an embarrassment for Britain, who would like to resolve the issue with Spain. It has formally endorsed the shared sovereignty formula; an outcome that both Spain and Britain agree is the best way forward. In reality the only solutions to the Gibraltar problem are either a continuation of the *status quo* or the introduction of some form of shared sovereignty.

The Spanish government has re-stated their position on Gibraltar many times and has invited the current Chief Minister of Gibraltar to participate in negotiations. Spain has made it clear that it intends to continue conversations with Britain to reach an agreement that satisfies all interested parties. Spaniards have been surveyed many times and ironically agree with the Gibraltarians on joint sovereignty:

- Only 6% support joint sovereignty status.

- 49% want Gibraltar integrated into Spain.

- 41% are not against Gibraltar achieving independence.

Today's Gibraltar

Gibraltar has an image of comprising English pubs, fish and chips shops, British retail outlets, together with Tax Free electrical and liquor outlets. Things are changing! Britain's fortress is dominant no more, and young Gibraltarians are being born into a community where the working partnership is no longer with Her Majesty's Armed Forces, but with leading European and International financial companies.

The Rock has moved on from servicing the former vast armies and fleets of Britain's Empire, to learning skills which exploit its unique position inside the EU. Gibraltar remains outside the EU VAT structure and the Customs Union. It has jurisdiction in its own right for sovereign and fiscal matters, but is subject to most EU directives and rights.

Trans-shipment of vehicles, offshore betting, e-commerce, industries that use qualified company status complement a finance centre dominated by banking, self-holding investment structures, trusts and insurance work. This is the new central pillar of work opportunity and the economy of the Rock.

The future? E-land, naturally. Seven years ago two computer enthusiasts took the plunge and set up Gibraltar's first Internet provider – Gibnet. Scepticism was promptly followed by addiction, and soon the most senior people were avid e-mailers. Then came Victor Chandler and

Ladbrokes with the offshore betting, its success causing a change to UK betting tax laws.

The most exciting move in recent years has seen a memorandum of understanding signed between the Gibraltar Government and a specialist in complex web hosting, increasingly described as net-sourcing. The project depends on their ability to provide high quality, secure and reliable management for websites. The base for this international hub of predominantly financial sites is at Lathbury Barracks, formerly the heart of the British Army. This 80 million Euro project will place the Rock at the heart of a worldwide industry expected to grow five-fold over the next few years.

Today most visitors to the Rock are on duty free shopping sprees, but there is plenty to fascinate the historically curious including the 32 miles of tunnels open to the public. Other visitors include migrating birds: they cross from Africa to Europe and back over a strip of land a few kilometres wide with Gibraltar to the east and Tarifa to the west. Migration takes place all year round but the key periods are spring for northward movement and autumn for southward movement.

MOROCCO

Ceuta with a population of around 70,000 is an enclave of Spain in north-west Africa, a seaport on the Straits of Gibraltar, bordered by Morocco. For administrative purposes Ceuta is governed as part of Cadiz Province in Spain. The city is on a headland consisting of seven peaks at the end of a narrow isthmus. Once a military and penal station, Ceuta became an important centre for the manufacture of brassware and for trade in slaves, gold, and ivory. The Portuguese captured the city in 1415 and then Spain in 1580.

Melilla too is a Spanish enclave, a port in north-west Africa, administered as part of Malaga Province. Bordered by Morocco, Melilla is an old, walled town on a peninsula with modern buildings to the south and west. The city is a rail terminus serving the mountainous Rif hinterland and exports iron, lead, zinc, fish and fruit. The chief industries in the city are fish processing, boatbuilding, sawmilling, and flour milling. It was conquered by Spain in 1497 and has a population of 57,600.

The majority of the population in both areas are native Christian Spaniards. Both cities have Jewish communities, synagogues and schools. Moslems constitute about one-third of the population and there are many Moroccan workers who cross the frontier daily to work.

The potential for conflict is great. Spain will not contemplate withdrawal from areas it considers to be part of its territory. What is at stake is nothing less than Spanish sovereign territory in the form of two major cities, their hinterlands surrounded by Moroccan territory and several small but strategic islands, the Chafarinas, Velez de la Gomera and Aihucemas, located a few kilometres from the Moroccan coast. The last three island groups are important for the maintenance of Spanish fishing rights, navigation, control of illegal migration and smuggling.

What makes this situation so difficult is the number of interested parties:

- A struggle to achieve independence for Western Sahara backed by Morocco.
- The UK's interest in reaching accord with Spain over Gibraltar.
- Periodic bouts of Arab nationalism and growing Islamic extremism.

The Basques watch with interest too, seeking precedents to establish their own independence claims.

Spain's campaign to recover Gibraltar would not countenance a loss of overseas territories in the same region and Spain views the predictable Moroccan demands to regain Cueta, Melilla and the islands with apprehension. Its insistence that the principle of territorial integrity justifies its claim to regain Gibraltar is a double-edged sword. Morocco claims the same right over the Spanish enclaves. Spain further insists that the territories were legitimately acquired, have been Spanish for 500 years and are much closer to the mainland of Spain than the Canaries or the Balearics.

Arab opinion has backed Morocco fully. How can Spain legitimately request Britain to return Gibraltar to Spanish control and yet adamantly refuse to return the enclaves to Morocco? Spain needs the support of the Arab world to soothe its dispute with Morocco and peacefully to resolve its withdrawal from the West Sahara territory. Arab countries most assured of Spain's friendship all have supported Morocco's open defiance of Spain to win control of the territory, and have further pressurised Spain into accepting that people of the Sahara territory should have the right to self-determination.

Like Gibraltar, the *status quo* remains, the issues too complex to resolve. These issues are for governments. The ordinary people of Spain are accustomed to seeing Moroccan families on the main road south. They work in the EU and return to their homeland for a holiday heading to the ferry port of Algeciras. A few weeks later they will make the return journey. They will tell their brothers in the souks of the wealth in Germany, the liberal ways of France, the warmth of Spain. They have a legal job and the necessary papers, but their brothers don't.

Consequently there is another type of immigrant to the EU and particularly Spain – an illegal immigrant, one who comes in the hope of securing a job and a brighter future. How do they get to Spain? They come in small open boats normally used for inshore fishing and powered by an outboard engine. Many die, as the Straits of Gibraltar is a dangerous place with strong currents, high winds and inclement weather.

Thousands of Moroccans do make it to the interior of Spain, though. Those who are not picked up by the police face an uncertain future with no documents and confined to low paid jobs. Those picked up are difficult to expel because they refuse to say where they come from.

PORTUGAL

Portugal is a country lying along the Atlantic coast of the Iberian Peninsula in southwestern Europe. It is bordered on the east and north by Spain and on the west and south by the Atlantic Ocean. To the west and southwest lie the Atlantic islands of the Azores and Madeira, which are both part of Portugal. As a member of the European Union and the North Atlantic Treaty Organization, Portugal plays a greater role in both European and world affairs than its size would suggest. Nonetheless it is one of the poorest countries in western Europe causing the country to have one of the highest rates of emigration in Europe.

At the height of its colonial endeavours in Asia, Africa, and South America, Portugal was the richest nation in the world. Because this wealth was not used to develop an industrial infrastructure, the country gradually declined. After 1974 the Portuguese economy was detached from its remaining overseas possessions in Africa and reoriented toward Europe.

Spain and Portugal have much in common. An imperial past, famous explorers and map-makers, a shared Iberian Peninsula, dictatorships followed by democracy, membership of the EU and NATO. Yet relations between the two countries have been marked by mutual suspicion, fear and scheming.

One starting point for this arose with the Portuguese revolution in 1910 which deposed a corrupt monarchy and established a republic. Overnight the Portuguese broke with the past by introducing a new flag, national anthem, separated church from state and adopted a new constitution, as well as ending the monarchy. This was directly opposite to the way Spain was governed and this difference was magnified by the way the two countries approached international relations during the World Wars. Spain was allegedly neutral, Portugal was orientated to the Allies with the strategic significance of the Azores.

Why did Portugal become an independent nation? One factor is probably the very rugged mountainous terrain and low population density that characterises the Spanish-Portuguese border region. Language is another consideration. The main difference however lies in its people, for the Portuguese character is more sentimental, ironic, mild, caring, and more melancholic than the ardent, arrogant and aggressive Spanish characteristics. This has given rise to a feeling of Portugal being a little brother to Spain, similar to the relationship Wales and Scotland have to England.

Spain has tended to ignore its little brother Portugal. Motorways radiate from Madrid to all its provincial capitals. They snake down the Mediterranean from France to Morocco. A new motorway is under construction along Spain's northern coast. But there is still no direct motorway link between the two EU capitals of Lisbon and Madrid.

In recent years the two countries have drawn closer together. Membership of NATO and the EU have helped. The 2003 war in Iraq was fully supported by both governments. Football events result in friendly camaraderie. Big brother still dominates however, for the Spanish press cover international events from all over the world but rarely make any mention of Portugal.

BASQUES

The Basque Country, a region in which the Basque language is spoken, comprises the Atlantic side of the Pyrenees, including the Pyrenees-Atlantiques of south-west France and the northern Spanish province of Navarra. Euzkadi, as it is known in the Basque language, is the homeland of the strongly nationalistic Basque people, who proudly maintain their distinctive culture, traditions, language, and religious style, with a sense of independence from both France and Spain.

The Basque Country has been independent throughout most of its history. The area came under Spanish and French control after the Basque people supported the Carlists in their 19th-century struggle with the monarchy and were later defeated with them. The fight to regain Basque autonomy began soon afterwards. The Basque Country was recognised by France in 1951, while in Spain, the 1979 Statute of Guernica granted a degree of autonomy to the Basque community of northern Spain.

The region boasts picturesque and varied scenery ranging from the high mountains, rivers, and pasture meadows of the Pyrenees to the beaches of the Bay of Biscay and Atlantic Ocean. The French coast of the Basque Country is a popular holiday destination with a rich history, beautiful old towns, and coastline. Tourism, however, has not reached its potential, possibly owing to the risk of terrorism in the region. The major industrial city is Bilbao, but much of the Basque Country is rural, the economy based upon agriculture and fishing.

ETA – Euzkadi Ta Azkatasuna

ETA is a Basque separatist terrorist organisation that aims to secure independence for the Basque country in northern Spain from the Spanish government. The words '*Euzkadi Ta Azkatasuna*' mean 'Basque Homeland and Liberty'. *ETA*'s aims, if not its methods, go back to 1894 when the *Partido Nacionalista Vasco* (*PNV*) was founded. Forced into exile during the years of Francisco Franco, the *PNV* was considered too appeasing by many of its members and in 1959 *ETA* was founded as a splinter movement.

From the outset *ETA* differentiated itself from the *PNV* by its belief that violence was legitimate in achieving its aims. In 1966 however differences within *ETA* itself caused the younger organisation to split. One side favoured the traditional aims of Basque independence; the other took a harder Marxist-Leninist line and placed more emphasis on the use of bombings and assassinations. The Spanish government responded with force, moving into the area and carrying out a brutal policy of beatings and torture. By 1970 the organisation was severely weakened and many of its leaders were in prison.

Franco's death brought about a change in government policy. The Basque region was granted partial autonomy and *ETA* members were pardoned. However, the most noticeable outcome was a tenfold increase in violence in the decade that followed. In the 1960s and 1970s *ETA* maintained close links with terrorist organisations such as the Irish Republican Army and sympathetic regimes such as Libya. As these links weakened *ETA*'s policy was to establish itself as an independent force financing its operations through robbery, extortion, and blackmail.

With falling support and notable police successes on both sides of the French-Spanish border, *ETA* waned in importance during the early 1990s. In 1994 the organisation officially renounced violence but in practice the terror continued. In July 1997 five million people took to the streets across Spain to try to prevent the killing of the town councillor Miguel Angel Blanco who had been taken hostage by *ETA*. His eventual shooting caused widespread popular outrage. Regular mass protests against *ETA* violence continue to take place across Spain. In December the entire political front of *ETA* was jailed for seven years on charges of collaborating with terrorists. In early 1998 further Popular Party politicians were murdered within the Basque country and across Spain.

In September 1998 *ETA* announced a unilateral ceasefire, though some commentators were sceptical about whether this would lead to a permanent end to violence. 14 months later, the ceasefire was declared to be at an end on the grounds that peace talks were failing to make progress following the government's refusal to discuss independence initiatives. In January 2000 a car bomb exploded in the Spanish capital Madrid, killing an army officer, and marking a return to violence yet again.

Several arrests by Spanish and French police failed to prevent a further surge of violence. During 2001 the Spanish government under José Maria Aznar took an increasingly hard line against *ETA* and Basque nationalism but despite a number of arrests several car bombs were set off in and around Madrid, including one at the airport. Killings of policemen and government officials, all regarded as legitimate targets by *ETA*, also continued, including the fatal shooting of a judge in Bilbao in November.

The Basque case is clear. They have a totally different language and a long period of settlement with little mixing with other people. The Basque country has been an integral part of the Kingdoms of Navarre and Castile for 1,000 years and as Spanish citizens they are entitled by the constitution to the same rights as other citizens. They have justified suspicions and concerns for their status in any political arrangement. Even in cuisine and habits the Basques are not typical of Spaniards for they prefer beer and cider to wine, eat dried cod rather than fresh fish and even wear a beret.

It was however the Spanish Civil War that allied the Basques against outside control. The Basque leadership chose to support the Republican cause and fight against General Franco. Their hatred of the Franco regime and international Fascism was cemented by the German Luftwaffe attack on the historic centre of Basque nationalism, Guernica, immortalised by Picasso's most famous painting. The following is an edited extract from *The Times* eyewitness account of the tragedy of Guernica.

A Town Destroyed in an Air Attack

BILBAO, April 27, 1938

Guernica, the most ancient town of the Basques and the centre of their cultural tradition, was completely destroyed yesterday afternoon by insurgent air raiders. The bombardment of this open town far behind the lines occupied precisely three hours and a quarter, during which a powerful fleet of aeroplanes consisting of German Junkers and Heinkel bombers and Heinkel fighters, did not cease unloading on the town bombs weighing from 1,000lb downwards and more than 3,000 two-pounder aluminium incendiary projectiles. The fighters, meanwhile, plunged low from above the centre of the town to machine-gun the civilian population who had taken refuge in the fields.

The form of its execution and scale of the destruction wrought by the raid on Guernica is unparalleled in military history. Guernica was not a military objective. A factory producing war material lay outside the town was untouched. So were two barracks some distance from the town. The town lay far behind the lines. The object of the bombardment was seemingly the demoralisation of the civilian population and the destruction of the cradle of the Basque race.

Monday was the customary market day in Guernica and in the country around. At 4.30 pm when the market was full the church bell rang the alarm for approaching aeroplanes, and the population sought refuge in cellars and in the dugouts prepared following the bombing of the civilian population of Durango on March 31, which opened General Mola's offensive in the north.

Five minutes later a single German bomber appeared, circled over the town at a low altitude, and dropped six heavy bombs aiming for the station. The bombs with a shower of grenades fell on a former institute and on houses and streets surrounding it. In another five minutes a second bomber threw a number of bombs into the middle of the town. About a quarter of an hour later three Junkers arrived to continue the work of demolition, and the bombing grew In intensity ceasing only with the approach of dusk at 7.45. The whole town of 7,000 inhabitants, plus 3,000 refugees, was slowly and systematically pounded to pieces. Over a radius of five miles round, the raiders' technique was to bomb separate farmhouses. In the night these burned like little candles in the hills. All the villages around were bombed with the same intensity as the town itself, and at Mugica, a little group of houses at the head of the Guernica inlet, the population was machine-gunned for 15 minutes.

The effect of the bombardment of Guernica, the Basques' holy city, has been profound and led President Aguirre to issue the following statement 'The German airmen in the service of Franco have bombarded Guernica, burning the historic town which is held in veneration by all Basques. They have sought to wound us, in the most sensitive of patriotic sentiments, making it entirely clear what Euzkadis may expect of those who do not hesitate to destroy us. We Basques must react with violence, swearing from the bottom of our hearts to defend the principles of our people with unheard of stubbornness and heroism if the case requires it. We cannot hide the gravity of the moment; but victory can never be won by an invader if we steel ourselves to defeat.'

With Franco's victory in 1939, severe measures were taken against the Basque country. The traditional use of the Basque language, cultural organisations and activities that smacked of Basque separateness was forbidden. More than 25,000 Basque prisoners were executed following the Civil War in revenge for their support of the Republic. An ineffectual underground resistance was abandoned after a few premature unsuccessful operations from 1946–57, and the Basque nationalist cause languished until the establishment of *ETA* in 1959.

Things began to change in the 1970s when *ETA* stepped up violence and blackmail, abandoning its policy of taking care to prevent injuries to innocent bystanders. They gradually became more and more anti-American and anti-Israel. They admired the *PLO* and other Arab terrorist groups. Eventually, extremist and mercurial Arab leaders, such as Libya's Ghaddafi became open supporters of *ETA*, supplying it with explosives and funds.

The Basques today have the same or more rights and freedoms as they had under the Republic – yet they want more and more and independence too. *ETA* is a terrorist organisation with its political wing *Batasuna*, now banned as a political party, only able to operate behind the scenes practising blackmail against many ordinary citizens in the Basque country, where supporters of the *status quo* are liable to be targeted and denounced as Spanish lovers.

Quite rightly the Spanish government will not move, so like Gibraltar, Morocco and Portugal, the *status quo* remains.

3
INTERNAL AFFAIRS

THE ECONOMIC MIRACLE GOES ON

From 1960 until 1974 Spain's economy grew an average of 6.6% per year: faster than any country in the world except Japan. Spain's economic miracle took place during a period of high western prosperity and was largely dependent on favourable external circumstances. Three factors were especially important:

- Investment. Foreign investment in Spain increased rapidly once the economy had been liberalised. The United States was the most important source, followed by West Germany.

- Tourism. General prosperity made foreign travel a reality for large numbers of Europeans and North Americans. Spain, with its many beaches, warm climate and bargain prices, became an attractive destination and tourism quickly became the country's largest industry.

- Emigrant remittances. From 1959 to 1974 millions of Spaniards left the country. The vast majority went to Switzerland, West Germany and France, countries whose growing economies were creating a massive demand for unskilled labour. There they joined Portuguese, Italians, Yugoslavs and Turks as 'guest workers'. These emigrants sent large sums of money back to Spain: more than £1.5 billion in 1973 alone.

The great dependence on external conditions made Spain's economic growth vulnerable to economic changes elsewhere. The oil crisis of 1973, which initiated an extended period of economic uncertainty in the Western world, brought Spain's economic growth to a halt. The clearest sign of change was the dramatic increase in unemployment. The unemployment rate stood at 4.3% in 1975 but by 1980 it was at 11% and in 1985 it peaked at 21.5%.

Economic growth returned during the late 1980s. Although growth rates were well below those of the 1960s, they were still among the highest in western Europe. Unlike the earlier boom, this one was accompanied by high inflation and continuing high unemployment. Inflation was 6.6% in 1989 and 6.4% in 1990 – below the figure for earlier years but still significantly higher than the EU average of 4.9 and 5.2%. Unemployment also began to drop from the official figure of 21.5% reached in 1985, but it remained extremely high – 17.3% in 1989 and 16% in 1990, almost double the average for the EU. Particularly hard hit by unemployment were young people trying to join the work force for the first time.

Spain's early industrialisation took place behind high tariff walls, and most industries remained small in scale. The liberalisation of the economy in the 1960s and the influx of foreign investment, however, added a number of large firms. It also made Spanish industry much more varied than it had been. The most striking example of this change was the automobile industry. Before 1960 Spain built few motor vehicles, but by the end of the 1990s it was producing 1.5 million annually in factories owned by Ford, Renault, General Motors, and SEAT (largely owned by Volkswagen).

Iron, steel, and shipbuilding continued to be important heavy industries in Asturias and the Basque Country, but in the 1980s they became subject to downsizing. Cotton and woollen textiles and clothing industries remain significant in Catalonia, as they have been since the early 19th century. Other leading manufacturing industries include chemicals, toys, shoes, and electrical appliances (televisions, refrigerators, and washing machines).

Spain's foreign trade grew rapidly during the 1990s, but the long-established pattern of imports outweighing exports continued. The largest share of Spain's foreign trade is conducted within the EU; its two largest trading partners are France and Germany. Outside of Europe the largest and most important trading partner is the United States. Spain also conducts significant trade with the United Kingdom, Italy, Portugal, Mexico, and Japan.

In the mid-20th century Spain was an exporter of agricultural products and minerals and an importer of industrial goods. This pattern has now changed, reflecting the increasing sophistication of the country's economy. At the start of the new millennium Spain's imports were dominated by crude oil, which accounted for about one-eighth of all imports. Other key imports were transport equipment, spare parts, computers, and coffee. The most important export was automobiles and mopeds, which accounted for more than one-sixth of the total. Other exports included fresh fruits, vegetables and nuts, chemicals, petroleum products, footwear, iron and steel bars, alcoholic beverages, electronic data-processing products and pearls.

Spain's economic issues are different now. A US survey of Spain, the UK, the powerhouse Irish economy and that of near neighbour France follows.

Spain

The Spanish economy boomed from 1986 to 1990, averaging five percent annual growth. After a European-wide recession in the early 1990s, the economy resumed moderate growth starting in 1994. Spain's mixed capitalist economy supports a Gross Domestic Product on a per capita basis 80% of the four leading West European economies. The centre-right government of former President Aznar successfully worked to gain admission to the first group of countries launching the European single currency (the euro) on 1 January 1999. The Aznar administration continued to advocate liberalisation, privatisation, and deregulation of the economy and introduced some tax reforms to that end.

Unemployment fell steadily but remains high at 10.4%. Growth of 2.5% in 2003 and 2.6% in 2004 was satisfactory given the background of a faltering European economy. The new socialist president, Zapatero, has initiated economic and social reforms that are generally popular among the masses of people, but are an anathema to religious and other conservative elements. Adjusting to the monetary and other economic policies of an integrated Europe, reducing unemployment, and absorbing widespread social changes will pose challenges to Spain over the next few years.

United Kingdom

The UK, a leading trading power and financial centre, is one of the quartet of trillion dollar economies in western Europe. Over the past two decades the government has greatly reduced public ownership and contained the growth of social welfare programmes. Agriculture is intensive, highly mechanised and efficient by European standards, producing about 60% of food needs with less than 2% of the labour force. The UK has large coal, natural gas, and oil reserves; primary energy production accounts for 10% of GDP, one of the highest shares of any industrial nation. Services, particularly banking, insurance, and business services, account by far for the largest proportion of GDP while industry continues to decline in importance. GDP growth slipped in 2001–03 as global downturn, high value of the pound and the bursting of the 'new economy' bubble hurt manufacturing and exports. Output recovered in 2004, to 3.2% growth. The economy is one of the strongest in Europe; inflation, interest rates and unemployment remain low. The relatively good economic performance has complicated the government's efforts to make a case for Britain to join the European Economic and Monetary Union (EMU). Critics point out that the economy is doing well outside of the EMU and they cite public opinion polls that continue to show a majority of Britons opposed to the euro. Meantime, the government has been speeding up the improvement of education, transport and health services at a cost of higher taxes.

Ireland

Ireland is a small, modern, trade-dependent economy with growth averaging a robust 7% in 1995–2004. Agriculture, once the most important sector, is now dwarfed by industry and services. Industry accounts for 46% of GDP, about 80% of exports, and 29% of the labour force. Although exports remain the primary engine for Ireland's growth, the economy has also benefited from a rise in consumer spending, construction and business investment. Per capita GDP is 10% above that of the four big European economies and the second highest in the EU behind Luxembourg. Over the past decade the Irish Government has implemented a series of national economic programmes designed to curb price and wage inflation, reduce government spending, increase labour force skills and promote foreign investment. Ireland joined in circulating the euro on 1 January 2002 along with 11 other EU nations.

France

France is in the midst of transition from a well-to-do modern economy that has featured extensive government ownership and intervention to one that relies more on market mechanisms. The government has partially or fully privatised many large companies, banks, and insurers. It retains controlling stakes in several leading firms, including Air France, France Telecom and Renault and is dominant in some sectors, particularly power, public transport, and defence industries. The telecommunications sector is gradually being opened to competition. France's leaders remain committed to capitalism in which they maintain social equality by means of laws, tax policies and social spending that reduces income disparity and the impact of free markets on public health and welfare. The government has lowered income taxes and introduced measures to boost employment and reform the pension system. In addition, it is focusing on the problems of the high cost of labour and labour market inflexibility resulting from the 35-hour workweek and restrictions on lay-offs. The tax burden remains one of the highest in Europe (43.8% of GDP in 2003). The lingering economic slowdown and inflexible budget items have pushed the budget deficit above the euro zone's 3% of GDP limit.

How wealthy is Spain?

Earlier it was stated that Spain has a Gross Domestic Product per capita of around 80% of the leading western European economies (UK, France, Germany and Italy). Another similar comparison, more favoured in Brussels, is Spain's GDP per capita compared to the average of other EU countries.

In the 1980s, when Spain was catching up on its European neighbours, the idea got around that it had been doing so, if only gradually, ever since the 1950s. This is not in fact the case. Its GDP per capita relative to the average in the countries which make up the European Union at that time fluctuated quite a lot. During the 1960s and the first half of the 1970s, it

Luxembourg	223	Slovenia	78
Ireland	139	Portugal	73
Denmark	122	Malta	72
Austria	122	Czech Republic	72
Netherlands	120	Hungary	61
United Kingdom	119	Slovakia	52
Belgium	119	Estonia	50
Sweden	116	Lithuania	48
Finland	115	Poland	47
France	111	Latvia	43
Germany	109	Croatia	46
Euro-zone	107	Romania	32
Italy	105	Bulgaria	30
EU25	100	Turkey	29
Spain	98	Norway	153
Greece	82	Switzerland	130
Cyprus	82	Iceland	116

Fig. 2. Gross Domestic Product per capita in 2004 for EU Member States, Candidate and EFTA countries. EU25 = 100

rose steeply, until by 1975 it was 80% of the EU average. But then it fell back sharply. 10 years later, when the recession in Spain ended, its GDP per capita was only 72% that of the average. By 1991 the figure was still only 79%. Since then things have slowly and steadily improved and while a straight line convergence between Spain and its western European neighbours may not be totally possible, progress is steadily being made.

Figure 2 tells it all. Based on these statistics the GDP per capita in Luxembourg was more than twice the EU25 average, while Ireland was nearly 40% above average, and Denmark, Austria, the Netherlands, the United Kingdom and Belgium around 20% above average. Sweden and Finland were about 15% above average, and France and Germany around 10% above average. Italy was about 5% above the EU25 average. Spain was just below the EU25 average, and Greece, Cyprus and Slovenia were about 20% below average. Portugal, Malta and the Czech Republic were around 30% below average, and Hungary 40% below. Slovakia, Estonia, Lithuania and Poland were around half the average, while Latvia was about 55% below the EU25 average.

So Spain has now closed the gap. It has a GDP per capita 90% of the leading western economies of the UK, France, Germany and Italy. Those of us who live along the Mediterranean coast have been aware for some time that we were living in a prosperous, expanding country. We witness the massive development of new industrial estates with hundreds of new business, new hospitals and schools, out of town shopping centres, hillsides covered yearly with new white houses and apartment blocks.

The economic miracle goes on, albeit with EU support. Things will however change again, for Spain accepts that it is far too wealthy to continue to qualify for EU development aid totalling a net 93bn euros in EU funds since joining the union in 1986, a cash injection that surpassed total US aid to Europe under the Marshall Plan after the Second World War. Since 1992 Spain has received a quarter of the EU budget. But from 2007 Madrid could lose up to 90% of its funding as money is diverted to help the EU's new East European members. Spain will become a net contributor to the EU budget by 2012.

Spain's new-found prosperity has resulted in other impressive statistics. Surprisingly, the number of passenger vehicles per 1,000 people is 390 in Spain and 370 in the UK. Unsurprisingly, the number of people per doctor is 320 in Spain and 560 in the UK.

OVERDEVELOPMENT

Many British, German, Scandinavian, Dutch, Belgian, Swiss, Irish and Russian people are now resident in Spain. Why? Ask anyone and they will tell you it is a desire to enjoy the sun and sea, a much more congenial climate, a much lower price for property, food, cheap alcohol and tobacco and an easy going, relaxed lifestyle. A growing number of retirees from the wealthy North European nations have sought out Spain's natural beauty, hospitality and booming economy to settle permanently in the country. Others are happy to buy a holiday home, perhaps for investment or to rent out until they can live there themselves when they retire a few years later.

Additionally, Spain is the unrivalled number one tourist destination in the world with 50 million tourists entering a country with 40 million inhabitants. Its prosperity, excellent health services, new roads and spotless beaches have outdistanced the more expensive, traditional resorts in France and Italy.

The economic boom has changed the country almost from head to toe. As was stated in the Preface, don't look for on old lady dressed in black carrying twigs on a donkey. She does not exist any more, except in old black and white photographs. Some commentators say the Spaniard has moved from donkey to BMW in one generation. Don't try to find unspoilt fishing villages along the Mediterranean for they have long been covered in vast swathes of concrete. As for food and drink, *paella* and *sangria* can now come frozen or in cartons: such is the change in Spanish lifestyle.

What does all this mean? It means overdevelopment. Hotels and houses built at an incredible rate. Where fishing boats were once moored the largest hotel in Europe now stands. Spaniards now clean beaches daily but let orange groves decline. Has development gone too far? The whole of the Mediterranean coastline between France and Gibraltar is now seemingly for hotels and apartment blocks only.

Look at beautiful stretches of the Spanish coastline or rolling hillsides and you will find dozens of properties that no planning officer has approved. By the time the council had obtained an injunction the work was done. And since no one has the heart to order a demolition (especially if the owner wields some influence in the area) the most that is likely to happen is that he or she will have to pay a fine. In the length and breadth of Spain there are hundreds of homes, blocks of flats or even urbanisations which nobody has ever agreed should be there.

Spain's new Socialist government has vowed to demolish illegally built houses and hotels in an attempt to preserve the parts of its coastline that remain unspoilt. Determined to prevent the Costas from disappearing entirely beneath concrete, a raft of measures has been announced to protect the country's 8,000 mile coastline. Chief among them is a commitment to enforce a 1988 law that banned the construction of any building within 100 metres of the shore conveniently ignored by local planning authorities. This initiative would guarantee public access to the entire coast; its recovery and transformation in spoilt and built-up areas. The government appears to have been spurred into action by a series of reports decrying the toll taken by excessive development. One study claimed that unchecked construction of hotels, houses and marinas, but approved by local authorities, had helped to blight 90% of the coast.

Concern has also been growing over the effects of a controversial land law in the Valencia region which has not only fuelled overdevelopment but has financially crippled thousands of homeowners including many Britons. The law, known as *La Ley Reguladora de la Actividad Urbanistica*, was introduced in 1994, ostensibly to regulate the acquisition and development of land, and prevent excessive speculation.

However, a report by the European parliament stated it had been misused by unscrupulous developers to force homeowners to sell their homes at well below market prices or to make them pay excessive sums towards the cost of local infrastructure. 'There is no doubt that the application of the land law has led to a serious abuse of the most elementary rights of many thousands of European citizens, either by design or by deceit,' the report concluded. 'They have had their land and their homes expropriated and had to pay for the experience, finding themselves in a surreal legal environment without any proper recourse to legal justice.'

The law was due to be amended as this book went to print.

MADRID V. BARCELONA

Manchester has few political problems with London. Edinburgh has few cultural issues with Glasgow. Perhaps old attitudes widen a gap between Belfast and Dublin. However the political, cultural and sporting rivalry between Madrid and Barcelona is something else.

The relationship between Madrid and Barcelona is a troublesome one. Swathes of literature exist on the subject but in none of it will you find any reference to strictly financial antagonism. One of the best descriptions of the Madrid-Barcelona syndrome is 'A story of lack of love'.

To begin with, Madrid and Barcelona are historically very different as cities. Madrid has always been more patriarchal, more bourgeois, although its resistance to Franco's troops in the Civil War has been played down in recent times, in favour of Orwell's view of Barcelona as the heroic centre of resistance; the bleeding martyr of Spain's republicanism. This is not to play down the Catalan cause, but a modern legacy of Spain's political history as viewed by Europe is that Barcelona is the goodie and Madrid the baddie.

Barcelona feels very different from Madrid. Its position at the centre of the European universe has ebbed a little since the heady days of the 1992 and the Olympics, but it remains a fashion sensitive and self-conscious city, with a fast-moving and innovative atmosphere quite unlike the rest of Spain. The Catalans speak a different language from the Madrid types, but the differences are not merely linguistic. Both communities have their strengths and weaknesses, but they are culturally very different from each other.

Franco was from Galicia but his disdain of any cultural tendencies other than his own stodgy Catholicism was widespread. He harboured a particular dislike for the Catalans, regarding them as haughty and untrustworthy. But, like Hitler's paranoia towards the Jews, he hated them most of all for their cleverness, for their ambition and for their success.

He was not the only right-leaning Spaniard to regard Catalans in this way. Well before he arrived on the scene, the relationship between Barcelona and Madrid was already uncomfortable. The political problem between the two communities was based on the fact that Catalonia was the country's major earner, yet the capital Madrid was the country's biggest spender.

From the Civil War and beyond, the antagonism between the two communities has also been reflected by hostility between the two cities' major football clubs; one that now drives the engine of Spain's politics and not *vice versa*. To understand today's rival politics and culture you simply have to understand its football and the adversarial relationship between the two sides. Very few players have dared to make the politically charged move from one club to the other. A few minor players and reserves aside, it is a remarkable testament that the list comprises a mere six players, covering a period of a hundred years: Josep Samitier, Alfredo Di Stéfano, Bernd Schuster, Michael Laudrup, Luis Enrique and Luis Figo. Nearly all of these players have come to regret their decisions to cross the Great Divide.

Camp Nou, one of Europe's largest football stadiums, home to Barcelona's famous football club with its fanatical, critical supporters and its magnificent sweeping structure, befits one of the world's richest clubs. Barcelona FC, more than anything else, is a symbol of Catalan nationalism pitted against the central government of Madrid. To fail to win the league is one thing; to come behind Real Madrid is a complete disaster. With these two clubs it's not so much a case of sport but mortal combat, dressed up as football.

CHANGING FACE OF AGRICULTURE

Centuries ago almonds, oranges and olives were a characteristic of rural Spain. Almonds growing on dry hillsides, olive trees growing slowly, planted in long straight lines on the rolling hills of Andalusia, living to a grand old age and harvested during the winter months for pickling, eating fresh or pressed for oil. Things are changing!

The decline of agriculture has meant the rural population has decreased and with that many farms have disappeared. Spanish agriculture has remained relatively backward by western European standards: capital investment per hectare is about one-fifth the average for Europe and the vast majority of farms are smaller than 10 hectares. Since it joined the EU, Spain's agricultural sector has had to respect EU policies with the result that many small-scale traditional operations, especially in grape, almond, olive and citrus growing has ceased.

The face of agriculture first changed with the Huerta. One hundred and fifty years ago, the Valencia region was the wealthiest in Spain. La Huerta, together with the nearby freshwater lagoon L'Albufera, combined natural wild beauty with high agricultural yields in one of the main wetland habitats for bird-life in Europe. It was the market garden of Spain with its principal crops of oranges and rice, much of which was exported.

This region grew to prominence as a top producing region of citrus fruit in Europe during the latter part of the 19th century through the use of spring water and irrigation ditches on flat terrain surrounded by high mountains. Later the construction of rail links to the ports of Valencia and Castellon aided exports. The Huerta is man made and needs constant supervision to maintain its correct water level.

Many crops are grown in the Huerta; cauliflowers, artichokes, potatoes, peanuts, onions, tomatoes, green beans, peppers, lettuce, flowers, melons and wheat. But oranges and rice dominate. Acres and acres of oranges, their destination the supermarkets of Europe. Rice cultivation is automated as fields are drained, planted, the crop grows, fields drained again and the rice harvested. This crop stays in Spain, for Valencia is also the home of *paella*.

One other crop needs to be mentioned. Cultivation of the *chufanut* took off spectacularly as a result of the demand for a popular drink called *horchata*. *Chufa* is a non-alcoholic drink unique to Spain being the juice of a plant called *chufa*. In Valencia *horchata* (another name for *chufa*) is very popular and can be drunk in *Horchaterias*, served with cakes and pastries. It can also be bought in bottles from supermarkets. Marketed in a similar way to sterilised milk it is sold in ice cream shops as an alternative to branded, chilled soft drinks.

Since the 1950s, the importance of the Huerta has declined. Migration to the now highly industrialised city of Valencia is one reason but realistically a decline in demand and a rise in early season produce grown in the plastic covered fields of Almeria are the true reason.

Almeria, a province of Andalusia in southeastern Spain borders the Mediterranean. A dry arid area of 8,774 square km consisting of mountains crossed by sierras and valleys of the Adra. The Almanzora and Andarax rivers provide the only fertile land. Despite a low rainfall, several important irrigation systems have increased cultivation. The infrequency of cloud cover over the province has opened opportunities in agriculture and for unusual projects such as the siting of a major Spanish-West German astronomical observatory.

Fruit growing is the principal agricultural activity, with large exports of oranges and white grapes. Olive oil, cane and beet sugar, almonds and esparto are also produced. These crops are not grown in open fields but protected under the cover of thousands upon thousands of acres of white plastic. Driving along the main north-south road near the coast, one could be forgiven for thinking the whole of Almeria was under plastic.

This, too, is the home of the migrant worker; the Moroccan employed casually to pick the fruit to be dispatched to northern Europe. This is where fresh strawberries can be picked in February and where brightly coloured peppers are available all year. By concentrating on all year availability, northern European markets, reducing the importance of almond and olive crops have been the key to Almeria's success in the changing face of Spanish agriculture.

... AND FISHING TOO

Spain has long had an important fishing industry with fishing grounds both in its coastal waters and far beyond. The main fishing ports are in the northwest, especially Vigo and La Coruna. The activities of the commercial fishing fleet have led to conflicts between Spain and a number of other countries, especially Morocco and Canada. On a number of occasions Spanish fishermen have been arrested for fishing illegally in these countries' waters.

With more than 8,000 kilometres of coastline, Spain is the number one fishing nation in Europe. It has the largest fleet with 18,000 vessels capable of plying waters far from home and it accounts for the largest catches. Around 40,000 people are employed on ships and in the allied industries of canning, processing, storage, transport and marketing. Spaniards eat more fish per head than any other Europeans. The most popular are octopus, cod, elvers, trout, scallops, mussels, lobsters, mussels, prawn, squid and salmon.

The UK is no stranger to fishing wars. Three such events took place with Iceland over its declaration to extend its fishing zones. These wars however were minor in comparison to Spain's long-distance fishing fleet which has involved the country in numerous disputes; such as wars over halibut with Canada, tuna with France, sardines and anchovies with Morocco, with the UK over access to waters around Gibraltar and around Britain itself.

Before Spain's entry into the EU, it was frequently at odds with other countries over fishing rights. Since its entry into the EU things have changed little. Other EU countries had to adjust to Spain's entry and the size of its fishing fleet by adjusting all their quotas. EU conservation measures designed to protect fish stocks from over-fishing have meant a drastic downsizing of the total industry. These measures are a greater burden for Spain than for any other member state. The EU has managed a Common Fisheries Policy to conserve decreasing stocks of fish for its member states by the use of fish quotas. Other measures are aimed at decreasing and decommissioning a part of the EU's fishing fleets. Part of the difficulty about over-fishing is enforcing quotas, and regulations over net sizes at sea in waters that are hard to define into exact geographic zones.

EU countries realise it is in their common interest to reduce the size of their catches but, in the short-term, most of them are constantly fighting for a bigger share. Large Spanish boats ply waters as far as the Pacific and Indian oceans to provide the home market. It is no wonder that the Spanish fishermen fear that EU regulations will reduce their catches and further limit their activities in the North Sea.

Fishing is especially important in Galicia where families rely on mussel beds for their livelihood. Fresh mussels are one of the most appealing items on a menu of fish restaurants. Mussel growing is a special form of fishing in the rich inlets of the Galician coast where, from thousands of floating rafts, mussels are suspended and grown in the cool, clear, clean waters of the Atlantic. Harvesters pull up ropes on which clusters of black mussels grow; the larger ones are plucked and the smaller ones left behind to mature. This industry is at risk from frequent oil spills from tankers *en route* from the Gulf to Europe.

WATER

There is more water consumed per head of population in Spain than in any other European country: a remarkable statistic! However most water is used in agriculture, leaving drinking water in some coastal areas both scarce and impure. Desalination plants are constantly being built. City Mayors fight for more supplies as irritated voters register their displeasure at having to buy bottles of *agua* because tap water is undrinkable.

Conventional crop irrigation takes place by gravity feeding water from tanks to cultivated fields through a complex system of stone or concrete channels. A series of doors, open or close within the channels diverting water to various outlets. The system has remained unchanged for centuries. Orange and lemon trees are watered once or twice per week by flooding the groves. The hot sun immediately evaporates the water. It takes millions of litres of water to supply a field for one year.

On the plains of La Mancha things do get slightly better. Massive sprays bring water to the long rolling wheat fields. But evaporation there is also a problem.

Crop watering is a very inefficient system. Spain has a long way to go in conserving water. Perhaps they should copy the farmers in Arizona USA, another dry area. They have pipes located about 20 centimetres under the surface of the soil, drip feeding water to the roots of plants for a few minutes per day. Water is conserved as it does not evaporate.

The River Ebro is the longest in Spain. Rising in the Cantabrian Mountains in northern Spain, it flows 910km in a southeasterly course to its delta on the Mediterranean coast near Tarragona, midway between Barcelona and Valencia. It has the greatest discharge of any Spanish river and its basin at 85,500 square km, is the largest in Spain. The river drains about one-sixth of the country. The Ebro receives water from more than 200 tributaries, the largest of which has been utilised for hydroelectric power and irrigation. A system of 35 major dams produces a significant proportion of Spain's hydroelectric power. This river, if the politicians can bite the bullet, can solve Spain's water shortage by bringing water via pipelines from the mountainous regions of the north to where it is needed most, along the Mediterranean coast and to the more arid southern part of the country.

There is no doubt that more water is needed in the south of Spain – for both agriculture and planned increases in population. This approach seems quite logical given the Mediterranean region has attracted enormous revenues through tourism and settlement from northern European immigrants. The largest single requirement is the massive construction of dams and canals to bring water from the Ebro River basin to the coastal regions of Murcia, Valencia, and the area around Almeria in Andalusia. Such a plan would however have ecological consequences for the Ebro delta.

The real social consequence of the plan is a growing resentment that too much consideration is been given to foreigners, to the detriment of Spaniards, who believe they are being called upon to assist at the expense of their own environment. The political scene is further muddied, for the water plan was proposed by one political party and with a change of government, opposed by the other party.

Pushing politics to one side; what about the economics, the real issues and the real alternatives? The capital cost of the water plan is around 25 million euros of which 40% would come from EU funding resulting in a cost of 0.3 euros per cubic metre of water. It's expensive. There are many objections centring on an erosion of the Ebro delta, an increase in salt levels and its effect on offshore fishing.

Perhaps the real issue lies with water wastage. Why subsidise the irrigation of crops that are already subsidised and are often produced in excessive quantities? Irrigation water for agriculture is very cheap whereas the cost of water for domestic and industrial consumption is much higher. The price differential could be reduced to encourage water conservation and growing crops needing less water. This would make more water available for population increases.

The only practical alternative is more and more desalination plants. As we have seen before in Spanish politics – the *status quo* prevails, for the present.

CORRUPTION

In the world wide corruption league, Spain ranks 18th. Finland is best at number one and Bangladesh bottom at 133. The UK is 10th, Ireland 14th, France also 18th, and Italy 36th. Scandal and corruption in Spain lies just below the surface.

The first civilian head of the *Guardia Civil* was caught stealing from secret funds used to pay informants and widows of slain policemen. The director of the Bank of Spain was locked up for financial irregularities. Suspicious links were shown between the interior ministry and a group of off-duty policemen thought responsible for numerous deaths of suspected *ETA* terrorists, resulting in the interior minister going to jail.

The former Mayor of Marbella was required to report weekly to the local police. The former Mayor of Pego now languishes in jail for draining nearby wetlands. In a nation with a large underground economy, tax evasion is a national sport.

The latest scandal to erupt in March 2005 was a huge money-laundering scam in Marbella. Details of organised crime, local corruption, money laundering and fiscal fraud, all wrapped up in real estate speculation has flooded the newspapers. Solicitors known to many overseas buyers on the Costa del Sol were arrested and charged, along with foreigners. Three Spanish notaries, of all people, were also temporarily detained. And at the centre of this scandal is Marbella's real estate market. Local corruption makes it the perfect vehicle for laundering dirty money. A side effect of this is that illegal developments of the lowest quality get built, destroying a beautiful natural environment and enriching some really unwholesome characters, including some British and Irish estate agents.

However several good things are emerging from this scandal. First of all it has galvanised the regional government in Seville to take action. The Minister for Public Works has made it clear that measures will now be taken to clean up the Costa del Sol's real estate sector. Action will finally be taken to sort out illegal developments in the municipality of Marbella. There could be as many as thousands of properties in Marbella that in one way or another fail to comply with regulations.

The taint of corruption which has clung to politics in recent years will need to be dispelled if the image of Spain is to be improved. Laws regarding corruption are full of holes that governments are unwilling to plug. All of Spain's major parties have been drawing funds from charging 'commission' to companies in exchange for promoting, or not obstructing, their projects. Construction firms are known to have been a prime target. Eventually, somebody has to pay for corruption. If the price of every property or public contract is inflated to allow for the cost of bribes someone has to find the extra to pay for it.

4
LOOKING BACK

The Iberian Peninsula, like most Mediterranean countries, has been invaded many times. The Phoenicians, the Greeks, the Carthaginians, the Celts, the Romans and the Visigoths, six different invaders, take us only to the year 711. Then the good guys arrive. They were the Arab and Berber invaders, now popularly known as the Moors, who called Spain 'Al Andalus'.

Visitors to Spain, unless historians, do not need to know about its early invaders but they will inevitably come across some of their interesting remains.

- Santa Barbara Castle, Alicante – an original site of a Carthanian fortress.

- Palm Grove, Elche – where the Dama de Elche was found, the grove originally planted by the Phoenicians.

- Segovia – a world famous Roman aqueduct.

- Tarragona – ruined Roman walls and amphitheatre.

HERITAGE OF THE MOORS

Arab invaders from northern Africa in AD 711 created a new society combining three distinct ethnic and religious groups. Muslims now joined

Christians and Jews. These Muslim settlers were known as 'The Moors'. Their powerful presence was established in Andalusia where mathematics, science and architecture flourished. Competent administrators, they also brought new crops such as rice and oranges to Spain.

Cordoba was the great shining light of Islamic culture. In time, it became a centre of learning, literature and the arts. Arabic numerals enabled the Spanish Moors to invent algebra. Great libraries sprang into being, the one at Cordoba containing 250,000 books. Poetry flourished. Fine art, silken garments, elaborate glassware and pottery were produced. Moorish surgeons used full anaesthetics to carry out brain surgery and eye operations, so that the wealthy from all over Europe used their services. Above all, the Moors built great mosques and palaces. The great Mosque in Cordoba and the mighty Alhambra in Granada bear witness to the magnificence of Moorish architecture.

The Moorish legacy to Spain is immense. Over 4,000 words of modern Spanish are of Arabic origin. The elaborate courtesy of many Spanish phrases reflects Islamic greetings. Spain's most impressive buildings, palaces and castles are Moorish. Many words used in the context of architecture, mathematics and the practice of medicine are traceable to Arabic.

One other group was to have their lives profoundly affected by centuries of Moorish occupation. The Jews of Spain enjoyed, for the first time in their troubled history, a respected role in daily life. Freed from persecution, they were highly valued as merchants, administrators, ambassadors and financiers. Cordoba attracted Jewish scholars from all over Europe. Salamanca created a school of languages at the famous University, where Jewish, Christian and Moorish scholars worked side by side, translating the Holy Books of all three religions into Spanish.

Although Moors established themselves principally in the south, their power stretched to every corner of the peninsula. However, Christian kingdoms flourished in the far north and were eventually responsible for a rebellion that became known as the Re-conquest. It took Christian troops seven centuries to achieve a definite end to Muslim rule in Spain,

1100 BC	Phoenicians began colonising Spain. Modern cities such as Cadiz and Malaga were founded by the Phoenicians around this time.
400s BC	The Carthaginians conquered much of Spain.
200s BC	Spain became an important part of the Roman Empire following the Punic Wars.
AD 573	The Visigoths completed their conquest of the Iberian Peninsula.
711–718	The Moors conquered most of Spain. Many Spaniards converted to Islam, and Moorish culture began to flourish.
1000s	The Christian reconquest of Spain began.
1479	Aragon and Castile were united under Ferdinand V and Isabella I. The following year the Spanish Inquisition was established.
1492	The Kingdom of Granada was conquered, ending Moorish rule in Spain. Christopher Columbus initiated Spanish claims in the Americas, where Spain quickly established a huge colonial empire.
1512	The Kingdom of Navarre was absorbed into the unified Kingdom of Spain. Spanish culture flourished and Spain became a world power.
1588	The English navy defeated the Spanish Armada, beginning a period of slow decline for Spain.
1714	Britain gained Gibraltar from Spain.
1808	Napoleon I of France invaded Spain and captured Madrid. Spanish, English, and Portuguese forces did not drive the French from Spain until 1814.
1810–1825	Most of Spain's American colonies won their independence.
1898	Spain lost the rest of its important overseas possessions following the Spanish–American War.
1931	King Alfonso XIII fled from Spain, and the country became a republic.
1936–1939	Spanish Nationalist forces led by General Francisco Franco defeated Republican forces during the Spanish Civil War.
1968	Buoyed by strong economic growth, the government eased censorship restrictions. Protests erupted in Barcelona and Madrid, and regional separatist groups gained strength.
1975	Franco died and was succeeded by King Juan Carlos. Spain became a constitutional monarchy.
1980s	Spain joined the North Atlantic Treaty Organization (NATO) and the European Community (now the European Union), increasing its ties with the rest of Europe.
1992	The Summer Olympic Games were held in Barcelona.
1994	Spain threatened to block expansion of the European Union until a compromise guaranteed protection of Spanish fishing rights.
1996	Following a general election the conservative Popular Party, led by Jose Maria Aznar, formed a new government, bringing to an end 13 years of rule by the Socialist Workers' Party.
1999	Spain became a founder member of the single European currency, the euro.
2000	Renewed campaign of violence by ETA. Popular Party won general election led by Jose Maria Aznar.
2002	Introduction of euro notes and coins.
2004	Madrid train bombings. Change of government. Troops withdrawn from Iraq.

Fig. 3. History at a glance.

a so-called triumph celebrated to this day by a fiesta known as 'The Moors and Christians'.

Far from being a simple conflict between Christians and Muslims, the Re-conquest was a see-saw of hostile encounters between Muslims and Muslims, Christians and Christians and only ultimately between Muslims and Christians. Within each warring camp there were opportunists, mercenaries and contending royal houses ready, willing and able to make a deal by temporarily enlisting the support of allies.

Charlton Heston played the magnificent, gallant and heroic Christian hero El Cid in the Hollywood film of that name. El Cid's title *Cid* is Arabic for gentleman or chief, and was given to him in recognition of his service to the Moors. He was, in fact, an adventurer and battled with equal heroism against Christians and Muslims to further his own ends. He was no more averse to destroying a church than a mosque and plunder was his expected reward. His name is, nonetheless, preserved in history as an ideal husband and father, gentle courageous soldier, a generous noble conqueror and unswervingly loyal to King and country.

The expulsion of the cultured Moors and the rich industrious Jews left great gaps in the agricultural and administrative expertise of Spain. The Moors had also been responsible for the intricate terraces and irrigation systems that had created exotic gardens and orchards that still exist today, and the Jews had been highly placed in court circles as advisers. Without the Moors and the Jews, Spain suffered a long slow economic decline.

CONQUERING THE WORLD

Christopher Columbus, an Italian, proposed voyages of exploration to the Catholic government to find the New World. His first voyage in 1492 was a modest affair comprising three ships and a total crew of 90. With his crew on the point of mutiny he landed in the Bahamas and later discovered Cuba and the Dominican Republic. Buoyed by success the second voyage, a year later, was a grand affair comprising 17 ships and a crew of 1,500. It lasted three years and discovered countless West

Indian islands. Fighting with the natives was common and five shiploads were sent back to Spain – the start of a slave trade.

The third voyage from Cadiz in 1498 was a failure. Columbus discovered Venezuela but he failed to find the westward passage to the Pacific. Politics within the monarchy ensured Columbus returned in irons, but he was soon released. Columbus was now a nuisance. There was a fourth voyage; the three ships searching vainly for the westward passage.

Columbus was a brilliant navigator and had a natural instinct for navigating by stars, sky and wind. He had an obsession to prove his ideas about a westward passage were correct. Although he was wrong, this does not minimise his achievements, for it was Columbus who introduced the Old World to the New World.

Soon after Columbus's discovery of the Bahamas, the Spanish invaded Central and South America, conquering Mexico, Peru and Chile. In doing so they destroyed many civilisations. The Spanish conquerors stood open mouthed when they first saw the capital city of the Aztecs, but when the conquest ended in 1521 they had destroyed the city and had started to build in its place what was to become today's Mexico City.

In the 16th century, vast quantities of gold and silver flowed across the Atlantic to Spain. Not only did Spain profit from the precious metals brought back from the Americas, but also from an amazing range of new crops. Potatoes, tomatoes and maize were introduced. Tobacco, spices and cacao were discovered.

The vast Spanish Empire in America which grew out of Columbus's voyages of discovery made Spain – and broke it. The phenomenal wealth in gold, silver, pearls and other precious stones which poured across the Atlantic brought unimaginable riches to a country only just emerging from centuries of warfare. But it also brought enormous expense for defence against its rivals, equipping fleets which brought the treasure home, support of the missionaries who went out to convert the 'heathen' natives and the cost of the large bureaucracy required to run the new colonies. The Empire did, however, give Spain an eminence it might not otherwise have acquired. Spain gained enormous prestige in Europe and became the prime champion of the Catholic Church.

This was Spain's most productive era known as the Golden Age; a time of great achievement. Such brilliance occurred, however, against a background of economic deterioration and ruinous wars with the Low Countries and France. Spain gradually lost its influence in Europe. The 133-ship Armada suffered a further major defeat when it attempted to invade England: the Spanish galleons, although sturdily built, were hard to manoeuvre and were no match for swifter English vessels.

THE SPANISH INQUISITION

The Inquisition was not peculiar to Spain, but the Spanish form was the most famous and most dreaded, due chiefly to the activities of Tomas de Torquemada a Spanish Dominican monk who revived the system in 1453. It was established in 1233 to punish heresy within the Catholic Church. The Spanish Inquisition was not abolished until 1834 by which time it had tried some 60,000 cases of heresy. Of these, Torquemada alone condemned some 2,000 people to be burned.

The Roman Inquisition in 1542 was in response to the Protestant Reformation. Originally those found guilty were sentenced to excommunication, a fate which was pronounced after a religious ceremony; the 'act of faith' as it was termed. In Spain, however, the act of faith was a preliminary to punishment by the secular authorities, and this usually involved burning. The ceremony included a procession, solemn mass and a sermon before sentence was pronounced. Apart from burning, penalties could include fines, flogging or imprisonment. Trials by the Inquisition were held in secret and the accused were customarily tortured to confess.

SPAIN V. USA

The Spanish–American War in 1898 was a conflict between the United States and Spain which ended Spanish colonial rule in the Americas and resulted in the US acquisition of territories in the western Pacific and Latin America. The war originated in the Cuban struggle for independence from Spain, which began in February 1895. Spain's brutally repressive measures to halt the rebellion were graphically portrayed to the US public by several sensational newspapers as American sympathy for the rebels rose. The growing popular demand for US intervention became an insistent chorus after the unexplained sinking in Havana harbour of the battleship USS Maine which had been sent to protect US citizens and property after anti-Spanish rioting in Havana. Spain announced an armistice on April 9 and speeded up its new programme to grant Cuba limited powers of self-government, but the US Congress soon afterward issued resolutions that declared Cuba's right to independence, demanded the withdrawal of Spain's armed forces from the island and authorised the President's use of force to secure that withdrawal while renouncing any US design for annexing Cuba.

Spain declared war on the United States on April 24, followed by a US declaration of war on the 25th which was made retroactive to April 21. The ensuing war was pathetically one-sided, since Spain had not readied its army or its navy for a distant war with the formidable power of the United States. George Dewey led a US naval squadron into Manila Bay in the Philippines on May 1, 1898, and destroyed the anchored Spanish fleet in a leisurely morning engagement that cost only seven American seamen wounded. Manila itself was occupied by US troops by August.

The Spanish Caribbean fleet was located in Santiago harbour in Cuba by US reconnaissance. An army of regular troops and volunteers landed on the coast east of Santiago and slowly advanced on the city to force the Spanish fleet out of harbour. The ships tried to escape westward along the coast but in the ensuing battle they came under heavy fire from US guns and were beached either burning or sinking.

By the Treaty of Paris signed on December 10, 1898, Spain renounced all claim to Cuba, ceded Guam and Puerto Rico to the United States and transferred sovereignty over the Philippines to the United States. The Spanish–American War was an important turning point for Spain's defeat, decisively turned the nation's attention away from its overseas colonial adventures and inward to its domestic needs; a process that led to decades of much-needed economic development.

MOROCCO AGAIN

Between the World Wars poison gas was used in colonial wars despite the Versailles treaty ban on the use of chemical weapons. Probably the least known of these chemical offensives was waged by Spain against the Moroccans in the Riff War of 1919–27.

Three years after the First World War, Spain reached a secret agreement with a German gas producer to supply chemicals and technicians to make the gas. Evading Allied controls, supplies were transported to Spain and factories were converted to produce mustard gas. Between 1921 and 1927 vast quantities of the gas were dropped on civilian targets in northern Morocco.

The deadly effects of mustard gas were well known to the European powers from its use in the First World War. Mustard gas survivors are prone to die of cancer, and evidence indicates that the cancer produced by the gas can be passed on genetically. Figures suggest the rate of childhood cancer is much higher in those areas bombed with mustard gas by the Spanish than elsewhere in Morocco.

FRANCO ERA

In July 1936 a military revolt against the democratically elected government took place. The country was soon divided between the rebel-led Nationalists generally located in the agricultural areas, led by General Franco, and the Republicans located in the industrialised areas. A three-year civil war ensued.

Both sides received help from abroad. Fascist Italy and Nazi Germany sent troops, arms and aircraft to aid the Nationalists. The USSR sent military equipment and advisers to the Republican loyalists who were also aided by idealistic volunteers from Europe and America.

The Nationalists won after three years. The savage war was followed by a vindictive peace. Franco made no attempt at national reconciliation. Hundreds of thousands of people were imprisoned and 37,000 executed during the four years after the war. The main political forces during this period were the Army and, surprisingly, the Church which had developed close ties with Franco.

What role did the UK play? Officially it was neutral, but murky dealings have since come to light. Franco was commanding the Canary Islands garrison when the right-wing military coup against the Spanish republic was launched. He was ferried to take command of the military revolt in a British De Havilland Dragon Rapid aircraft chartered from Olley Air Services at Croydon aerodrome and flown by Captain Cecil Bebb.

That much has been known for some time but recently declassified documents at the Public Record Office at Kew, England show a far deeper involvement. On the plane with Franco was Major Hugh Pollard who was an experienced intelligence officer who later, in 1940, was stationed in Madrid working for MI6. Pollard spoke Spanish and was a firearms expert who had served in wars and revolutions in Ireland, Mexico and Morocco. Since Special Branch at Croydon monitored all international flights at that time they must have had knowledge of its purpose, which ultimately was to help to overthrow a democratically elected government.

At the end of the Second World War, Spain was an international outcast. The UN ostracised the Franco regime and many countries cut off diplomatic ties. But with the outbreak of the Korean War in 1950, Franco was seen as an important ally against communism, and a slow re-emergence took place in the next decade as Spain attempted to integrate itself into the world economy.

From 1961 the economy boomed because of rapid industrial growth and a substantial rise in tourism. Owing to a labour shortage, wages increased, trade unions developed and agriculture was mechanised. Greater prosperity brought rapid social change. There was massive migration from rural to urban areas bringing in its wake a government-sponsored housing programme. During this period social pressures brought a change from an oppressive rule to one more liberal.

OLIVE OIL SCANDAL

Twenty-five years ago the Spanish 'cooking oil' disaster began as a mystery illness. Years later the toll was more than 1,000 deaths and more than 25,000 seriously injured, many of whom were permanently disabled. It was the most devastating food poisoning in modern European history.

The epidemic is officially deemed to have started on May 1, 1981 when an eight-year-old boy, Jaime Vaquero Garcia, suddenly fell ill; he died in his mother's arms on the way to La Paz children's hospital in Madrid. Learning that his five brothers and sisters were also ill, doctors brought them in to Hospital del Rey, Madrid's prestigious clinic for infectious diseases where doctors began treating them for pneumonia.

The Vaquero family proved merely the first of many. The initial symptoms were flu-like: fever and breathing difficulties, vomiting and nausea and patients soon developed a pulmonary oedema (the build-up of fluid in the lungs), skin rashes and muscle pain.

More than a month after the epidemic first struck most of those in power had no strategy other than to hope something would turn up. Finally, it did. Dr Juan Tabuenca Oliver, director of the Hospital Infantil de Nino Jesus told the government that he'd found the cause of the epidemic. The government accepted his theory and on June 10 an official announcement was made on late night television informing the public that the epidemic was caused by contaminated cooking oil.

The cooking oil theory was persuasive. To protect its native olive oil industry the Spanish government had tried to prevent imports of the much cheaper rapeseed oil by adding an inedible aniline to restrict its use to industry. The illness was attributed to aniline poisoning caused by unscrupulous dealers selling the oil illegally for consumption.

Throughout all this time one man ignored the official lines of inquiry and spent months pursuing his own. Having eliminated cooking oil, Dr Muro and his colleagues turned their attention to other salad products and concluded that, without any doubt, the contaminated foodstuff was tomatoes and that pesticides were responsible for the epidemic.

The tomatoes, they established, had come from Almeria. Although exactly what happened may never be known, it is likely that one farmer had used chemicals too liberally or had harvested the crop too quickly after applying them.

For the various political and industrial concerns there was a common interest in hiding the truth. For the multinational chemical companies, the revelation that a mass poisoning had occurred would have been scandalous and financially disastrous. The Spanish administration had entirely congruent interests. Democracy itself depended on the government being seen to deal capably with this national tragedy. At that time Almeria represented an economic miracle for Spain, providing produce that went to all parts of Europe. Had it been acknowledged that those deaths had been caused by pesticides on tomatoes, the effect on the entire Spanish export trade would have been incalculable.

TENERIFE AIR DISASTER

The Tenerife disaster took place on March 27, 1977 when two Boeing 747s collided on the Island of Tenerife killing 583 people. The Tenerife disaster had the greatest number of casualties of any air disaster until the September 11, 2001 terrorist attacks and remains the deadliest aviation accident in history.

On March 27, 1977 Pan Am Flight 1736, N736PA, had taken off from New York's JFK International Airport bound for the Canary Islands. Upon approaching its final destination – Las Palmas – it was told that the airport was temporarily closed due to a bomb attack by Canary Island separatists, and was ordered to divert to Los Rodeos airport on the neighbouring island of Tenerife.

KLM Flight 4805, PH-BUF, a 747 flying as a charter full of holiday makers was getting ready to head back to Amsterdam. KLM had instructions to depart first. The Pan Am 747 would follow. Following the tower's instructions the KLM jet taxied to the end of the main runway and waited for takeoff clearance. What happened next would turn out to be a fatal chain of events.

With KLM ready to go, Pan Am was instructed to taxi along the same main runway until they reached exit 3, then to head on to the take off point via a parallel taxiway. Due to heavy fog they missed exit 3 and decided to go on to exit 4.

Air traffic control gave the KLM plane clearance for the route it was to take after takeoff, but the KLM crew mistakenly thought that it was permission for the takeoff itself. Since there was dense fog the KLM's pilots were unable to see the Pan Am 747 ahead of them. In addition neither of the 747s could be seen from the control tower and the airport was not equipped with runway radar.

Later investigation showed that the KLM pilots misinterpreted some of Tenerife's instructions. This was partly caused by squelched radio messages (calls from both planes to the tower and vice versa cancelled each other), partly by non-standard phrases used by the tower, and partly by the Dutch captain Jacob Veldhuyzen van Zanten seemingly jumping to conclusions.

Captain Veldhuyzen van Zanten, impatient because the flight had been delayed for hours and thinking that they had permission to take off, applied full power. The co-pilot expressed his concern about the level of clearance they had obtained but he was immediately overruled and hesitated to further challenge the captain who was not only senior in rank, but also one of the most able and experienced pilots of the company.

As soon as the Pan Am, still taxiing along, spotted the KLM 747, the pilots tried to take a sharp turn away from the runway, but collision was only seconds away. The KLM plane, by now already partially airborne, slammed into the side of the Pan Am plane ripping apart the centre of the fuselage. The KLM plane rolled 180 degrees and slammed into the ground belly-up near the Pan Am jet. All 234 passengers and 14 crew members in the KLM plane were killed and 321 of the 380 aboard the Pan Am flight perished too. The Pan Am captain was among the survivors.

As a consequence of the accident, sweeping changes were made to international airline regulations and to aeroplanes. A worldwide rule was made that all control towers and pilot crews had to use English standard phrases. Aeroplane manufacturers began installing equipment that helped pilots see through fog. Cockpit procedures were also changed. Hierarchical relations were played down. More emphasis was placed on decision-making by mutual agreement. This is known in the industry as crew resource management and is now standard training in all major airlines.

MADRID TRAIN BOMBINGS

Summary

The 11 March 2004 attacks consisting of a series of 10 explosions occurred at the height of the morning rush hour aboard four commuter trains. Thirteen improvised explosive devices were used and all but three detonated.

The attacks were the deadliest assault by a terrorist organisation against civilians in Europe since the Lockerbie bombing in 1988 and the worst terrorist assault in modern Spanish history. The number of victims in this attack surpassed Spain's previous worst bombing incident at a Hipercor chain supermarket in Barcelona in 1987, which killed 21 and wounded 40; on that occasion, responsibility was claimed by the Basque armed terrorist group *ETA*.

Official statements issued shortly after the Madrid attacks identified *ETA* as the prime suspect but the group which usually claims responsibility for its actions, denied any wrong-doing. Since then evidence has strongly pointed to the involvement of extremist Islamic groups with the Moroccan Islamic Combatant Group the focus of investigations.

A further attempted bombing of the track of the high-speed *AVE* train took place on April 2 but was unsuccessful. Shortly afterwards police identified an apartment in Leganes, south of Madrid, as the base of operations for the individuals suspected of being the organisers of the Madrid and *AVE* attacks. The suspected terrorists committed suicide by setting off explosives, killing themselves and one of the policemen in the blast.

It is generally presumed that the terrorists killed at Leganes were, indeed, the individuals responsible for both attacks.

The attacks

The explosions occurred during the morning rush hour, targeting a busy commuter rail line that runs just south of downtown Madrid. Four bombs (planted at the front, middle and rear of a single train) exploded at 7:39 at Atocha station, and three bombs planted on another train went off simultaneously just outside Tellez Street, near Atocha station. Two more bombs on a further train detonated at 7:41 at El Pozo station. One further bomb exploded on a train at Santa Eugenia station at 7:42. Most of the casualties occurred at Atocha/Téllez (89 dead) and El Pozo (70) with another 17 at Santa Eugenia. By 23 March, 191 people were confirmed dead, 177 at the scene and 13 while under medical care. More than 1,800 were wounded.

Security forces carried out a controlled explosion of a suspicious package found near the Atocha station and subsequently deactivated the two undetonated devices on the Tellez train. A third unexploded device was later brought from the station at El Pozo to a police station and became the central piece of evidence for the investigation. It appears that the El Pozo bomb failed to detonate because a cell-phone alarm used to trigger the bomb was set 12 hours late.

All of the devices are thought to have been hidden inside backpacks. Despite claims by the Spanish Government that the explosive used was Titadine, a type of compressed dynamite used by *ETA* in recent years, forensic analysis of one of the remaining unexploded devices found at El Pozo revealed the explosive used to be Goma-2, manufactured in Spain and not used by *ETA* since the 1980s. A van was found parked outside the station at Alcalá de Henares containing detonators, audio tapes with Muslim verses, and cell phones.

Responsibility

ETA has a history of mounting bomb attacks in Madrid, planting delayed-action bombs to kill rescue workers and using booby traps such as explosives in wallets. The 11 March attacks however were on a scale far exceeding anything previously attempted by a European terrorist organisation. Observers noted that *ETA* customarily issues warnings before its mass bombings and that there was no warning for this attack.

Al-Qaeda had certainly shown an interest in Spain in the period preceding the attacks. In November 2001, Spanish authorities arrested eight men suspected of being *al-Qaeda* operatives, one of whom reportedly had past links with Basque *ETA*. Osama bin Laden issued a public threat in October 2003 to carry out suicide bombings against any countries joining the US-led invasion of Iraq: 'We reserve the right to retaliate at the appropriate time and place against all countries involved, especially Britain, Spain, Australia, Poland, Japan and Italy.' At the time, Spain had some 1,300 soldiers stationed on Iraqi soil.

Information made public on 12 March by the Norwegian Defence Research Establishment revealed intelligence agencies had known for two months that a terrorist attack was being planned against a country entering into an election period. However, they mistakenly believed that country to be Iraq. Documents found over the internet described in detail the tactics and strategies to be employed. The tactic was to break the US-led occupation of Iraq by performing successive strikes on the co-operating member states, starting with the one which would most easily lose its resolve to keep its troops stationed in Iraq, and then following on with the rest. As the Iraq war was very unpopular in Spain, this would make a likely first target.

The attacks came on the morning of the penultimate day of campaigning before the Sunday elections.

The investigation

Although the Spanish Government initially blamed Basque separatist group *ETA*, the investigation took a different turn with the discovery of an abandoned white van containing detonators of a type not used by *ETA*, and a tape recording with verses of the Koran.

Another breakthrough came when an unexploded bag bomb was found and defused aboard the wrecked train at El Pozo station. Investigators discovered the bombers used mobile phones to set off the devices, and traced the recovered phone's sim card to two Indian salesmen who had sold 13 other identical cards to three Moroccan men – Jamal Zougam, Mohamed Chaoul and Mohamed Bekkall. Zougam was also identified by survivors of the blasts as a man seen loading bags onto the trains at Alcala de Henares. He was arrested on 13 March and provisionally charged with multiple counts of murder and terrorist offences.

Serial numbers on the outside wrapping of the explosives found in the bag were traced to a mine in northern Spain. On 18 March, Jose Emillo Suárez Trashorras was arrested and charged with supplying some of the explosives to the bombers. On 16 June, a 16-year-old boy was also arrested and charged with stealing 20kg of explosives. The boy, who cannot be named and is known only by his nickname 'El Gitanello' (the little gypsy) later stood trial and was sentenced to six years in a juvenile detention centre.

On 3 April in an effort to trace other phone sim cards believed to have been used by the bombers, investigators raided a flat in Leganes in the suburbs of Madrid. Before any arrests were made seven men inside blew themselves up. Moroccan brothers Mohammed Oulad Akcha, and Rachid Oulad Akcha were among the dead. Police later named them as prime suspects in the train attacks. Also killed in the flat siege was Serhane ben Abdelmajid Fakhet, known as 'The Tunisian', a man police named as the ringleader of the bombings.

In the months after the attacks, police arrested dozens more suspects in an investigation spanning six countries. To date some 70 people have been arrested. Investigators believe a network of mainly Moroccan Islamic militants orchestrated the attacks although members of the former government, now in opposition, have continued to voice an opinion that *ETA* also had some involvement.

A year after the train blasts, Spanish investigators believed they had clarified the key aspects of the country's worst terrorist attack. Judge Juan del Olmo released a 40,000 page report which stated that three groups were involved in the preparation and execution of the bombings. In December he charged the alleged leader of a Moroccan Islamic Combat Group thought to be linked to *al-Qaeda* with 191 counts of murder. The Moroccan Islamic Combat Group is also blamed for the May 2003 Casablanca bombings.

At least five suspects in the Madrid blasts are thought to remain at large. Investigators are now looking at suspects who have been charged in other cases with belonging to *al-Qaeda* or the Moroccan Islamic Combat Group. Despite the progress that has been made in dismantling Islamic terrorist cells in Spain and elsewhere in Europe counterterrorism experts stress that the threat of similar attacks remains. Experts are said to believe the full extent of the terrorist network involved in the 11 March bombings has yet to be determined both in Spain and internationally. They are correct, for 16 months later a similar attack took place on the London Underground with equally devastating results.

Terrorism is no different in Spain, London, Bali, New York or any other country.

5
DIVERSE CULTURES, DIVERSE LANGUAGES

CASTILIAN OR …

Spanish is spoken by more than 250 million people in Spain, the Americas, and Africa. Spanish is also known as Castilian after a dialect from which the modern standard Spanish language developed. That dialect formed in the 9th century around the town of Burgos, in north central Spain (Old Castile) and, as Spain was re-conquered from the Moors, spread southward to central Spain (New Castile) around Madrid and Toledo by the 11th century. In the late 15th century the kingdoms of Castile and Leon merged with that of Aragon, and Castilian became the official language of all Spain. Castilian contains a large number of words of Arabic origin.

Outside the Iberian Peninsula, Spanish is spoken in virtually all of Central and South America except Brazil (where the closely-related Portuguese language is spoken), as well as in the Canary Islands, parts of Morocco, and the Philippines. Latin-American Spanish has a number of regional dialects; all are derived from Castilian but differ in several points from European Spanish.

Catalan, modified French, is spoken in the north east along with Valenciano, Basque and Galician. To be absolutely correct, Catalan, Basque and Galician are recognised languages, whereas Valenciano is a regional dialect. All of these languages except Euskera (Basque) are Romance languages, i.e. they evolved from Latin. Euskera is what is known as a language isolate; it is totally unrelated to these or any other languages of the world.

In today's Spain the Constitution grants the autonomous regions of Cataluna, Galicia and the Basque country control over their own languages, cultural identity and education. The result is that there are three official Spanish languages recognised in different parts of Spain alongside that of Castilian, which foreigners recognise simply as Spanish. The alternative languages are recognised by local government as equal to Castilian. Local officials are also trying, with some success, to turn Valenciano into an official language.

Many people who encounter the Catalan and Galician languages for the first time immediately see a close similarity with Castilian Spanish and jump to the conclusion they are regional dialects blending with French and Portuguese respectively. Nothing is calculated to infuriate their speakers more, who point out they are official Spanish languages, designated by law and on an equal footing with Castilian.

Spain has always been a multi-lingual country and always subject to continual controversy over the language issue, even although the Castilian language abroad continues its rapid growth. Tension exists between the centralised state and autonomous regions and this has led to conflicts over the degree of local autonomy. The Spanish constitution is liberal, according a large measure of autonomy to the autonomous *comunidades* and in the cases of Cataluna, Galicia, the Basque Country and Valencia, special privileges designed to enhance cultural identity.

Children acquire regional languages or dialects in the first few years. The town in which the author lives has two primary schools; one teaches in Castilian with the compulsory second dialect Valenciano and the other teaches in Valenciano with a second language Castilian.

A good example of the complexities of a regional dialect and its pronunciation is given below:

- *Jalon* – the name of a town spelt in Castilian and written on national maps;
- *Xalon* – the same town spelt in Valenciano dialect seen on signposts;
- *Halon* – how to pronounce it in any dialect.

English is the business language of Madrid and Barcelona, but is rarely spoken or understood in rural mainland Spain. English is understood on the Costas and Islands where waiters and shop assistants often manage some English words which they have been taught at school. Builders, repairmen, installation engineers, petrol attendants, postmen, policemen and nurses generally speak only Spanish, or Catalan, or Valenciano or …

WHY LEARN THE LANGUAGE?

It has become customary to point the finger at ex-pats who fail to learn Spanish, a chore for insular Brits who have not been accustomed to speaking or hearing a language other than their own. They now reside in their new Spanish ghettos having a more than satisfactory existence without speaking a word of Spanish. If surrounded by fellow Brits, then why speak Spanish? This means most elderly Spaniards and most elderly Brits have had little or no incentive to learn a foreign language, so for the first time Brits have to deal with people who have the same attitude as themselves. For the younger generation, schooling now gives Spaniards a taste of English while British schools still focus on French.

A foreigner away from the areas of mass tourism may well be stared at as an object of curiosity, but it is easy to turn this round by attempting to overcome the language barrier by starting a simple conversation with the odd phrase and expressive gestures. Spaniards are generally pleased when a foreigner makes an effort to speak their language. They are remarkably patient with someone who is trying to communicate, and they listen carefully in an attempt to make sense of the mangled grammar and odd vocabulary. Exactly 'how' it is said is less important than 'wanting' to say it.

It is just about possible to live in Spain without speaking Spanish. Interpreters or friends can be used as an aid to discussion. The use of body language, pointing, nodding and shrugging can also assist. Enhancement of communication with a few key words such as *si, una, por favor, gracias* (not necessarily in that order) is a step in the right direction.

But the non-linguist needs one other major phrase: *Hable Inglés, por favor?* (Can you speak English please?). Fifty or 100 or even 200 key Spanish words are used by many Brits to get by. Meals can be ordered in restaurants, goods bought in shops, neighbourly greetings exchanged and the weather discussed.

There can be no substitute for learning the Spanish language. If choosing to live in Spain, we can surely be polite and respectful by learning more than a few words of the language. For a student or someone wishing to work in a professional occupation then learning the language is an absolute necessity.

How do you learn the language? Home study courses by book and audiotapes are heavily advertised. These courses are an intensive learning medium with timing best suited to an individual. Intensive language schools operate in Spain with prospectuses aimed at a variety of levels. One of the best learning methods before leaving home is an old fashioned adult evening class at a local school or college. A bit of fun and a common purpose, together with some effort for 20–25 evenings, will get the average person to a decent standard.

WHICH REGIONAL LANGUAGE?

Catalan

By the mid-nineteenth century Barcelona rather than Madrid had become a symbol of progress and change. It pioneered its own way rather than following Madrid. In Madrid old prejudices against merchants and manual workers still prevailed among the elite who were out of touch with the new way of life. The Catalans made the transition to a modern economy and became the dynamo of Spain. Today's Catalans stop short of demanding independence, but they will never yield their identity as being more industrious, more ambitious, more progressive and more hard working than other Spaniards.

Catalans justifiably point out that more people speak Catalan as their native language than the national language of some European countries; yet their language is not accorded the same official status outside Spain. There is considerable pressure over the issue of language and a constant struggle to ensure that Catalan receives priority in every sphere of public life. Catalan has witnessed remarkable growth but there is considerable resentment that the majority of people make little effort to learn it unless forced to do so. Outside the region the value of the language is very limited.

Shop and public services post bilingual signs, but Catalan is often the only language used to warn the public of fines for traffic violations and for smoking on the metro. There is legislation that provides generous subsidies for Catalan language films, books, choirs, lectures, radio and television programmes.

Basque (Euskera)

The Basque language (Euskera) is currently used in a narrow area of approximately 10,000 square kilometres in Spain and France. The number of Basque speakers outside that territory, in Europe and in the Americas, however, is far from insignificant. In Spain the Basque-speaking region comprises the province of Guipuzcoa, parts of Vizcaya and Navarra a corner of Alava, and in France the western region of the Pyrenees-Atlantiques. Although few statistics are available the number of speakers, who are largely bilingual, might be estimated at 1,000,000. Most of them live in the highly industrialised Spanish part of the Basque country.

Euskera is the most distinctive of languages spoken in Spain. It is neither a Romance nor an Indo-European language, and it predates the arrival of the Romans in Spain. Until the end of the 19th century Euskera was spoken mostly in the countryside, and, unlike other peninsular languages had no significant literary tradition.

In the 20th century – and especially since it was made the official language of the Basque Country in 1978 – it has been used in literature and journalism. The language issue is emotionally tied to the demand for Basque independence. Many Basque adults have had to go to special schools to learn the rudiments of a language their grandparents had stopped using a century ago. Few migrants from other areas in Spain see any point in trying to learn it unless under pressure to do so at their workplace.

Before the outbreak of the Civil War there was a blossoming of Basque cultural expression through Euskera in literature, poetry, the theatre, dance, singing, and traditional sports. In the post-war period the Franco regime tried to woo opinion in the Basque country by permitting an expression of cultural activity, but deep suspicion remained of any attempt to develop literature or make semi-official use of the language. Franco believed in one language: Castilian.

Basque is the language of instruction in some schools and is a required subject at all schools in the region. This means that practically 90% of pupils in the elementary schools in the region study bilingually or wholly in Euskera but the percentage drops to 40% for those completing high school and studying for entrance to university.

Gallego (Galician)

Gallego has many similarities to the Portuguese language. It is spoken in the autonomous community of Galicia, Spain – where almost 90% of the population spoke Galician at the turn of the 21st century – but also in adjacent regions of Portugal. It is the ancestor of modern Portuguese.

Galicia was liberated from Moorish rule with the help of nearby Asturias-

Leon before the independence of Portugal. The early development of the great pilgrimage centre in Santiago de Compostela tied Galicia to other parts of Spain even though the original language was basically Portuguese. After a long decline, a renaissance of Galician took place in the 19th century modelled on the movement to revive and promote Catalan.

Galicia fell quite early in the Civil War to Nationalist forces, so Franco took a more relaxed attitude towards what was simply considered a dialect of the poor semiliterate rural population, all of whom also spoke Castilian. Franco was also born in Ferroll on the Galician coast.

About two million Galician's out of a total of 2,700,000 speak the language along with Castilian, and are essentially bilingual, but few use it for any purpose outside the home. Many Spaniards have no difficulty at all understanding Gallego. Television comedy and drama productions can be received outside the region. Most Galician artists, actors and writers are adept at speaking and writing the language with a maximum of clarity so that Castilian speakers can readily understand more than 95% of any dialogue.

Valenciano

In the *Comunidad* of Valencia a variety of Catalan is spoken which local nationalists say qualifies as a language, rejecting the label of dialect. South of a line near Alicante, Castilian is used for all official purposes. In the northern area Valenciano is used.

Nothing can be more frustrating for northern Europeans retiring to the Costa Blanca, having made an attempt to learn Spanish back home to find they have settled in an area which speaks a different language altogether. The multi-language issue can often be seen in the cut and thrust of local politics where the use of Valenciano is a petty mechanism to freeze out councillors of British origin representing towns with more ex-pats than Spanish residents. The language issue does indeed create tensions!

SAYING HELLO

Irrespective of dialect the most common Spanish greeting is *Hola* (Hello) and *Buenos dias/tardes/noches* (Good morning/afternoon/evening). It is polite to use these terms together when entering a shop or if passing someone on the street.

If you are introduced to someone you have a choice of expressions; a choice that hinges on the appropriate level of familiarity. If you are introduced to an unknown adult it is best to err on the side of formality, shake hands and say something simple such as *Encantado* or *Con mucho gusto* (pleased or delighted).

It is common to hear Spaniards saying *Hola, como esta usted?* (Hello, how are you?) The standard response is *Bien gracias* (Good, thank you). When introduced to a young person, such greetings may suggest unnecessary formality. *Hola* or *Que tal?* (How are you?) is a more normal greeting.

The rules about greeting with a kiss on the cheek are somewhat ambiguous. The safest advice is to shake hands rather than kiss older women. It is usually quite acceptable for younger people, when they are presented to each other, to kiss on the cheeks. It should be noted that this 'kiss' is the slightest of actions. Quite often lips do not even touch the skin, but rather the touch of cheek to cheek.

6
WHY GO TO SPAIN?

A NEW AGE OF DISCOVERY

Why have so many northern Europeans discovered modern Spain? First there was the cheap package holidays of the 1960s, a tourist attraction different from rivals Italy and France. Then visitors slowly discovered that the country's old image as a backward, under-developed, economically poor country dominated by the Catholic Church was no longer true. Before any one realised it, by the 1990s Spain had taken on the mantle of a prosperous modern European nation with many benefits and advantages not available back home. It had sun! Not only sun, but a relaxed lifestyle and a cheaper cost of living too.

HOLIDAYS FROM NORTHERN EUROPE

Most Europeans obtain direct experience of foreign countries from tourism. Since the 1960s, there has been remarkable growth in foreign holidays. This has been fuelled by reductions in real prices and the increased understanding of foreign holidays as 'positional goods'. The two dominant nationalities of European holidaymakers are British and

German. In 1965 the number of British people going abroad was five million: the number increased by 140% in 1980 and doubled again by 1995. Equally impressive are the statistics for the proportion of the UK population taking a holiday abroad – 13% in 1971 and 35% in 1995. Well over half the British population has taken a foreign vacation at some time. Those who holiday abroad tend to be younger, more prosperous and of higher socio-economic status than those who holiday in Britain. The growth in international tourism from Germany has been even more rapid. Whereas only 5.8 million went abroad in 1962, this rose to 18.3 million in 1985 and to 40.7 million in 1995 (partly boosted by reunification).

There are four major types of tourists seeking a different experience from their travels:

- The organised mass tourist who takes an inclusive holiday which offers protection within an environmental bubble. Familiarity dominates novelty.

- The individual mass tourist who is more autonomous and follows a flexible itinerary. Familiarity dominates, but some novelty is sought.

- The explorer investigates new areas and tries to get off the beaten track. Novelty is sought, but if it becomes stressful this tourist will retreat into the familiarity of the environmental bubble.

- The back to nature drifter, who avoids any kind of commercial tourism establishment, seeks contact with native culture and tries to live the same way as locals.

One other relevant feature has been the growth of winter sun holidays. Some 12 million British holiday visits are made between October and March each year to various overseas locations. In general overseas winter holidays have been expanding at about twice the rate of summer sun holidays. Older people constitute an important element of this market, with 23% being aged 55 and over. There have also been other changes in the Mediterranean tourism market, notably an increase in self-catering. The experience of renting a villa or apartment may lead to the purchase of a holiday home to be used later for retirement.

The traditional Spanish package holiday, still enjoyed by many, consists of sand, sea and sun. Holiday reps efficiently escort people from the airport to a three or four-star hotel with half board accommodation, offer trips and sort out any problems. Tourists stay in their self-imposed environmental bubble. This type of holiday will always be the core of Spain's tourist industry, but it has now peaked. It has spawned a massive expenditure to keep its visitors happy and to encourage them to visit again and again.

The Spanish holiday market is now segmented. Firstly into different types of accommodation such as hotels, timeshares, rented properties and holiday homes. Secondly into the traditional family holiday. Thirdly for special interest groups looking for culture, rural, walking, sporting or adventure holidays. Fourthly to encourage tourists away from the Costas to rural inland areas. To do this the Spanish Tourist Board have developed a number of concepts:

- Traditional sun, sea and sand.

- *Espana Verde* (Green Spain) covering the northern regions of the country embracing Asturias, Galicia, Cantabria and Pais Vasco.

- The Gold and Silver routes that are old Roman roads through the Spanish heartland.

- Eight Spanish cities recognised by UNESCO for their artistic and cultural legacy. They are Avila, Caceres, Cordoba, Cuenca, Salamanca, Santiago de Compostela, Segovia and Toledo. They are not major cultural cities such as Granada, but smaller, rural cities each with a wealth of history and culture, and a variety of customs.

- Short city breaks promoted to Alicante, Barcelona, Madrid, Palma, Granada, Salamanca, Santander, Santiago de Compostela, Seville, Toledo and Valencia.

A UNIVERSITY VIEW OF RETIREMENT

Most of Spain's visitors are holiday makers, but many northern Europeans become permanent residents. The early trickle of migrants has become a steady flow, forming one of the main retirement locations for people from northern Europe. For this group of people climate is important, but another important reason is grounded in personal finances as there are considerable house price differentials between northern and southern Europe. Reasons given by people wishing to move permanently to Spain and researched by Sheffield University are published in their book entitled *Sunset Lives*:

- Climate and other aspects of the natural environment, such as landscape and clean air.

- The pace of life, feeling healthier, more relaxed, opportunities for golf, sailing and active sports.

- Lower living costs, housing costs, cheaper food, lower heating bills and lower taxes.

- The presence of a British community, many friends, a good social life, the opportunity for relatives to visit, and a friendly local population.

- Admiration for Spain, the country's society and culture.

- Childhood or family links, including marriage to a Spaniard.

- Antipathy to the UK caused by high crime rates or poor social values, a general wish to live abroad or long-term expatriates with no wish to return to the UK.

- English is widely spoken with easy travel to the UK.

A BUILDING SOCIETY VIEW

More recently a report issued by an international branch of a UK Building Society stated an extra six million Britons will venture abroad to work or live by the year 2020. Their motivation is to reduce stress as many are working long hours in highly pressurised occupations. These Brits are already looking and researching destinations that can give them a more relaxed lifestyle and more leisure time. A breakdown of reasons indicates:

- 39% are searching for a better quality of life;

- 38% are searching for new experiences;
- 25% are searching for a new challenge.

Brits also have a growing appetite for overseas holidays, with Spain as their number one destination. This has increased their exposure to new experiences. People are becoming more dissatisfied with their lives and a trend for television programmes such as *A Place in the Sun* and *No Turning Back* emphasises the point. The TV experience is aimed at despondent Brits who want to make a new life with new challenges in another country.

The research forecasts that Britons will constantly be on the lookout to change their lifestyle. In the past, people may have moved abroad because of high unemployment levels in the UK – now they move to experience something new.

The concerns and biggest worries Brits have about moving and living overseas are:

- 59% said they would probably miss their family;
- 47% said the logistics of moving home;
- 45% said that healthcare would be a concern;
- 37% said language was an issue.

As Europe has easy border controls for entry, and travel is becoming cheaper, opportunities will increase for Britons moving abroad thus allowing more people to fulfil their dream of a new experience. The research also shows substantial differences of opinion between classes, with senior managers citing Spain and France as joint favourites whereas finance workers, manual staff and middle managers name Spain as their favourite.

PROS AND CONS OF LIFE IN SPAIN

Climate

It is hardly surprising that the overwhelming attraction of Spain is its excellent climate. Summer everywhere is hot, in some places very hot. In winter anywhere south of Valencia is mild, but surprisingly around Madrid it often drops to below freezing. Some parts of the Costa Blanca have been described by the World Health Organisation as having one of the healthiest climates in the world.

Climate should be a balance. Not too hot, not too cold, a little bit of rain to grow the crops, but not too much to deter people. Some snow in the mountains for recreational purposes, but not enough to affect communications. The influence of the Atlantic, the Mediterranean and Africa produces a varying climate. Northern Spain has lush green pastures. The Costas offer sun and sand coupled with the clear blue waters of the Mediterranean. The southern rolling hills of Andalusia are blisteringly hot in the summer. The Balearic and Canary Islands are always pleasant, the latter very mild in winter. Madrid, the capital, is either freezing or roasting. Cordoba in the south is known as the 'frying pan' of Europe.

The Mediterranean region has an ideal balance:

- 320 days of sunshine per year;

- 11.5 hours of sunshine per day in summer;

- 14 inches of rain per year;

- Average spring temperature seven to 27° centigrade;

- Average summer temperature 17 to 36° centigrade;

- Average autumn temperature nine to 30° centigrade;

- Average winter temperature one to 23° centigrade.

While northern Europe is being deluged with rain, battered by wind, its roads closed by snow and ice, you can almost guarantee that Alicante and Malaga will be bathed in sunshine. But not all of Spain enjoys a Mediterranean climate. Here are some less attractive statistics:

- San Sebastian – 41 inches of rain per year;

- Madrid – average lowest winter temperature: –5° centigrade;

- Extremadura – average highest summer temperature – 41°
  centigrade.

While there may be other reasons for coming to Spain, climate is the big, big number one. It is healthy and makes one feel good. But despite Spain's excellent climate, things occasionally go wrong. Once per year rainfall can be heavy and prolonged. Water runs off baked, hard soil into dry riverbeds and finally out to sea. As there are few urban drains, roads flood. Opposite is an extract from a recent newspaper article.

		Jan	Feb	Mar	Apr	May	Jun	Jul	Aug	Sep	Oct	Nov	Dec
Costa Brava	Max	14	14	16	17	20	23	27	26	25	21	16	15
	Min	6	6	8	9	12	16	18	21	17	13	9	7
Costa Dorado	Max	13	14	16	18	21	25	28	28	25	21	16	13
	Min	6	7	9	11	14	18	21	21	19	15	11	8
Costa del Azahar	Max	15	16	18	20	23	26	29	29	27	23	19	16
	Min	6	6	8	10	13	16	19	20	18	15	10	7
Costa Blanca	Max	16	18	20	22	26	29	32	32	30	25	21	17
	Min	7	6	8	10	13	15	19	20	18	15	10	7
Costa Calida	Max	15	16	18	19	23	25	29	29	27	24	20	17
	Min	5	5	8	9	13	17	20	20	18	14	10	7
Costa del Sol	Max	17	17	19	21	23	27	29	30	29	23	20	17
	Min	9	9	11	13	15	19	21	22	20	16	12	9
Costa de la Luz	Max	15	14	18	21	23	27	29	30	29	23	20	17
	Min	8	7	11	12	15	18	20	20	19	15	12	9
Santander	Max	12	12	15	15	17	19	22	22	21	18	15	12
	Min	7	7	8	10	11	14	16	18	15	12	10	8
Galacia	Max	14	15	16	18	20	24	25	26	24	20	16	14
	Min	3	4	5	7	10	12	13	13	12	9	6	5
Sevilla	Max	15	17	21	23	26	32	35	36	32	26	20	16
	Min	6	6	9	11	13	17	21	20	18	14	10	7
Balearic Islands	Max	14	15	17	19	22	26	29	29	27	23	18	15
	Min	6	6	8	10	13	17	19	20	18	14	11	8
Canary Islands East	Max	21	21	22	23	23	24	25	26	26	27	24	22
	Min	16	16	16	17	18	19	21	22	22	21	18	17
Canary Islands West	Max	20	21	22	23	24	26	28	29	28	26	24	21
	Min	14	14	15	16	17	19	20	21	21	19	17	16
Madrid	Max	9	11	15	18	21	27	31	30	25	19	13	9
	Min	1	2	5	12	10	14	17	17	14	10	5	2

Fig. 4. Temperatures (degrees centigrade).

Emergency services from Castellon to Almeria have been placed on red alert this weekend after meteorologists forecast similar torrential downpours and gale force winds to those that caused millions of euros worth of damage on Tuesday when flash floods claimed two lives. Downpours of up to 300 litres per square metre fell in Javea, Gata and Pedreguer. Floods in Javea left the area completely isolated by road and about 100,000 people were without electricity for eight hours as rainwater flooded a sub station. A four-storey building in Alcoy collapsed due to torrential rain and high winds.

Cost of living

Spain is no longer the cheap and cheerful country it once was. The cost of living has increased considerably over the last decade. However, with the exception of large cities, the cost of living is still lower in coastal and rural areas than it is in the United Kingdom, Ireland, Germany and France. It is significantly lower than the cost of living in the Scandinavian countries and is on a par with Florida.

A dominant factor in such a comparison is the relationship between the Pound Sterling and the euro. Ex-pats who were paid in Sterling during the first few millennium years received unprecedented exchange rates of 1.7€ to the £. However these are unlikely to be repeated as European monetary integration continues.

Spain's sunny geographical location, too, affects the cost of living. There is an abundance of locally-produced food and wine, not only fresh from the market garden of Europe, but also cheap and plentiful. The beneficial effect of sunshine on day-to-day living costs is truly amazing. Utility bill unit charges for electric and gas may be slightly high, but low demand more than compensates.

Something for everyone

There is more to life in Spain than the sun, sea and sand of the Costas. Only a few miles inland, traditional Spain opens up. The transformation is remarkable as high rise modern buildings, set in clean cities, are quickly left behind to be replaced by small white-walled villages and then, even further inland, by individual white houses scattered over hillsides. One such example is typified on the Costa del Sol where, a few miles from the city of Malaga, the white village of Competa is completely surrounded by thousands of individual white properties nestling on hillsides or sheltering in valleys.

Some beer and sandwich resorts, which in the past have received negative publicity, recognise their prime source of income is from tourism. They have now embarked on programmes to attract family groups. Spain, once home of the package holiday now has international entertainment, theme parks and top class restaurants. There really is something for everyone in Spain.

The people

Anyone who has spent even a short time in Spain will know that its people are friendly, polite and welcoming. If you are polite, smile, and offer locals a greeting in their own language it will go a long way towards establishing and maintaining relationships.

Some people have been known to say this friendliness is superficial, asking the question 'Have you ever been invited into a Spanish home?' In some communities there is resentment to the new foreign invaders. This is valid and it would also be fair to say that in tourist resorts the desire to extract the maximum cash in the minimum time has eroded the natural charm of Spaniards. But it would be wrong to characterise the whole country with the behaviour of a few.

As one might expect there is a contrast between the older and younger generations. Elderly Spaniards will have endured the repression of the Franco years, may be illiterate and have worked in agriculture. In contrast younger Spaniards will be vibrant, computer literate and have a city based mentality that embraces new cosmopolitan values.

Today, social customs are changing. People are much less formal, but familiarity is still a hallmark of Spanish life. Old fashioned courtesy and formality are still the custom in rural areas. Great store is set by personal loyalty and friendship, but it is also very important to take account of the Spanish sense of honour and pride, which is easily offended. The extended family is the main social unit, with strong family ties.

Medical facilities

Medical and dental facilities are among the best in Europe. There are many new hospitals staffed by highly qualified doctors and nurses. A high percentage of the cost for this service is provided from private resources. In addition to the doctor's surgery, the chemist occupies a unique position in the medical hierarchy by providing remedies for simple ailments.

Crime

Spain does have a high petty crime rate. Homes have to be protected by security grilles on doors and windows. Cash, passports and electrical goods are the main targets. The theft of motor scooters is so high that insurance companies do not accept this risk. The police seem unable to reduce these incidents, so homeowners need to ensure protection of their property.

Pickpockets, operating in gangs, are active at all open-air markets, indoor markets and within some supermarkets, particularly when thronged with people during the busy summer season.

It is wrong to point the finger at any nationality, social or occupational group. While murder, bank robbery and crimes of passion are reported in the popular press these are a rarity. As long as sensible precautions are taken the streets of Spain are safe for both adults and children.

Red tape

Unfortunately Spain is a nation of bureaucrats. Red tape stifles simple daily transactions and frustrates all nationalities including Spaniards themselves. While it is not necessary to obtain permission to wallpaper a room, Spanish officialdom can be all pervasive. When something has to be done, approved or achieved it usually follows a standard pattern – fill in a form and get it approved. It all takes time.

First, there is a queue for the application form. Then a queue to hand it in, only to find the application is not valid unless accompanied by two other documents which can only be obtained from other departments in different parts of town. Once obtained, queue again only to discover that the application will not take effect until stamped by the head of department and they have gone home for the day.

The whole process is made more difficult by the opening hours of the little grilles behind which Spanish bureaucrats confront their public. Not only can the opening hours vary from department to department, but they are always as short as possible. Then there are fiestas, local and national holidays and … !

Culture

Festivals, cultural events and sports events crowd the Spanish calendar. Even small villages have at least one traditional fiesta, lasting a week or more, when parades, bull running and fireworks replace work. Rural and coastal towns celebrate their harvest or fishing catch with a gastronomic feast where local produce can be sampled with liberal quantities of wine. Music, dance and drama festivals are held in the major cities throughout the year. It is called Spanish culture. If however fireworks go off at midnight, a band is playing at four o'clock in the morning and all shops are unexpectedly closed due to a local holiday then patience, among other things, is required.

Manana

The last major downside of Spain is a feature called *manana* – never do something today if it can be put off to tomorrow, or the day after, or perhaps never to be done at all. To live successfully in Spain it is necessary to come to terms with its culture. Coping with *manana* is a necessary skill that just has to be acquired. It is most prevalent with builders, repairers, mechanics or indeed in any situation requiring a commitment to a time or date. A shrug of the shoulders, an upturned hand, a slight bow of the head, a moment of silence is *manana* in progress.

It is argued in large cities *manana* does not exist. They work as hard as their European counterparts. Builders work hard, for long hours with full order books. Supermarkets have extended opening hours. The old Spanish proverb 'It is good to do nothing and rest afterwards' (*es bueno descansar y no hacer nada despues*) is no longer applicable. All this is true, but somewhere, under the surface still lurks *manana*.

7
A ROOF OVER YOUR HEAD

WHERE TOURISTS STAY

Hotels

Tourism is a vital industry for Spain which has resulted in thousands of hotels of all grades. Hotels are government regulated. They must fulfil certain requirements according to their star rating. A five star hotel will have air conditioning and central heating in all public rooms and bedrooms and all bedrooms will have *en-suite* bathrooms. Three or four stars hotels are of a quality associated with package holidays. One and two-star hotels will have central heating but not all bedrooms will be *en-suite*.

An unusual fact! With the recent construction of four new macro hotels, Benidorm is currently third in Europe behind London and Paris in offering tourist accommodation rooms – and cheaper too. The newly opened Gran Hotel Bali is the tallest building in Spain at 210 metres and the tallest hotel in Europe.

Here are some useful hotel-related phrases:

- Do you have rooms? – *Hay habitaciones?*

- For an individual room ask for *una habitacion individual*. It may well be that there are two single beds in the room but the charge will only be for one.

- Intending to share a room? Ask for a *una habitacion doble*, which will be a room with two single beds.

- If you want a double bed, ask for *una habitacion con cama matrimonial* (a room with a double bed).

- A room with a bath is *una habitacion con bano*, and one with a shower is *una habitacion con ducha*.

Paradores

The Spanish tourist industry is proud of its unique network of 86 hotels called *Paradores*. They range from three- to five-star, the majority of which are restored historic monuments such as castles, monasteries, convents or palaces. Great care has been taken to preserve their decor and distinctive characteristics while converting them into high-quality modern hotels. Even the modern, purpose designed *Paradores* reflect regional styles and have unique decor and furnishings. Their restaurants too pride themselves on regional cuisine and wine. Travelling around Spain staying in *Paradores* is a special way of seeing the country.

- There is a high standard of service and cleanliness.

- The cuisine is excellent, normally to international standards and caters for all tastes.

- The buildings are usually interesting and the facilities are modern.

- They are frequently located in beauty spots off the beaten track.

- They are expensive.

Balneario (Spa)

There are numerous spas. They take you back to the last century with a leisurely way of life and treatments which range from a rest cure to a full twice daily programme controlled by doctors and staff. Fourteen of

Spain's 17 regions have spas. They can be like expensive hotels. *Te ensenamos el poder del agua thermal* (We teach you the power of the thermal waters).

The history of spas is interesting, for Spain was once rich in medicinal baths and spas, a strong Mediterranean tradition. Most have fallen into decay but a few of these ancient baths still survive in Granada, Jaen, Cordoba, Ronda and surprisingly in Gibraltar. The Moors still practise the art of bathing for pleasure in their home country Morocco with each town having several public baths known as *Hammans*. Of course it was these invaders who built and developed the spas of Spain.

Hostales and *pensiones*

These are usually defined by the letters *MS* or *P* on a blue background outside the establishment. They are more modest forms of accommodation, but like hotels they are graded according to the facilities offered. The star rating is based on facilities, so a two or three star hostel can be better in terms of furnishing than a low-rated hotel. *Hostales* and *pensiones* are good value for money.

Guesthouse

A basic form of accommodation, consisting of a room with only a simple bed and washbasin can be found in *fondas* or *casas de huespedes*, which are both forms of guesthouse or lodgings. They can be identified by signs with the letters *F* or *CM* in white letters on a blue background, and are usually to be found in the older sections of a town.

Farmhouses and cottages

This accommodation offers a chance to see rural life without losing the basic comforts of a hotel. The houses are not necessarily in the country – indeed, the majority are in villages. Government money has been granted for improving a home or a house not in use in order to make it suitable for receiving guests. This has the effect of conserving and modernising country dwellings and thus offering the possibility of holidays away from the traditional centres of tourist activity.

Wayside inns

Many wayside restaurants, often called *ventas*, have accommodation which they advertise with the sign *camas* (beds). If the sign is not visible, but the establishment looks large enough to have rooms above the restaurant ask: *Hay camas?* (Are there beds?). These places are useful on a long drive, if there is a need for a meal and an overnight stop without diverting to search in the nearest town or village.

Campsites

Spain has hundreds of registered campsites. These sites can be found close to major cities, next to beaches, by rivers and lakes and throughout the whole of Spain. Considering the range of facilities offered by most sites, camping is particularly good value. Prime sites have showers, launderette facilities, bars, restaurants, first aid/medical facilities, shops, swimming pool, telephone, post box, safes for valuables, electricity and water supply for caravans and a range of sporting facilities.

Off-site camping is permitted in Spain, subject to the permission of the landowner, but not in the mountains or on beaches.

Caves

Andalusia is home to thousands of cave dwellers. The structure of the rock at Guadix near Granada means caves can be excavated and turned into homes. They are not natural caves. Many have eight rooms, electricity supply, sewerage disposal, television and garage. They can be two floors high, converted into bars, restaurants, discos or churches. Caves are quiet, do not leak or collapse, have a constant temperature of 17 degrees all year round and can be easily modified.

Cave houses have become tourist attractions. Government subsidies are available to preserve them. Coach tours are commonplace. Rent-a-cave is a fact. *Cuevas Pedro Antonio de Alarcon* is a hotel cave complex in Guadix, with richly furnished rooms, all mod cons and excellent food.

A cave home can be bought and sold in the normal way. As the younger Spaniards leave a cave to work in the town or city, so demand has decreased and therefore cave houses are very cheap.

Timeshare

A classic timeshare investment is where the co-owner pays a sum of money which is an entitlement to use a specified property for a number of weeks at a certain time of year. Additionally there is an annual fee for the management and upkeep of the property. The main principal of timeshare is that it gives quality accommodation for less than the equivalent hotel rate.

It is however an industry that has a bad reputation for unscrupulous practices. This is changing. Spain introduced timeshare regulations in 1999. The highlights are:

- Restrictions on high pressure selling tactics in public places and tourist spots.

- Introduction of a cooling off period of 10 days during which the buyer can withdraw from the contract with no penalty.

- Written information must be supplied in the mother tongue of the buyer.

- Spanish law governs contract disputes.

Holiday homes

Anyone looking for a holiday home will invariably come across the town of Torrevieja the fastest expanding town in Spain where, since the mid 1980s houses have been built at a prodigious rate. In the last 10 years the town's registered population grew by a staggering 135%. In the next five years new homes are planned at the rate of 6,000 units per year. What is the attraction? Properties around Torrevieja are cheap, the climate excellent, and communications good. On the other hand there is a profusion of Irish bars and Chinese restaurants and it can be a bit tacky. In summer it is packed with people, the beaches are crowded and the restaurants full. In winter, the urbanisations are mostly uninhabited.

Holiday rental

There are many self-catering properties for rent in Spain. Properties have been built for that purpose and are available from absentee owners. They will mainly be apartments near the sea or near a golf course, or a villa in the mountains. Detached villas with a swimming pool or rustic country houses are also available through up-market letting agents.

Short-term holiday rental companies advertise their wares more effectively through websites rather than by thousands of very expensive brochures. Information can be assimilated very quickly making the web ideal for accessing the up-to-date availability of any holiday rental. Viewing the alternatives on a screen, checking price and availability, booking and paying by credit card are but a few clicks away. E-commerce is rapidly taking over as the most effective method of booking a holiday rental.

Holiday rental contracts are called *Arrienda de Temporada*. The property is furnished. The straightforward, standard contract is in Spanish or English. With a returnable deposit required to cover any damages caused by the temporary tenant, the contract is for a specific period of time at a stated price. The renewal of the contract is at the agent or landlord's discretion.

WHERE PROSPECTIVE EMPLOYEES STAY

Long-term property rental

Properties available for long-term rental are found mainly, but not exclusively, in a city. Long-term rentals can be found out of season in tourist areas. They can be furnished or unfurnished. It is an expensive method of accommodation. Over a five-year period it is generally cheaper to buy and then sell than it is to rent.

Like most countries, Spain has its letting law. It is called *Ley de Arrendamientos Urbanos* and commenced in 1995. The contract for a long-term rental is called *Arrienda de Vivienda*. The law provides for long-term rentals to be up to five years' duration, thus giving the tenant a degree of security. If the landlord offers a contract of three years' duration, which is accepted, and then the tenant wishes to stay on for another two years it is automatically renewed on the same terms. If the tenant wishes to leave after three years then the contract is terminated.

Annual rent increases in line with inflation take place during the contracted term. A new level of rent is set at the commencement of a new contract.

WHERE SPAIN'S NEW RESIDENTS STAY

Urbanisations

Spain is a land of urbanisations, which is a continental name for housing estates. They may line the beach, be in the country, attached to towns, villages or resorts, they may be on flat land, on hills or around sporting facilities such as golf courses. They can be high-density estates of identical white properties, or small individual developments of big detached houses spread over a hillside. More likely, they will be various combinations in between.

A property on an urbanisation is easy to buy and maintain having all the necessary facilities, ready-made social contacts and greater security than a detached home in a more remote location. Disadvantages can be the inflexible and restrictive community rules, difficult neighbours, a lack of privacy and a lack of control over the future of a development.

Life on an urbanisation can, however, be popular whatever the type of house. Sitting by the swimming pool meeting new friends, passing the time of day with a glass of wine in hand is an agreeable way of life. Little Spanish is spoken. Sharing experiences bonds the community together. Informal groupings take place. Golfing partners come together. Coffee mornings just happen. Family problems are shared. The siesta is forgotten as people assemble in the local bar to escape the searing heat of the afternoon sun. Life is easy. However it is very important for mind and body to stay active or a slow soporific mental decline may occur.

Some urbanisations are closed communities where people meet up at night and know each other's business. Others are less intrusive. Some are entirely of one nationality while others are more mixed. In some, most of the residents are elderly. Some urbanisations are a group of holiday homes scarcely having any permanent residents and becoming virtual ghost towns in winter. Standards of behaviour need to be set. An urbanisation is a community by itself, where the level is set by the standard of the lowest.

The prevalence of urbanisations is due to the popularity of living in planned communities that provide shared facilities such as swimming pools, on-site parking, maintenance, electronic entry and exit gates, cable television and year-round landscaping. Such communities, mostly of apartments, offer the newcomer from northern Europe a much easier lifestyle than buying and maintaining a private house and garden. Estate agents project their advertising to attract buyers, many of whom prefer these advantages plus the additional factor of being able to communicate easily with others of a similar background and shared language. Although urbanisations exist for Spaniards there is a tendency for each national group to congregate.

Community property

A community property is one that involves homes with a shared element. An example would be apartments or a grouping of individual homes. Urbanisations have a shared element in the swimming pool or gardens. Apartments have a shared element in the lift. Detached properties may have a shared access road.

The cost of maintaining these elements is shared between the owners. The most expensive shared element is normally a swimming pool, followed by gardens and satellite TV. Spanish town hall services are limited, with elements such as street cleaning part of the community costs.

A *comunidad de propietarios* can be run by an independent company on behalf of the owners or, in a well organised community, by the owners themselves. Germans have a talent for this, the Spanish an eye for detail, the Scandinavians laid back. The British and Irish seem happy to leave it to others. Annual meetings are certainly long and sometimes argumentative as many nationalities, resident and non-resident, seek to have a voice. There is a Spanish law that surrounds communities. It has a strange title – the Law of Horizontal Property.

By the sea

This is a pleasant experience with cool afternoon breezes taking the sting out of the searing summer heat. But nearly all Mediterranean towns are tourist areas. In July and August with temperatures around 30°C, people pour in on package holidays. Spaniards too have their summer holiday then, as they rush to the coast in their thousands from the torrid heat of the big cities. For two frustrating months beaches are packed, roads jammed, car parks full and tempers frayed.

Mention should be made of Spain's 'Law of the Coasts' which empowers local authorities to restrict the number, height and density of buildings within 100 metres of the high water mark and to establish a zone of influence as far inward as one kilometre. Despite this, properties continue to be built close to beaches. They do, however, command a hefty premium, the price only kept low by high density designs.

In the country

Living in the country has many attractions and is more like living in the real Spain. Large plots of land give peace, with privacy assured.

Neighbours, although far apart, are normally friendly. Some of these properties have no electricity, no water, no sewage disposal, no gas and no telephone. All can be compensated for by other means. Electricity can be supplied by a generator, or by solar panels. Water can be delivered by tanker or from a well. A septic tank takes care of sewage. Gas can be supplied in bottles. Communications can be by mobile or radio telephone and internet.

Many country properties are large and set in beautiful locations – often at the end of a pot-holed dirt track. When it rains the dirt track turns into mud and a 4x4 is necessary just to reach the house.

Inland

Living inland is a balance. It gives access to both coast and mountains; a view of the Med and the smell of the country. The best of both worlds, as many people are starting to realise. Inland properties normally cost less than coastal properties, but things are changing with inland property values now increasing at a faster rate as people discover the real secret of Spanish living.

What do people really buy?

People moving to Spain for the first time often purchase a new property near the coast from an international property company of some repute, giving a sense of security in a country where the customs and laws are unfamiliar to the purchaser. There may well be an 18-month wait for the property, which can be built to standard or individual design and is usually located on an urbanisation. This type of purchase is simple, with no debt issues to worry about. The property company is on hand to deal with any outstanding problems.

In many parts of the country a resale property is a common purchase. Slightly older properties in mature areas where new buildings are not so prevalent are an attractive proposition away from the concrete, the coastal hustle and bustle. People have in mind life in a rural town or on an individual plot thus avoiding the disadvantages of an urbanisation. They seek to blend into Spain.

Discerning buyers look for something unique, something different. They are in the minority. They know the country well. They understand its culture, customs and procedures. They may have lived in Spain for a few years or may be buying a second house inland. Buying a plot of land, a ruin for renovation or perhaps building your own, are all possibilities.

SELECTING THE CORRECT LOCATION

Although it is easy to choose a region of Spain that is attractive, deciding on a particular town, village, development or hillside involves a whole series of much more individual choices. The key to a successful property purchase is definitely its location. It is by far the most important decision to be made. Location will also be a major factor in the price paid for a property. A villa by a golf course will cost far more than an apartment inland.

Age comes into it too! A spectacular mountain track that provides the only access to a restored farmhouse may seem an attraction when in full health, but is not so good 20 years later in poor health. Access to public transport and medical services will become more important too and the closeness of other ex-pats, who were avoided in earlier years, may become more comforting.

Some basic questions have to be asked.

- How far away from the summer crowd do you really want to be? Tourist towns can become massively crowded. If you do not want this, look away from the beach and go inland. Most people find a 30-minute drive to a reasonably sized town convenient.

- You may wish your property to be close to local shops, bars and restaurants, public transport, a good beach, golf and other sports facilities, arts and entertainment.

- Is the choice city, rural life or perhaps Green Spain?

- Do you seek a remote location? This can be a problem. Where are the nearest bus, coach and train services? How good are the roads? How easy is it to connect to the motorway network?

- How many local facilities stay open in the winter? This is particularly important if you are considering moving to a tourist area where there is a great difference between high and low season.

- Is being close to beach and holiday entertainment important? If that's what you want, then look no further than the Mediterranean Costas and the two groups of islands, the Balearics and the Canaries.

- How much sun do you need? For reliable mainland sunshine stay south of Valencia or in the Canaries.

- How close to neighbours do you want to be? So many Spanish properties are in apartment blocks or on a high-density urbanisation. In some holiday home urbanisations, no neighbours exist at all for long periods.

- How close do you really want to be to compatriots? There are British communities that allow their inhabitants to isolate themselves from every aspect of Spanish life. On the other hand there are towns and villages just inland with smaller, more mixed, foreign communities.

- Do you have any special outside interests or hobbies and are they catered for in this location? What is the social life like in the area and will it suit you?

SELECTING THE TYPE OF ACCOMMODATION

Apartments

An apartment offers easy living in secure surroundings. Apartments are always built to a high standard with outside balconies included. Some economy flats exist where low cost living is a priority in large cities or for holiday rental. Apartments are cheap, easy to resell but often attract high community charges. Living in an apartment will probably mean Spanish neighbours. Nice people they may well be, but they tend to be noisy and have a different 'body clock' to other nationalities. Normal behaviour is to rise late, have lunch at 14.00, an evening meal at 21.00 and go to bed at midnight or after. Family discussion is often loud, very loud, Spanish voices having a unique ability to penetrate all bricks and mortar.

Linked, terraced and town houses

Some of the most attractive new designs are for linked and terraced houses. These houses are on two levels with a third floor roof utilised as a solarium. They too are cheap and easy to resell, but lack privacy. Town houses are available new, but can also be older, restored, traditional properties in the narrow streets of a Spanish town where car parking is a problem.

Corner properties

Corner housing is mostly found in a duplex design, but can also apply to single level homes. It is a cheap form of building having few external walls. Services, although individual to each home, do have some common elements. Corner duplexes are noisy, but they mainly function as holiday homes, with neighbours rarely meeting.

Detached

These properties offer privacy at the expense of security. They can be expensive. Built to an individual design they are sometimes perched precariously on hillsides, so much so that insurance companies charge a premium for cover. Windswept plots make dust a perpetual irritant. Even with some disadvantages a detached property is desirable, particularly one that overlooks the sea or the mountains or even a lush green golf course.

Traditional homes

Older Spanish properties exist. In most cases they have been modernised or rebuilt. In the country they are called *fincas*. In the town they are simply called town houses.

A restored town house is in many respects an ideal property since it gives easy access to a town with the benefits of living in new modern surroundings. Found in the narrow streets of small towns and villages these properties have a number of cool, shady rooms. Built on a slope they often have several floors, balconies and internal courtyards.

But the classic is a *finca rustica,* located in the country. It is where dreams are made. It can be a labour of love and a marriage of considerable skill, determination and money to rebuild an old, crumbling building and turn it into an individual property of pride and charm. Renovating a property, or indeed maintaining it, demands very good DIY skills. Living in a rural location needs patience, tolerance and enthusiasm.

New or resale?

Most people prefer to buy a new property. It can be good value. In some parts of Spain, an off-plan property is the only type available. It is rather like buying a car. Why buy second hand if you can buy new? A resale property is slightly more expensive: drives have been laid, gardens are mature and often furniture and fittings are included. A resale property built within the last ten years will still carry a guarantee.

8
EMPLOYMENT

MAKING A START

There has traditionally been a link between an employment contract and a job for life. This situation has changed dramatically in recent years during which Spain's labour problems have been exacerbated by the unions' uncompromising defence of rigid employment terms. Spain has the most rigid labour market in Europe and is a major headache to employers. In spite of an agreement reached between the employers and unions in 1997 when unions reduced their entitlement to redundancy payments in return for permanent contracts, employers still hire 90% of new employees on a temporary contract.

Spanish job centres are called *INEM* (*Instituto Nacional de Empleo*). *INEM* operates 700 offices throughout Spain advertising both local and national positions. Vacancies in the local area are advertised on a bulletin board, together with some national positions requiring experience, training or qualifications. *INEM* offices provide a comprehensive career resource library including Spanish company listings, trade publications and a wide range of reference books. In addition to offering a job placement service, *INEM* also provides assistance to those wishing to start a business or be self-employed.

The most important requirement for anyone seeking employment or planning to set up a business is the ability to speak good Spanish. Regional languages and dialects cause problems for foreigners and Spaniards alike, but if seeking to earn money, learning the language *Castellano*, or a regional variation, is the only option. Lack of a second language restricts business opportunities to the English speaking community. While English may be the language of international business, dealing with Spanish people or fitting into a multi-lingual work environment requires an ability to converse in Spanish. Working in Spain for a multinational company, a UK company, or for one whose name is recognisable worldwide, can offer security. However teams of Spanish nationals run Spanish branches of multinational companies and most of the work is conducted in their language. There is a need to fit in.

WORK PERMIT

For European Union nationals

An EU national does not require a permit to enter Spain for work. Enter Spain as a tourist, register with the Spanish national employment office *INEM* and then you have 90 days to find employment. It is possible to obtain an extension after that date or leave Spain and re-enter for a further 90 days. Once a job is secured, an employment contract is necessary to apply for a *residencia* (residence card). In fact it is a *tarjeta comunitaria* which is a combined work permit and *residencia*. It also comes with a *NIE* (*Numero de Identificacion de Extranjero*, see page 148 for more details). Surprisingly this is provided by an employer.

For non-EU nationals

A non-EU foreigner who wishes to work in Spain must obtain a visa before moving to Spain. Work permits can be obtained from the Foreigners' Office (*Oficinas de Extranjeros*) or the provincial office of the Ministry of Labour (*Delegacion Provincial del Ministerio de Trabajo*), if the foreign applicant is on Spanish territory. The Provincial labour offices

(*Direciones Provinciales de Trabajo, Seguridad Social y Asuntos Sociales*) decide whether a work permit will be issued. If the foreign applicant is not in Spain the work permit is obtained from the Consular office of the applicant's home country at the same time as obtaining a visa.

WHICH JOB?

Casual and seasonal work

This type of work is ideal for anyone who has not yet firmed up a long-term life plan, or who seeks a few euros while enjoying life in the sun. It is not too easy to come by, involves asking around and may need personal recommendation. Casual work is more likely to be found in tourist regions where there is a seasonal demand for labour. It is likely to be paid in cash by an employer not wishing to incur any social security costs. When business demand is low there is no work, but the employer will be happy to welcome the employee back when tourists return.

It can be easy to get carried away by the seemingly casual lifestyle, a laid-back approach and amicable sales methods in tourist areas, but remember it is profit and customer service that count. Don't assume that working for an English-speaking northern European gives added security. Spain is full of ex-pats who for one reason or another have decided to make a living running a bar or shop where business is often fragile or seasonal.

Examples of casual or seasonal work are:

- Villa servicing and cleaning.

- Promotional work.

- Nursing and auxiliary nursing in hospitals, clinics and nursing homes.

- Bar, restaurant and hotel work.

- Holiday rep with a major tourist company. This is one of the best sources of seasonal work for foreigners. Competition for jobs is fierce and some Spanish fluency is usually necessary. Most companies have an age requirement.

Part-time and full-time work

For someone staying long term, some help may be found from the few, relatively new, employment agencies, but asking around is also essential. Without a command of the language, employment is again restricted to holiday regions. Procedures for finding a job are exactly the same as back home. Starting points include newspaper adverts, employment agencies, direct contact with companies, word of mouth and personal contact. A good CV in English and Spanish to sell your skills is helpful. Working full- or part-time involves a different working day, correct business etiquette, payment of social security and income tax. Examples are;

- Office work.

- English type supermarkets.

- Journalism and advertising with local English newspapers and magazines.

- Teaching English.

- Working in an estate agent's office.

- People who are fluent in Spanish and English can find work in the major cities as translators where the task involves business correspondence or assisting northern Europeans with some Spanish paperwork, or even at police stations on busy market days where petty theft is common and an interpreter necessary.

British entertainers often joke about a lack of motivation and an authoritarian style while working for Spanish employers. Other people question the less than democratic skills and employment practices of Spanish companies. 'Unquestionably sharp' is a phrase often used to describe abuse of employment contracts in a situation where an unsuspecting foreigner does not fully understand employment law.

Professional qualifications

Professionals whose training consisted of at least three years' degree level education plus job-based training, require their qualifications to be recognised, subject to any professional codes and limitations in force. For example a doctor must have his qualifications accepted by the medical college of the province where he intends to practise. He must also show that he is in good standing with the professional authorities in his country of origin.

All EU member states issue occupation information sheets containing a common job description with a table of qualifications. These cover a large number of trades and are intended to help someone with the relevant qualifications looking for employment in another EU country. A starting point for information regarding the official validation of qualifications and addresses of Spanish professional bodies is obtainable from the education department of Spanish consulates.

Teaching

Staying long term in Spain? Then the chances of finding teaching work are considerably better than any other profession, although this obviously depends on qualifications and experience. Teaching English is big business. Spanish nationals wish to have a second language. For commercial reasons it has to be English. There is a constant demand for teachers. People with Teaching English as a Foreign Language (TEFL) qualification or English as a Second Language (ESL) certificate can find a job quite easily. Where demand outstrips supply in the big cities, a graduate native English speaker can get a job without other qualifications. Some of the opportunities are:

- Private language schools in Spain offer English classes for both adults and children.

- English teachers and teachers employed in language schools supplement their income by giving private lessons.

- The British Council in Madrid recruits English language teachers and supervisory staff for two-year placements in its language centres in Barcelona, Bilbao, Granada, Las Palmas, Madrid, Oviedo, Palma de Mallorca, Segovia, Seville and Valencia.

- Being a Language Assistant enables students from Britain and more than 30 other countries to spend a year working in a school or college in Spain, assisting language teachers.

CONTRACT OF EMPLOYMENT

Spanish employees now have an affluent lifestyle compared to their parents in the 'Years of Hunger' They enjoy high salaries (particularly executives and senior managers) and good working conditions. Women have professional and wage equality with men, although they still fill most low-paid jobs. Employment security has been eroded in recent years with an increasing number of workers employed on short-term contracts giving some flexibility in the labour market. Some low-paid people hold down two jobs, rather like their civil service forefathers in the 1960s.

Although employment conditions vary throughout Europe the main area for comparison lies in salary level, fringe benefits and job security. Spanish employees are near the bottom of the European earnings league but good fringe benefits, lots of holidays, job security and strong protection under dismissal legislation are undoubted plus factors.

Spain has lost more production days due to strikes in the last 15 years than any other country in the EU. Contrary to the UK, the government can enforce an imposed settlement if a strike impairs public services or disrupts important sectors of the economy. Employees are guaranteed the right to strike under law and cannot be dismissed for striking.

The contract

Employees in Spain, like other parts of Europe, have an employment contract (*contrato de trabajo*), stating details such as job title, salary, working hours, fringe benefits and terms of employment. There are three types of employment contract:

- An indefinite term contract.

- A short-term temporary contract for a specific duration and reason. For example a contract for a specific project or service, or for six months to deal with peak demand, or to substitute for another employee entitled to return to work.

- A verbal or written contract for casual or seasonal work which has few legal rights.

All employment contracts are subject to Spanish labour law and references may be made to other regulations such as collective agreements. Anything in a contract contrary to the statutory provisions and unfavorable to an employee is deemed to be null and void. If there is no written contract, the law assumes a verbal agreement is for one year. At the end of that year, or at any other time, the employer can dismiss the worker, giving at least seven days' notice and paying seven days' salary for each full year worked.

Salary

A salary is stated in the employment contract together with any salary reviews, planned increases and cost of living reviews. Salaries can be paid weekly, fortnightly or monthly, by cash or into a bank account. A pay slip itemising salary and deductions is issued. Spain has a minimum wage. At around 3€ per hour it is a meaningless figure in the labour market, useful only to trade unions seeking a marker for annual wage increases.

Extra Months' salary and bonuses

Employers in Spain pay their employees two extra months' salary – one in July before the annual summer holiday and the other in December – which are intended to ensure that employees have extra money for their summer and Christmas holidays. Taking statutory, local fiesta days and annual holidays into account Spanish employees get 14 months' salary for 10 months' work.

Working hours

The standard working week in Spain is 40 hours. The average with overtime is around 42 hours. Working hours vary dependant on the type of work and the time of year. The standard working day is from 9.30 to 13.30 and from 16.30 until 20.30; although from June and September it may be continuous from 7.00 to 15.00 with a short break for lunch. In line with their European counterparts many companies now operate from 8.30 or 9.00 to 17.30 or 18.00. There are no scheduled coffee breaks but it's common for office workers in a town or city to pop out for breakfast or a cup of coffee, twice a day during business hours.

Overtime

Overtime is not compulsory and cannot exceed 80 hours a year. It must be paid at a premium of not less than 40% of the normal hourly rate and 100% for Sunday and statutory holidays. Employees are not obliged to work on Sundays unless a collective agreement states otherwise, although when an employee agrees to work on a Sunday, normal overtime rates are applicable. Overtime may be compensated for by time off rather than extra pay, providing there is a written agreement to that effect.

Social security

All employers and their employees, including foreign, temporary and permanent employees, must contribute to the Spanish social security system (*seguridad social*). Social security for employees covers health care (including sickness and maternity leave), injuries at work, unemployment insurance, retirement benefit, invalidity and death benefit. Pension benefit starts only after 15 years' contribution. Unemployment benefit is paid if someone has worked for at least one year during the last six years and has registered with the *INEM* within 15 days of unemployment.

There are special social security programmes for agricultural workers, seamen, self-employed workers, civil servants and military personnel, coal miners and students. For everybody else there is a general social security programme where people are classified under a number of professional categories in order to determine their social security contribution. Payment is based on a *nomina*, the official salary for a classification of work with the employee's contribution deducted at source by the employer. Social security contributions by the employee are around 5% and the employer 23%.

Spain has treaty agreements with other countries ensuring someone who has worked in two or more countries does not retire with a pension deficit. These agreements ensure the total number of years paid into social security systems in the various countries are added together to enable the employee to qualify for a pension which is paid proportionally by each country.

Public holidays

The government allows 14 national and local public holidays a year. Of these, two are regional or municipal holidays celebrating dates of local importance. All public offices, banks and post offices are closed on public holidays. In addition most regions and towns have their own carnival and fiesta days.

Annual holidays

Under law a full-time employee is entitled to a minimum of 23 working days (one month) paid annual holiday. When both annual and public holidays are taken into account Spain has the greatest number of holidays of any EU country. August is the traditional month for summer holidays with many businesses closing down entirely. Some businesses close for two weeks over Christmas and New Year, and many restaurants in holiday areas close for the month of February.

Dismissal and redundancy

In addition to reasons such as mutual agreement, death, expiration of the contractual term and retirement, an employment contract can be terminated for technological and economic reasons and for objective or disciplinary reasons.

An employee can be made redundant on technological and economic grounds only in relation to the collective restructuring of a company's workforce. Technological and economic causes are legally defined terms when the employer may decide dismissal unilaterally. Termination of employment due to redundancy attracts generous compensation. Eight days' pay for each year worked under temporary contracts and 33 days' pay per year for indefinite term contracts. If a company goes bankrupt, employees are entitled to 20 days' pay for each year of service.

Objective reasons for dismissal include employee ineptitude and an inability to adapt to technological change. Legal grounds for dismissal for disciplinary reasons include insubordination or disobedience, repeated absenteeism or lateness, physical or verbal abuse, fraud, disloyalty, poor performance, working for a third party without the consent of the employer and habitual drug or alcohol abuse.

An employee dismissed for objective or disciplinary reasons may challenge the decision in the labour courts. Equally an employee can leave and seek compensation if they feel an employer has not held to the terms of a contract. Disputes about these matters are taken to the *Magistratura de Trabajo*, the labour court, who will arbitrate and make judgment accordingly.

BLACK ECONOMY

Illegal working is common in Spain and neighbouring Morocco. The black economy (*economia sumergida*) accounts for a significant proportion of the country's generated wealth. What causes this situation?

- Influxes of illegal Moroccan immigrants seeking to better themselves in Spain are keen to accept low cash payments for unskilled work. It is illegal for non-EU nationals, such as Moroccans, to work in Spain without a work permit (the application is made by the employer). Unscrupulous employers bypass this procedure and use this labour, paying low wages for long hours in poor working conditions. This occurs in industries traditionally employing casual labour such as building, farming and food services.

- Illegal working avoids payment of additional costs (particularly social security and *IVA* (VAT) payments). This can make the difference between a fair product price and one too expensive or the difference between profit and loss.

- Many casual, seasonal workers (or indeed full time workers) choose to work illegally. They do not pay tax or social security contributions, and while there is no entitlement to state benefits for work injury, health care, unemployment benefit or pension, this is viewed as a small penalty for failure to pay social security contributions.

HAVING YOUR OWN BUSINESS

Spain is traditionally a country of small companies and sole traders. There are nearly two million families running businesses employing about 75% of the working population. The majority of businesses established by foreigners in Spain are linked to leisure and catering or to property sales. Why? Low entry cost and providing a service in one's mother tongue are key factors. People choose to be self-employed for the lifestyle and freedom it affords, but small businesses in Spain often exist on a shoestring with their owners working extremely long hours, particularly those running bars or restaurants. Many foreigners start businesses in Spain with little research, little business acumen, no knowledge, no capital and no linguistic ability. It is asking for trouble.

The first step is to conduct appropriate market research to establish whether there is a real need for a business in the area, and secondly to check that all necessary licences for the proposed venture actually exist or can be obtained. These could include the Opening Licence and, if appropriate, a licence for serving food (see pages 115–116 for more details). The purchase of an existing business to be run exactly as before will not require a new opening licence, but if the nature of the business is changed, a new one is required.

Before establishing a business, it is important to talk to a number of people to obtain legal advice and to take advantage of any tax benefits or grants. This advice is usually obtained from a lawyer (*abogado*) or an accountant (*asesor fiscal*).

POPULAR BUSINESSES

Bars, cafés and restaurants

Many people dream of running a bar or a restaurant in the sun. Some have been successful, but for every successful catering establishment there are many more that have ruined their owners. Competition is fierce. The hours in the height of the tourist season are very long. A normal bar or restaurant in the summer months will be open until the small hours of the morning and then be open again for lunch the next day, seven days a week. In peak season it cannot close for even a day since its customers will go elsewhere. A catering business also suffers from world events, disasters, climate and the economy.

Computer sales and service

While most people use computers, few know what to do when problems arise. Many ex-pats need an English-speaking expert to sort it out; someone to stop computers crashing, get our programs running smoothly and somewhere to buy bits and pieces including user friendly English language software. Anyone skilled in graphic design can also find a niche for web design and short-run print work – advertising, posters, banners, flyers, programmes, menus, invitations, etc.

Construction work

Painting and decorating, plumbing, building, carpentry and similar skills are in demand from ex-pats who want to use the services of tradesmen to whom they can describe the required task without any language problems. Many offer their services as part of the 'black economy' and are paid in cash. However, moving into large contracts will mean dealing with a different customer base – people who want IVA receipts to reduce their liability to income tax.

Estate agents

Opening an estate agency business is easy. Unlike many other European countries, the estate agency market in Spain is not regulated. There are many people working in Spain in real estate without any background or qualifications, although some are registered through a professional association. A booming property market means a very good standard of living. On the debit side it is a results-orientated business with a hard-sell approach and a poor reputation.

Hairdressing

Good hairdressing and beauty salons flourish. Many women go to a hairdresser on a regular basis, preferably to one where they can at least chat to the operator. Hairdressers offering additional beauty treatments have an advantage. Independent mobile hairdressers can also make a good living.

Hotels, guesthouses and B&B

This is yet another area where people dream of having a successful business in the sun. With a good establishment, in a good location, look at a capital cost of one million euros. Too much? Compromise on location by going to the country and renovating a ruin! Income from a modernised premises is only 50€ per night for a double room. The holiday season is short, so the room-occupancy rate is only 25% over the year. Most visitors to the coast will rent an apartment or stay in a budget hotel on a package holiday. Guesthouse and B&B demand is mainly in the inland areas for independent travellers where it would be unusual for guests to stay more than two or three days before moving on unless the location had something really special to offer.

Kennels and catteries

While finding the right premises may be difficult, demand is high. If someone wishes to go on holiday or back to the UK to visit friends and family – where does the dog or cat go? People who live in Spain welcome a good English-run kennel or cattery for their animals. Opening a kennel or cattery means a place in the country, but a word of caution – just because a person has bought land in the country does not give them a right to open a business. Planning permission is necessary.

Property management

This covers property cleaning, pool maintenance and gardening. This is relatively low paid, unskilled and seasonal, but if correctly managed can be a successful business.

Satellite television installation

This is one business where there is little Spanish competition – the language barrier in reverse. Demand for English language TV is high – or to be more direct, demand for a SKY package is high. While new urbanisations and apartments have communal satellite receivers, there is demand from owners of individual properties.

Shops and boutiques

Selling the right product in the right area can be very successful. Examples are a flower shop, an English bookshop, a butcher, a small supermarket with British products and second-hand furniture shop.

WORKING ON YOUR OWN

An EU national

EU nationals can now work in Spain without any restriction. They can work under the same conditions as Spaniards, the only thing they are required to do is to obtain their residence card (see Chapter 11).

A non-EU foreigner

Non-EU autonomous workers must have the required residence permit and work permit. Non-EU residents in Spain with a work permit and an employment contract cannot re-establish themselves to work on their own account until they obtain a corresponding work permit.

BUYING AN EXISTING BUSINESS

It is easier to buy an existing business than it is to start a new one. Taking over an established business is less of a risk than starting something new. Buying an existing business that is profitable is not easy. Most people do not sell a thriving business without good reason. Traditional Spanish businesses are usually passed down within the family.

- What is the reason for selling? Is there a hidden motive?

- Check at the local planning office for any development that may affect the business.

- Have two independent valuations been obtained?

- Make sure sales turnover and profit claims can be substantiated, while accepting the declared turnover for tax purposes is usually lower than actual turnover.

- Remember when buying a business property in Spain, all debts against the property are automatically transferred to the new owner.

- It is important to obtain all necessary licences and approvals before signing any lease or purchase contract, or alternatively that such leases and contracts are signed subject to the licences and approvals being obtained.

- Never sign anything that is not fully understood.

LEASEHOLD OR FREEHOLD?

Business premises are most commonly purchased as leasehold because it is easy to terminate the lease if required. Buying freehold (purchasing a property) may be worthwhile for a secure business venture. Some contracts offer leasehold with a view to purchase which allows the buyer to agree a price with the vendor at the start of a lease.

A Spanish lease is known as a *cesion*. The landlord owns the shell of the building for which they receive a fee and a monthly rent, but the tenant owns everything else. The lease can be anything from five to 25 years or for an indefinite period. However, five to 10 years is a normal lease period.

Lease agreements have no set formula. The exact lease terms are stated in the contract. During the agreed period of lease, rent can only be increased by the annual cost of living index. The leaseholder is responsible for services such as electricity, water, personal taxes and social security payments. *IBI* (a local tax) must be paid by the landlord.

In the UK, a leaseholder is responsible for the full term of the lease regardless of what happens. In Spain only two months' notice is required to terminate a lease. A landlord cannot terminate a lease for any reason other than non-payment of rent.

The cost of leasehold comprises a one off, up front fee, for which a 10% deposit will be required and the balance is usually payable in 30–60 days. The rules are similar to buying a property – should the potential leaseholder default the deposit is lost. Upon completion the landlord must be paid a security deposit of two months' rent with further rent instalments paid monthly in advance. A normal business transfer will cost 1,250€ for legal fees which includes preparation of a new lease contract, licence transfers and census registrations.

STARTING A NEW BUSINESS

What type of company?

A self-employed person (*trabajador autonomo*) or a sole trader (*empresa individual*) does not have the protection of a limited company should the business fail. It may be advantageous to operate as a limited company but 'limited companies' cannot be purchased off the shelf. A *gestor* (a person who specialises in dealing with administrative and legal work) can do this, but it usually takes some time.

A business may assume various legal titles. Most small business people operate as sole traders and must register with the appropriate trade association, pay a small joining fee and a monthly subscription. They are taxed as an individual. A small company is usually a private limited company (*Sociedad de responsabilidad Limitada*) designated *SL*. It is the simplest and most common form of limited company, does not have any public shares and is subject to corporate taxation. A large limited company is a public company (*Sociedad Anonima*) designated *SA* which is similar to a British Plc or an American Inc. To form an *SA* requires significant share capital, at least 50 employees and one director.

In order to create a new business entity the most important prerequisite is patience. It is necessary to visit a range of offices and officials. The hurdles are too great for some, so 40% of businesses remain unlicensed. There is little doubt setting up a company is a specialised task – even a small *SL*. It is important to appoint someone who has experience in doing it. The core document is a Deed of Incorporation which must be signed before a Notary (see page 171 for more information on *Notarios*). However, registration of the company name, registration at the tax office and payment of share capital deposit into a bank account, are all necessary before a business is up and running.

Business considerations

• Is there a business plan in existence?

• Most people are too optimistic about the prospects of a new business.

- Lack of capital is the most common reason for business failure.

- All banks are wary of lending to a new business.

- Borrowing money? Is it the euro, the dollar or the pound?

- When starting a retail business, people traffic is governed by location.

- Is access to motorways and rail links important?

- Is access to a popular tourist area or local attractions important?

- Are any housing developments or new shopping centres planned nearby?

Grants

Investment incentives are available from the Spanish government and the EU. Incentives include investment subsidies, tax relief, low-interest or interest-free loans, social security rebates and reduced local taxes during the start-up period. There are also regional government incentives for investment in economic promotion zones, declining industrial zones and urgent re-industrialisation zones.

LEGAL REQUIREMENTS

Opening licence

A business having premises such as a shop, workshop or offices, requires an opening licence (*licencia de apertura*) from the local town hall before starting. For a new building it is necessary to employ the services of an architect to submit a project to the town hall. The council will visit the premises to make sure that they fulfil all legal and sanitary obligations, but it is not unusual to take six months before examining a project and issuing a licence. Many people operate on the basis of a stamped application for a *licencia de apertura*. This is usually tolerated by the authorities.

If a business is likely to inconvenience the local community, such as noise from a bar or discotheque, the council will insist on certain requirements before granting an opening licence. A licence application is not necessary if the business premises are to be used for the same purpose as previously. The serving of alcohol and food also requires a health licence.

A licence issued for a business owned by a non-EU national may be conditional on the employment of a minimum number of EU citizens. A non-EU citizen wishing to start a business in Spain must also make an investment of around 120,000€ in order to be granted a work permit.

Special authorisation

To be able to carry out certain business activities it is necessary to obtain other relevant authorisation. This will depend on which sector a company is going to operate within. For example, in order to be able to open a bar, restaurant or hotel an authorisation from the Delegation of the General Directorate of Tourism in the region where the business activity is going to be performed must be obtained. There are also several regulated activities which require additional approval, such as travel agencies, security and toxic substances storage.

Building work

When work must be carried out on premises or land where the business activity is going to take place the relevant Works Licence (*Licencia de Obras*) must be requested from the town hall. Details required include the plans, relevant application form, layout and sketch of the project, description of the works to be carried out and its total valuation.

Declaration of opening a workplace

The opening of the workplace must be declared to the labour authorities – *Declaracion de Apertura del Centro de Trabajo* within 30 days following the commencement of a business activity. The official form obtained at the *Direccion Provincial del Ministerio de Trabajo y Seguridad Social* gives information about the company, employees and activity.

Social security

All self-employed people, even those who work part time, must contribute to the social security system. Not only are social security contributions under this scheme higher than for employees, there are also fewer benefits. There are various levels of social security payable, depending on the size of pension on retirement and if aged over 50. The *autonomo* scheme will cost a minimum of around 230€ per month.

Impuesto sobre Actividades Economicas (IAE)

All self-employed people and businesses must register at the *Hacienda* (equivalent to Inland Revenue) to pay a tax known as *IAE*. It is payable if business turnover exceeds 600,000€ per year and is a tax on economic activities. The high sales threshold is designed to help small and medium businesses.

Impuesto sobre el Valor Anadido (IVA)

All self-employed people and businesses must register for valued added tax (*IVA*) and levy this tax on all services or goods.

Taxation

Small businesses pay an estimated quarterly tax with a refund made or an additional payment demanded at the end of the tax year. Limited companies must file corporate tax returns to the provincial tax headquarters in the area where the business is registered. Various returns must be made including corporation tax, personal income tax and value added tax. Procedures for keeping the books are also defined.

9

GETTING THE FACTS ON RETIREMENT

No one can offer a blueprint for perfect retirement. Life's experience, knowledge, preferences, capabilities and what is expected from retirement are some factors to be considered. It is a period of change, a transition from one stage of life to another. At retirement people are faced with a change of role, responsibility, relationships, ways to use time, challenges to personal philosophy and changes in financial position. The major changes can be summarised as income, health and lifestyle.

PLANNING YOUR INCOME

Sources of income at retirement are usually:

- State retirement pension;
- Company and personal pensions;
- Investments and savings.

State retirement pension

The UK state retirement pension is made up of the following components:

- Basic pension.
- Graduated pension.
- Additional pension.
- SERPS – State Earnings Related Pension.
- Any extra pension for dependents.

The size of pension depends on the contributions made to the National Insurance Scheme during a person's working life in the UK and how many of those years were qualifying years. Retirement pensions are paid to beneficiaries at the rate prevailing in the UK if resident in Spain, although this is not the case with all countries.

Company and personal pensions

The principal of pensions is straightforward, but constant changes in the law have allowed a greater number of options. In an occupational pension one or more parties have invested money over a number of years. The pension is paid out, usually with an inflation element, according to the rules of the scheme as set by the trustees, based on final salary and the number of years in the scheme.

Annuities however are a bit more complicated. An annuity is a regular income bought with a lump sum. In the last 10 years annuity rates have fallen by 50%. They are based on the average life expectancy and long term yields on government bonds. Life expectancy has increased and yields have fallen which is bad news for annuities.

There are three types of annuity. Level annuities are paid at the same amount each year, but the purchasing power is eroded by inflation. Escalating annuities ratchet up by a set percentage each year, but the bigger the escalation, the lower the income to start with. Lastly, index linked annuities can follow routes such as the Retail Price Index. Recent changes in UK pension law have allowed greater flexibility with regard to annuities.

Some pensions are best left alone. Some better converted to annuities. A flexible pension, taken out in the later years of life according to one's need is excellent. A choice of pension is a major decision. Once done, that is it, for the rest of your life.

One final thought. 'People need to appreciate that they cannot work from 25 to 55 then live the life of Riley to 95,' so stated the Chairman of the National Association of Pension Funds. He may be right, or he may be wrong. Appendix 4 provides a template for a do-it-yourself ready reckoner to calculate income before and after retirement.

Investments and savings

Investments are more flexible, although each one should be entered into with a long-term strategy. Investments are about risk, with risk being relative to each person. Reward follows risk. It is the law of economics.

Risk can be categorised, ranging from low to high, but most investments focus on geographical, sectional and equity risk. Geographical risk involves a part of the world such as the UK, Europe, or the USA. Sectional risk involves investing in a sector such as technology, retail, or food. Equity risk relates to the investment type such as bonds, shares or unit trusts.

At the lower end of the risk ladder are building societies, corporate bonds and government stocks. Going up the risk ladder are tracker funds that mirror stock exchange performance and shares in companies. Near the top are overseas investments or themed investments such as technology stocks. At the top are volatile futures dealings.

Inheritance trusts

Protection from taxation and inheritance legalisation can be achieved by setting up an offshore trust fund which initially sounds expensive and complex, but in practice can be achieved simply by organisations specialising in this type of work. Protection of a Spanish property from inheritance tax is not possible under a trust.

Getting professional advice

Financial advisers based in the UK may be independent and able to choose from any company's services. They may be tied agents who only offer the range of products from the investment house that employs them. Insurance companies too have their representatives, but they may also employ others on a freelance basis to represent their products.

In most European countries these agents will be members of a recognised professional organisation, be independent and subject to legal scrutiny. Before choosing an adviser, do they know about Spain, Spanish taxation, offshore investments, and Spanish inheritance tax? If not then find an alternative adviser. It is a waste of time undertaking financial planning embracing the laws of another country when it is the laws of Spain that have to be understood.

Spanish financial advisers are not as well regulated as those in other countries. They even sell their 'own label' products. It does not mean they are bad. It simply means that one has to be that little bit more cautious when dealing with money matters in Spain. When dealing with investments, the quickest way to double your money is to fold it in half, put it back in your pocket and not to be seduced by newspaper advertisements offering exceptionally high returns.

Investing offshore

The term 'offshore' has no legal definition.The reference to offshore infers that private investors are making financial transactions in a jurisdiction different from their normal residence for tax purposes. It is thought that half of the world's capital is invested within International Offshore Financial Centres also known as tax havens.

The best-known close offshore centres are the Isle of Man, Jersey, Guernsey, and Gibraltar. Land-based popular offshore centres are Luxembourg, Switzerland and Liechtenstein. The more distant well-known offshore tax havens are Bermuda, Bahamas, and British Virgin Islands. There are more than 50 well-established international tax havens.

Why invest offshore? The most common reason for private investors to place capital offshore is to reduce income tax. Banks and financial institutions invariably pay less tax in respect of subsidiaries based in offshore locations. For example, identical insurance investment funds based in London and the Isle of Man would not perform the same. This is because UK based companies deduct tax at source on income and make allowances for capital gains tax on unrealised gains. The same fund located offshore would suffer little or no tax.

A word of warning! The law of Europe is changing. Offshore banks are now obliged to disclose any interest gained in bank accounts to the tax authorities in the country where the account holder resides. Luxembourg is exempt from this legislation for a number of years. It is speculation that further legislation may occur limiting the benefits of offshore investments.

KEEPING HEALTHY

Physical health

An individual is responsible for his or her own health and the need to maintain it. Fitness is how efficiently the heart works, how strong muscles are and how easy it is to bend and stretch.

- Can you walk uphill or run for a bus without getting out of breath?
- Can you walk up two flights of stairs or carry a load of shopping home without getting tired?

- Can you bend down to weed the garden or reach up to clean the windows without difficulty?

- Is your body mass index in the range 20–25? For the uninitiated the index is calculated by dividing body weight in kilogrammes by height in metres squared.

It's never too late to start getting more exercise. Get moving, move a little more, build up gradually and keep it going. Exercise does not have to be physical jerks or jogging in a tracksuit. Do something enjoyable. Walking and swimming are very good non-impact exercises.

There's no shortage of advice about what to eat and what not to eat. The guidelines are clear. Cut down on fat, sugar and salt. Eat lean meat, fish and fibre with plenty of fresh fruit and vegetables. But knowing it is one thing, doing it is another as we learn our eating habits very early in life.

Mental health

To keep happy we probably need to be with other people at least some of the time, to be involved in warm and friendly relationships, to have someone to talk to and to play a part in what's going on inside the family and the community. As we get older it becomes more important to think about maintaining and strengthening friendships, keeping in touch with people we like and making opportunities for meeting new friends.

Stress and strain can spoil happiness. Losing a close friend or relative, losing a job, or changing familiar surroundings can make people ill. We can't avoid stress. What we can do is be aware of how we react to it, notice our own warning signals, and take some positive action to keep it in check.

It's important in retirement to maintain a sense of purpose. Motivation for working – whatever that may have been – at least gave a sense of purpose. Transferring energies towards enjoyable activities, or new commitments, is a way of maintaining that sense of purpose.

NEW LIFESTYLE

Men and women have traditionally followed different life and career patterns. Retirement of one partner needs to be thought about in terms of how the relationship will be affected by this change. Each person's expectations may be different.

Whether the choice is early retirement, voluntary redundancy or retirement at the normal age or unexpectedly being in this situation there is a number of issues to explore. Any change in personal circumstances presents an opportunity positively to reassess lifestyle. To stagnate or to go forward is the choice.

FREQUENCY OF MOVING HOUSE

In affluent countries most people entering retirement find their income and physical capabilities are reduced. These changes alter housing requirements and preferences. Men who attain 85 years of age on average move 1.06 times after their 55th birthday and women 1.14 times. While most are local moves, a minority are long-distance changes.

Since the 1920s retirement migrations have become commonplace and have passed through several phases. During the 1930s and 1950s, railway-influenced holiday destinations guided retirement moves from the UK's large cities to numerous resorts in Devon, Dorset, Somerset, Sussex, Kent, Essex, Lancashire, Yorkshire and North Wales. From the 1960s the destinations favoured unspoilt market towns and well-serviced villages in Dorset, the Cotswolds, Central Wales and most recently to Lincolnshire and Yorkshire. In the 1990s the choice was resort and rural settings in France, Spain and other southern European countries.

Some reasons for staying put

If you enjoy your home, it fits your needs and you can afford it, then why move? If you stay in a place where you have friends, neighbours and children living close by and you know your way around, then why move? If the facilities and services are good, then why move? After all, moving is a lot of trouble and expense.

Some reasons for moving

If your house is too big, too expensive, or the capital tied up in it could provide income if invested, then consider moving. If the area is deteriorating or the community does not offer social, cultural and physical activities and lacks services, then consider moving. If your health would benefit from warm sunshine, then move. If your children and friends have moved away, then why stay?

Who buys a home abroad?

A wide range of people buy a home in the sun, particularly if it is near an airport, faces the sea or a golf course and the area has plenty of facilities. If it is a permanent retirement home then the average profile is of a couple, mid-fifties and upwards, whose children have flown the nest. At least one partner will be an extrovert capable of dealing with the upheaval and change, so together they can look forward to their golden years with some enthusiasm. The responsibilities of children, grandchildren and elderly parents are issues that have been dealt with.

Moving abroad is a challenge, an adventure, a new culture and a different lifestyle. As life expectancy increases moving abroad is now commonplace. In the last 20 years the number of retirees living abroad has doubled. However the number of people from the UK retiring to Spain has doubled in the last ten years.

Most people who retire abroad are fully fit, active and in possession of all their faculties. Unfortunately as age increases health may fail and we become partly dependant or totally dependant on partners, friends, and special housing or welfare facilities. Care for the elderly in Spain falls upon the family unit with sheltered housing rare.

INTERNATIONAL PASSENGER SURVEY

The UK International Passenger Survey samples between 0.1% and 5% of the passengers that enter or leave through seaports, airports and the Channel Tunnel. It establishes the age, sex and citizenship of a traveller, and asks both emigrants and immigrants whether they are moving for work or study. Unfortunately, neither retiring abroad nor joining a family abroad is identified.

Since 1980 on average 11,300 men and 6,600 women in their late working years (45–59 years for women, and 45–64 years for men) have emigrated from the UK each year. In this age group the main categories are:

- UK citizens moving to another country for work;

- Non-UK citizens returning to their countries of origin or moving elsewhere;

- UK citizens retiring early abroad.

There have been sharp annual fluctuations in the total number of emigrants. The total increased during the mid-1980s to 23,000 but in 1988 the housing market boom in southern England collapsed and the number of emigrants decreased. There was another emigration peak in 1993. The following three years' total hover around 17,000 and in 1999 it rose sharply to 24,500.

Since 1980 the annual average number of departures from the UK of people of state pensionable age (60 and above for women and 65 and above for men) has been 2,320 men and 4,660 women. The numbers have a high female-to-male ratio; the principal explanation being that many of the emigrants are widowed, divorced or single women, leaving to live with or near relatives and friends who settled abroad earlier.

STATISTICS FROM NEWCASTLE

The Pensions and Overseas Benefits Directorate in the UK, based at Newcastle, record a second source of information on the number of people living abroad. Beneficiaries fall into three categories: those receiving state pensions, widows' benefits and 'unclassified'.

It is well known the British population in various Mediterranean locations is not clearly differentiated between tourists, seasonal residents, temporary residents and permanent residents. It is difficult for these categories to correspond tidily with legal and administrative statuses such as resident foreigner or non-resident foreigner. Further confusion arises as many people retain a property and bank account in the UK, finding it convenient to maintain a base back home.

There has been a substantial increase in the number of overseas state pensioners. Starting at a quarter of a million in 1981 they have now more than doubled at an annual growth rate of 8.95%. Growth was high at 10% during 1988–89 at the end of the 'Lawson boom' when the exceptional inflation in UK house prices fuelled a high rate of overseas property purchases. During the 1990s growth moderated to 3.5% per annum.

The average age of overseas pensioners is younger than the corresponding home population. The differential is more pronounced among women. Younger male overseas pensioners (aged 65–74 years) outnumbered the older (75+ years) by 60%, compared with 46% in the 1999 home population. Among women the younger outnumbered the older by 48%.

The ratio of women to men pensioners resident abroad was 1.26, whereas according to the 1999 mid-year estimates, the ratio in the UK resident population was 1.42.

British pensioners receive their state benefits in more than 200 countries. Of the 814,000 who receive their pension abroad, nearly a quarter live in Australia and a substantial number in the USA, the Irish Republic and Canada. Surprisingly these four countries account for nearly two-thirds of the total. But the countries with high growth rates are southern European countries with Sun Belt retirement locations such as Spain, France, and Italy, neighbours of the UK who have strong economic, social and working links. The highest rates of increase during 1994 to 1999 were Italy, Spain, France and the USA.

MORE THAN PLEASANT AMENITIES

Contrary to a widespread view, British and other overseas-retired populations are not predominantly composed of those who work and live in their own countries until their late fifties or sixties and then undertake a pleasant and agreeable move to a sunny location on the Spanish Costas. The path to overseas retirement involves greater consideration than a move to the sun-drenched resorts.

Widespread multinational processes and specific historical factors are involved. The growth rate in each destination country is subject to the vagaries of political events, local economics and, in some cases, the legacies of a military and imperial past.

Other people return to the 'old country', a sequel to the extensive and increasingly global labour migrations that began in the 1950s. A large numbers of British pensioners are evident in the Republic of Ireland.

The substantial number of UK pensioners in Germany reflects the British population's changing overseas employment and family connections through higher education, skilled labour demand, armed forces and temporary work placements. When a country has numerous opportunities for retirees to join their family and has an attractive environment, then migration is obviously high; as is the case with the Mediterranean countries.

While the number of older migrants may be few in comparison to the number of economic migrants and political refugees, there is huge potential for growth as ageing, the falling cost of international air travel, and rising affluence all combine to increase the number of amenity seeking migrants.

10

50 MILLION VISITORS EACH YEAR

TWO GREAT MEN

Pedro Zaragoza Oils – Benidorm

'This is the very spot where I was born, on May 15, 1922', says Pedro pointing downwards to an imaginary bed that occupied a spot in the family home. The house eventually made way for the block of shops, offices and apartments that became part of an urban plan that took a village of 1,500 souls to a city that is now the major holiday destination of Europe.

As a young man Pedro Zaragoza intended to follow in the footsteps of his father who captained one of the ships of the Transatlantica Line. He soon discovered his heart was not in the shipping industry and began travelling over Spain. With the death of his father, he returned to Benidorm. 'This is the land of my family, the fields, the houses, it's the Mediterranean way, it's important for us. We like to be in a place where all the family is in the cemetery.'

At the end of the 1940s there was no such thing as elections: officials were appointed and on December 10, 1950 the Civil Governor of the province asked Pedro to take over the position of Mayor for three months. Guidebooks state that Benidorm was originally a fishing port, but this was never the case, although villagers did live off the sea. 'When you have no fresh water and the land is only fit for olives and almonds, you eat a lot of fish!' exclaims Pedro. 'Many of the men in the village travelled the world on the liners and cargo ships. They had seen things and knew that they could make a better way of life for us.' So why tourism? 'What else? All we had was the sun, the sea and the beaches.'

By the 1960s, visitors from northern Europe were beginning to arrive in droves. In the late 1950s the icon of liberty was the bikini, its roomy bottom and bra top barely recognisable by comparison with today's string and handkerchief affairs, but in Spain, still held in the firm grip of the Catholic Church and state, this scanty garment was a tool of the devil.

In one famous incident, a British tourist, sitting in a bar opposite the beach wearing only a bikini was told by a *Guardia Civil* officer that she wasn't allowed to wear it there. She hit him and her strike for social justice cost a fine of 4,000 pesetas, no mean sum when the average wage was just over 100 pesetas a day. Step forward Pedro Zaragoza. 'If you want people to come to your town for their holidays you have to be ready to accommodate not just them but their culture as well. People have to feel free to be able to wear what they want if it helps them enjoy themselves. If they enjoy themselves they will not only come back but will tell their friends to come too.'

When Pedro Zaragoza took his 'War of the Bikini' to General Franco everyone thought he was mad, but he gained his audience with Franco who decreed visitors could wear the bikini in the streets and plazas of Benidorm, the first town in Spain where they were allowed to do so.

Other stories of Pedro's promotional ploys are endless. The marketing skills of this small-town boy would put many of today's business innovators to shame. He sent boxes of turron (almond nougat) and bottles of wine labelled 'Bottled in the sun of Benidorm' to Queen Elizabeth, talked the airlines into flying branches of almond trees, still in bloom in early December, to sub-zero Stockholm, and invented the Benidorm Song Contest which eventually became one of the biggest in Europe.

Pedro Zaragoza's reputation as a pioneer of Spanish tourism is widely acknowledged but for him his life's greatest achievement is the *Plan General de Ordenacion de Benidorm* which he brought into being in February 1954. 'This was an urban revolution. I knew the town would develop and I wanted it to develop in a human way. Many of the landowners were very shortsighted and couldn't understand why, for example, I wanted an avenue 80 metres wide. Their objections were hardly surprising considering there were only seven cars in the town at the time. They thought 10 metres was enough, so we eventually settled on 40.'

The essence of the plan was that every building would have an area of leisure land surrounding it in direct relationship to the built area, so that whilst Benidorm gained a reputation as being a high rise development, seen from the highest point in the city, it is in fact very green and open. The plan is still in use today, and has been adopted by a number of developing towns on the Costa Blanca.

When he decided to retire as Mayor of Benidorm, Pedro Zaragoza went on to become president of the *Diputacion de Alicante*, *Director General de Empresas y Actividades Turisticas* for the Ministry of Information in Madrid, Civil Governor of Guadalajara, Member of Parliament and held high office with many banks and major business.

Pedro Zaragoza feels that his ideas have been justified. Benidorm boasts more hotel stars than the whole of Greece; is arguably the most important holiday destination in Europe and has the highest level of return visitors. And you can still go fishing!

Jacinto Alarcon – Mojacar

The depopulation of Mojacar began in the mid-nineteenth century and started to assume alarming proportions after the Spanish Civil War. By this time drought had become chronic and fishing boats were gradually disappearing from the foreshore. By 1960, Mojacar had a population of less than 1,000 whereas at the turn of the century it had been around 8,000. Before leaving, the emigrants had ripped out doors, windows and beams from their houses to help pay their travelling expenses. Their homes stood like empty skeletons in the deserted streets.

Mojacar would have ended there if it were not for the Mayor, Jacinto Alarcon, who set about publicising the attractions of the region. In this, he was helped by a group of writers and artists who, captivated by its charms, had chosen Mojacar as their home. They dug wells in their search for water to irrigate the fields. The ruined houses were gradually demolished and plots of land were given away on the condition that houses were built immediately. All kinds of amenities were extended to those who wanted to become residents. There was constant publicity both in the national and foreign press and on radio and television.

There was only one problem. Would enough people come to see Mojacar? Jacinto knew that so long as people came, Mojacar itself would do the rest. And so it was. The village's charm captured all those who visited it. In 1962, Mojacar was a curious sight. Everywhere were mounds of cement, sand and lime. In the streets, lorries lumbered ceaselessly up and down the hill with their loads of building material, donkeys trundled along in unbroken lines carrying water, workmen's voices relayed orders from one construction site to another, cranes and pulleys creaked incessantly at work. Nothing quite like it had happened since the tourist boom first hit Spain.

The result of this hard work and determination was a fairy tale village which received a prize for the 'Most beautiful and improved village in Spain' from the Ministry of Information and Tourism.

And so Mojacar rose from the shell of its former self. Attractive white houses now cover the hill which give a honeycomb effect. Artists, writers, musicians, archaeologists, businessmen and diplomats now have their summer residences in Mojacar. One of the streets is appropriately called Ambassadors' Row.

Meanwhile, because of Jacinto Alarcon, Mojacar continues to make progress and is rightly called 'The Pearl of Almeria'. Golf courses, apartment blocks and major development now takes place around a town which 40 years ago was crumbling into extinction.

TOURIST INFORMATION

Tourism is promoted at three levels:

1 By the overseas Spanish National Tourist Offices;

2 By regional and provincial governments;

3 By local municipalities.

Spanish tourist offices are excellent sources of information. They are well equipped with free publications and information. Offices exist in cities, towns, and airports or near beauty spots. One very quick and effective method of obtaining information on accommodation, festivities and places of interest is simply click on to each *Comunidad*'s web page. Everything you could possibly want to know about a region is instantly available – in English, worldwide, before you even leave home.

Look at the following websites. These addresses use the name of the *Comunidad*, the province or the town. There are many more. The Internet code for Spain is .es. A good browser and the intelligent use of some key words will result in information from all parts of Spain suitable for a visitor or a new resident seeking to explore the country.

www.tourspain.es	The main Spanish tourist website.
www.comunidad-valencian.com	A very good *Comunidad* website.
www.ayto-valencia.es	*ayto* is short for *ayuntamiento*.
www.costablanca.org	The Costa Blanca site.
www.xabia.org	A popular town site.
www.cullera-turismo.com	A small site which even sends a CD-ROM!

VISIT STUNNING NATIONAL PARKS

Few countries in western Europe have such unspoilt scenery as Spain. More than 200 nature reserves protect a broad range of ecosystems. The most important areas are the 11 national parks, the first of which was established in 1918.

Mountains

Some of Spain's finest scenery is to be found in the two national parks in the north where rivers have carved stupendous gorges between the high mountain peaks.

The National Park of the Picos de Europa is now Europe's largest national park straddling the three regions of Asturias, Cantabria and Castilla y Leon. In some parts deep gorges cut through the rocks. Elsewhere green valleys support dairy farming. The Picos offer superb hiking, rock climbing and caving.

The National Park of Ordessa y Monte Perdido situated in the high Pyrenees is accessible only on foot. In autumn and winter, snow makes it inaccessible to all, except those with specialist climbing equipment. In the high summer many way-marked trails can be tackled by the reasonably fit. But Pyrenean weather can change quickly. In case of need there are several *refugios* providing basic food and shelter.

Wetlands

The wetlands, including coastal strips and freshwater marshes, are ever-changing environments. Seasonal floods rejuvenate the water, providing nutrients for animal and plant growth. These areas are rich feeding grounds for birds.

The national park of Donana in southern Spain covers in excess of 185,000 acres. It is a massive wetland of marshes and sand dunes. As the land is not suitable for human settlers, wildlife is able to flourish. In

1969, this large area became the protected home to threatened species and thousands of migratory birds.

Volcanic landscapes

Three very different parks protect parts of the Canary Islands' amazing volcanic scenery:

- Caldera de Taburiente on La Palma is a volcanic crater surrounded by woods.

- Mount Teide in Tenerife, a high mountain usually covered in snow, has unique alpine flora.

- Lanzarote's Timanfaya is composed of barren, but atmospheric lava fields.

Islands

Cabrera off the coast of Mallorca is home to rare plants, reptiles and seabirds. The surrounding waters are important for their marine life.

ATTRACTIONS OF A TRADITIONAL FAMILY HOLIDAY

The eastern coast of Spain bordering on the Mediterranean, together with the Balearics and Canaries are Europe's holiday playground. As tourism has developed, so too have the amenities. Commercialism is on a terrifying scale, but all designed to let people enjoy, relax and realise a sun soaked holiday.

Costa Blanca

One of the big attractions on the Costa Blanca is Terra Mitica (Land of Myths), a theme park inspired by the ancient myths of Egypt, Rome,

Iberia and Greece. It is possible to step inside the Pyramid of Cheops, experience Triton's Fury with a good soaking and a white-knuckle splashdown, or experience the Flight of the Phoenix – a heart stopping 54m sheer vertical drop. There are activities for all ages, themed restaurants and costumed hosts.

In Benidorm itself there are performing dolphins, parrots and sea lions at Mundomar which also has many woodland paths to explore. Next-door is a huge water park called Aqualandia. A taste of Africa can be obtained at the two drive-through safari parks – Safari Park Vergel and Safari Aitana.

Close by, the sun's heat is escaped in the cool Canelobre Caves which feature weird and wonderful stalactites.

Costa Dorada

Is a jaunt round the world a bit much for a single weekend? Not at Port Aventura in Salou. The giant theme park divides into Mexico, China, Polynesia, Far West and Mediterranean areas and is part of Universal Mediterranea, an even greater resort encompassing a pair of 500-room hotels and Costa Caribe Water Park. There are life-sized Mayan temples in Mexico; coconut fronds wave menacingly as you climb to the lip of a bubbling volcano on Tutuki Splash water flume in Polynesia.

Despite the global theme, Universal Mediterranea also has a decidedly Spanish feel with late dining and entertainment plus a siesta-time lull and some excellent lunchtime alternatives to fast food.

Costa del Sol

The largest and best of Spain's animal parks is the recently opened Selwo Nature Park at Estepona, home to some 2,000 animals many of which roam free in semi-wild conditions, amidst various eco-systems. Spot the lions and tigers, rhinos and zebras, hippos in the lake and even rare albino kangaroos. Walk over a bridge, gaze down to the animals below or drive in special safari vehicles.

There are more wild animals in semi-natural conditions at Cocodriles Park, Aljaima, up in the hills behind Malaga. Come face to face with 'Big Nose', a full-grown 77-year old monster crocodile or coo over his just-hatched descendants.

Tivoli World at Arroyo de la Miel is one of Spain's longest-established theme parks, set in landscaped gardens. White-knuckle rides include roller coasters, the terrifying Tivoli Dragon and the biggest flume ride on the Costa del Sol.

At La Gueva de Nerja, a fantastic cave of cathedral-like proportions, the world's longest stalactite is featured.

Mini Hollywood near Almeria was the film location for over 100 movies, including *The Magnificent Seven*, *A Fistful of Dollars* and *The Good, the Bad and the Ugly*. Shoot outs, hangings and bank hold-ups – all carefully orchestrated – still take place.

The Isla Magica, Sevilla is the world's only major theme park right at the historic heart of a great city. Isla Magica stands next to the Guadalquiver River on the site of Expo 92. The park is themed around Spanish exploration of the New World with seven sections surrounding a lake. The Amazonia, set in the Peruvian rainforest, the high-speed El Jaguar roller coaster whirls through 360-degree turns, while in 'Port of the Indies' there is a mammoth 68-metre freefall drop.

Madrid – Movie World

This enormous Warner Brothers Park has five separate areas – Hollywood Boulevard, Cartoon Village, the Wild West, DC Super Heroes World and Warner Brothers Studio. Each offers rides based on the sets and characters of Warner Brother's films and cartoons – from Hollywood icons of the 1940s through to the present day. There are five roller coasters including the looping, cork-screwing Superman Ride of Steel, three water flumes and a host of spectacular shows featuring cartoon favourites such as Bugs Bunny, Daffy Duck and Batman.

Gibraltar

Everyone enjoys being whisked to the top of the Rock by cable car and then exploring the well interpreted Great Siege Tunnels. Of course, there are those famous Barbary Apes, which pose like actors for photos. Do not feed them or try to handle them. A short walk away is St Michael's Cave – a huge natural grotto, with beautifully illuminated giant stalactites and stalagmites.

Mallorca

Forget all that sun, sea and sand. Immerse the mind in the surreal, eerily lit stalactite and stalagmite-filled world of the Coves del Drac (Caves of the Dragon) on Mallorcas' East Coast.

The trip finishes with an unforgettable concert set on the cave's magical underground lake.

In the sunshine, near Palma Nova, dolphins are the star performers at Marine land, while sea lions and parrots are given supporting roles. There are also penguins, sharks and tropical fish, monkeys, a reptile house and a large aviary. Creatures without cages roam the Auto-Safari at Cala Millor, with giraffes, zebras and monkeys.

Aquacity at S'Arenal claims to be the biggest water park in Europe and also boasts go-karts, falconry demonstrations, a mini-zoo, mini-farm and the obligatory parrot show. Splash around at the Hidropark, Port d' Alcudia and the Aquapark at Magaluf.

Tenerife

Top of the attractions is the excellent Loro Parque, in the north of the island at Puerto de la Cruz, which began life as the world's largest collection of *bros* (parrots), then added more with the biggest dolphinarium outside the USA and the world's longest underwater tunnel. Sea-lions and parrots also perform; there's a gorilla jungle, bat cave, tigers, crocodiles, king penguins, chimps and a 180-degree cinema – all set in glorious subtropical gardens.

Down south, near Los Cristianos, also in a beautiful subtropical setting, the best wildlife attraction is Las Aguilas del Teide, featuring mostly birds of prey.

One of the island's most fascinating sights is its Drago Milenario a 1,000 year-old Dragon Tree. With a girth of around seven metres and height of 17m it's impressive by any standards.

Aquapark Octopus is the island's best water park – famous for its *trompe l'oeil* giant orange water tap! It too has a dolphinarium.

Gran Canaria

Wildlife, the Wild West and wild driving are three of the big attractions on Gran Canaria.

Palmitos Parque features over 1,000 exotic birds, including performing parrots, a butterfly house, hummingbirds and an orchid house. Crocodilos Park offers more than just 300 crocodiles, with Siberian tigers, performing parrots, snakes, reptiles, an aquarium and a monkey house. There are more snakes, reptiles and assorted creepy crawlies at Reptilandia Park, Galdar.

Sioux City was built as a Western set in the 1960s and has been developed as a small theme park. Cows stampede through the town, the bullets fly and the saloon resounds to the sound of 'yeehahs'!

Holiday World, in the centre of Maspalomas, is a permanent funfair with white-knuckle and gentler rides. Parrots and sea lions do their bit here too. Aqua Sur, near Palmitos Parque, is the largest water-park in the Canaries with 29 different rides. Ocean Park at Maspalomas and Aqua Park at Puerto Rico are two other splash-a-minute favourites.

Lanzarote

There is much less in Lanzarote than on the two main Canary Islands. However everyone will enjoy the incredible moonscapes of the Montanas de Fuego (Fire Mountains) National Park, and the guide's party trick of turning a bucket of water into a whooshing geyser. There are also camel rides. Until recently camels were beasts of burden on the islands, but today they are harnessed for tourism and safaris.

SPANISH CITIES

Selling visitors the idea of a short break to Spanish cities is very much a preoccupation of the Tourist Board. Barcelona and Madrid are the most popular. Seville is next, followed by Valencia and Palma. Bilbao, familiar with ferry passengers has now entered the tourist agenda because of the Guggenheim Museum, together with smaller cities such as Cordoba in Andalusia and Santiago de Compostela in Galicia.

Art and culture are the two most important factors drawing people to Spanish cities. Visitors enjoy the museums, art galleries, opera, ballet and concerts. Shopping is a secondary attraction, with outlets ranging from flea markets to major stores offering quality and choice at a price likely to be far lower than in the UK.

Spanish cities are alive almost around the clock, and because a large number of people still live in the city centre it is possible to experience typical bars, cafés, shops and markets within walking distance of major museums and other attractions.

Spanish food is gaining a higher profile in the UK with a proliferation of *tapas* bars and, while they might not be authentic, they have raised interest in experiencing the real thing. The *tapas* bars in Spanish cities are a good choice for the busy tourist, offering delicious snacks at any time if you don't want to wait for lunch after 14.00 or dinner after 21.00.

A good choice for solo travellers is Barcelona – a very cosmopolitan city where it is easy to make friends and the nightlife goes on until dawn.

GREEN SPAIN

Wild, rugged northern Spain offers visitors the chance to experience a rural countryside with a unique pace of life. Espana Verde – Green Spain – brings together four of the country's autonomous regions. Galicia, Asturias, Cantabria and The Basque Country, situated between the Cantabrian Sea and the Cantabrian mountains. These areas offer an individual identity that reflects a very traditional Spain – nature at its most wild, gourmet food, interesting trails and other activities such as horse-back riding, trekking and canoeing.

In Galicia, for example, 1,300 km of rocky coastline is broken by 13 estuaries and dotted with over 700 beaches, whilst the principality of Asturias – established in the 14th century – has one national park, three natural parks, 10 natural reserves and 10 protected landscapes.

RUTAS

Ruta via de la Plata and *Ruta via de la Oro* are two old Roman pathways in the north west of the country. They were built to establish an adequate communications system with the central plateau, crossing the Cantabrian Mountains that separate northern Spain from the rest of the country. The creation of these roads put an end to the isolation northern Spain was suffering and facilitated commercial exchange with its neighbouring regions.

Today the remains of these tracks can be visited: follow the authentic road as it winds its way from north to south linking the cities of Gijon, Astorga, Salamanca, Caceres, Merida and Sevilla. Along the route Roman bridges, arches and theatres are to be visited, city walls passed and mediaeval cities entered. As mountains, valleys and ravines are traversed the heritage of one of the most important parts of the Roman Empire is revealed.

WORLD HERITAGE SITES

Spain's World Heritage sites, recognised by UNESCO due to their artistic and cultural wealth are yet another example of tourism being diverted away from the coastal areas. The cities involved are:

- **Avila**: A 1,000-year-old walled city standing at over 1,100 metres high on the southern boundary of the Castilian plateau.

- **Caceres**: In the middle of Extremadura near Portugal, this city was home to the Romans, Arabs and Christians. It has thousands of coats of arms all evoking heroic deeds and legends carved on house walls.

- **Cordoba**: Situated on the banks of the River Guadalquivir, this city reached great importance with the arrival of the Moors and became the capital city of Al Andalus. It was a seat of learning. Today thousands of tourists visit, usually stopping at the vast mosque.

- **Cuenca**: Its hanging houses are famous world wide, but its setting on imposing limestone rock is equally unusual.

- **Salamanca**: Not far from Portugal this dynamic, cosmopolitan city is home to young students filling its prestigious University.

- **Santiago de Compostela**: Its proximity to the sea in northeast Spain gives a mild and wet climate for those who wish to undertake a pilgrimage to its historic cathedral.

- **Segovia**: The Romans recognised the strategic nature of this location, building an aqueduct some 2,000 years ago. This true wonder of engineering is over 700 metres long, has 166 arches and is still off the tourist trail.

- **Toledo**: A city located in the centre of Spain, its origins go back to the remote past. It has a maze of narrow streets, synagogues, mosques, museums and the River Tagus. It is famous for steel swords.

55 PLACES TO GO

5 cities to visit

Alicante A fine industrial, commercial and tourist city.

Barcelona It rivals Madrid. Bustling, colourful, and full of vitality.

Granada Home to the rich heritage left by the Moors.

Madrid The capital, worthy of its title.

Seville Orange trees line its streets and river.

5 places of historic interest

Cordoba The home of more than just bull fighting.

Gibraltar A legacy of imperial power.

Ronda Sits on top of a massive rocky outcrop.

Salamanca A university town.

Santiago de Compostela Its towering cathedral has welcomed Pilgrims for centuries.

5 tourist hot spots

Benidorm Something for everyone.

Ibiza Day and night party life.

Mallorca It has to be done – the top holiday island.

Playas de las Americas Tenerife's modern, cheerful, sun, sea and sand location.

Torremolinos Tired and past its best.

5 restful locations

Cullera	A river, a wide beach, but only known to the Valencians.
Marbella	Where the rich and famous come to play.
Port de Soller	A French influence in Mallorca.
Puerto Morgan	Unique planning in Gran Canaria.
Santander	The south of France in Spain.

5 mountain retreats

Ainsa	A gateway to the Pyrenees.
Alcoi	In the heart of the Costa Blanca's walking region.
Competa	Set in high, rounded hills close to Malaga.
Pollensa	A base for exploring Mallorca's rocky west coast.
Potes	Set in an amphitheatre of the Picos de Europa.

5 places off the beaten track

Arenas de Cabrales	Try the local black pudding.
Cuenca	See the overhanging houses.
La Coruna	Exposed to the Atlantic at the northwest tip of Spain.
Oliva	The best camp sites in Spain.
Ruidera	A line of lakes formed by a rift in the Meseta.

5 places to treat with caution

Extremadura	An area of Spain remote from the modern world.
Fuengirola	Demolish it.
Loret del Mar	Give this Blackpool with sun a miss.
Orihuela Costa	In summer it's wall to wall with people.
Playas del Inglés	Flats, hotels and neon developed in Gran Canaria in the 1950s.

10 museums to visit

Museo Nacional del Prado, Madrid	Number 1 in Spain and Madrid.
Museu Dali, Figueres, Costa Blanca	Number 2 in Spain.
Museo Nacional Centro de Arte Reina Sofia	Number 2 in Madrid.
Museu d'Art de Catalunya, Barcelona	Home to art.
Barcelona Museum of Contemporary Art	New.
Guggenheim Foundation, Bilbao	New, futuristic art gallery.
Picasso Museum, Malaga	He was born in Malaga.
Science Museum, Valencia	New spectacular visitor site.
Gibraltar Museum	Charts its history.
Maritime Museum, Santander	Fishing history.

10 great beaches

Javea, Costa Blanca	Tranquil, sapphire waters and the jewel of the Costa Blanca.
Calella, Costa Brava	Quaint fishing village with boats and sand.
La Pineda, Costa Dorada	Soft, clean, wide and safe.
Tarifa, Costa de la Luz	Premier site for wind- and kite-surfers.
Estepona, Costa del Sol	Promenade, beach huts and clean.
San Sebestian, Basque Country	Shell shaped signature of the town.
Gijon, Asturias	Fine reddish sand.
Jandia, Fuerteventura	14 km of fine golden sand.
Alcudia, Mallorca	Very popular shallow beach.
Cala Portinatx, Ibiza	No ravers here.

Home in Spain
© 2005 Arno Staub

Ronda Bridge, Costa del Sol
© 2005 Pablo Schmittner

Lake Zahara de la Sierra, Andalusia
© 2005 milalala

Gaudi's House, Park Guell, Barcelona

Moonscape on Spanish beach
© 2005 Dainis Derics

Casa la Pedrera, Barcelona
© 2005 Dainis Derics

Butron's Castle, Bizkaia
© 2005 Elena Aliaga

A Balearic cove
© 2005 Elena Cruz

Sunset
© 2005 Pilar Lorenzo Riesco

Fruit market, Barcelona
© 2005 Willem Dijkstra

Mallorcan windmill
© 2004 Nicolas Metivier

11

KNOWING THE
ESSENTIALS FOR A
NEW LIFE

IMMIGRATION

Tourist status

The EU allows free movement in its member states for all its citizens provided they have a National Identity Card or a Passport. The UK is one of the few countries in Europe which does not, at the time of writing, issue an ID card. UK citizens need a valid passport to enter Spain and for internal identification purposes thereafter.

A person on a short-term stay is classed as a tourist and can enter Spain for a period of up to 90 days with:

- A passport;

- European Health Insurance Card (EHIC) for temporary reciprocal medical cover;

- A driving licence;

- Some euros;

- A credit card. Since the introduction of the euro virtually all *Bureaux de Change* have disappeared, but ATMs (cash dispenser machines) take all international cards with instructions in English.

A 90-day extension called a *permanencia*, can be obtained once per calendar year. With this extension it is possible to stay as a 'tourist' for a total of six months. To apply for a *permanencia*, which is stamped in the passport, go to the foreigners' department of the nearest police station with a passport, two photos, and some evidence of your ability to finance a stay in Spain for a further 90 days. The *permanencia* is a little used procedure, but it technically bridges the gap between a 90-day short-term stay and permanent residence over 180 days. A tourist is a person who spends less than six months in Spain in one calendar year.

Anyone who stays more than six months must apply for a *residencia*.

Fiscal identification number

All residents or non-residents with financial dealings in Spain must have an identification number – *Numero Identificacion de Extranjero* (*NIE*), the significant word *extranjero* meaning foreigner. *Numero de Identificacion Fiscal* (*NIF*) is the equivalent for Spaniards which, in their case, serves as Fiscal, Identity and Passport Number.

To get an *NIE* go to the foreigners' department of a police station with a passport (and one copy of the passport), and two photographs and complete the relevant form provided. Foreigners will quickly become accustomed to a way of life dependant on personal identification by an *NIE* number. An *NIE* is required for:

- Purchase of a property, a car and other expensive items;

- Dealing with the tax authorities;

- ID for other documents such as insurance policies or bank records.

Permanent status

Intending to live permanently or to spend more than six months each year in Spain? Then no later than 90 days after arriving, begin the process of applying for a *residencia* (this is effectively an identity card). To do this, again visit the foreigners' department at the designated police station with the following documents:

- Copy of a valid passport and *NIE* number;
- Three passport-size colour photographs;
- The completed form.

At the police station fingerprints are taken. In about six months a new style plastic *residencia* card is issued which is renewed every five years. The passport goes into the file at home to be used for international travelling. Obtaining a *residencia* also necessitates a visit to the bank to change personal details and account numbers reflecting a change from non-resident status. It also means paying income tax in Spain rather than to a 'home' country.

Someone entering Spain as a student or as a tourist and then taking up employment or self employment should read Chapter 8 – Employment, where details of a combined work permit/*residencia* application are outlined. A person entering Spain as a potential employee should still obtain a *residencia*.

Other documents

When moving to Spain permanently it is wise to have the following documents available:

- Birth and marriage certificates;
- Credit facilities to open a new bank account if seeking a business account;
- CVs translated into Spanish, if seeking employment. Pre-approved work permits are no longer required for EU nationals;

- Vehicle documents, if temporarily driving a car registered outside Spain;

- A UK pensioner should obtain form E121 from The Pension Service, Newcastle upon Tyne, which shows a pensioner has been in the UK National Health system and is entitled to entry into the Spanish Health system. An E form means European, demonstrating a uniformity of approach within the EU.

BRITISH EMBASSY AND CONSULATE

The British Embassy has overall responsibility for representation and promotion of the UK in Spain. The consular section provides services for British citizens in Spain and visas for those who require them to travel to the UK. The British Consulate General is in Madrid and is the issuing authority for all UK passports and visas in Spain. Other British Consulates in Spain can issue emergency passports valid only for a one-way journey to the UK.

Application forms for passports and visas are available by post or to personal callers, or can be downloaded from their website. The site also offers information on subjects ranging from timeshares to victims of crime and child abduction as well as a range of travel information.

The Madrid Consulate also registers the births and deaths of British citizens resident or visiting Spain. The Consulate can:

- Issue emergency passports;

- Contact friends and relatives to ask them to help with money and tickets;

- Tell you how to transfer money;

- In an emergency, cash a sterling cheque up to £100, if supported by a valid bankers card;

- As a last resort give a loan to get you back to the UK;

- Help with local lawyers, interpreters and doctors.

The Consulate cannot:

- Intervene in court cases;

- Get you out of prison;

- Give legal advice or start court proceedings;

- Investigate a crime;

- Pay hotel, legal, medical or any other bills;

- Pay travel costs, except in special circumstances;

- Find somewhere to live, a job or a work permit;

- Formally help if you have a dual nationality in the country of your second nationality.

The main website is www.ukinspain.com It is well worth a visit as it demonstrates links with the British Council and the British Tourist Board. How your country is presented abroad is interesting.

AYUNTAMIENTO

To the ordinary Spaniard, politics start and stop at the *ayuntamiento* (town hall). Situated in the Plaza Mayor of each village, town or city the building is bedecked with a national flag together with flags of the *Comunidad* and the province, signifying its importance as a focus in everyday life. The town hall is the home of the *municipio*, a council headed by a mayor (*alcalde*) and a number of councillors (*concejales*) all of whom are elected. The *ayuntamiento* is responsible for keeping the streets clean, collecting garbage, street lighting, water supply and sewerage, roads, cemeteries, schools, planning, parks, libraries, markets, social services, fire prevention and public sports facilities. It is here where local taxes are paid, where licenses are issued, applications for building permits are lodged, the right to vote is granted and births, marriages and deaths are recorded.

Signing on the Padron

Your first encounter with the *ayuntamiento* will probably be to register as a new resident of the town and consequently be allowed to stand and vote at elections:

- Visit the town hall with a passport and evidence of residing in the town (*copia simple* or *escritura* – see Chapter 12, Buying a property – or *residencia*);

- Complete some details. Provided more than six months each year is spent residing in the municipality, and you are not registered in another municipality at the same time, you will now be on the census of inhabitants residing in the area administered by that *ayuntamiento*;

- An *empadronamiento* certificate (census registration certificate) is issued.

One method of communicating with the *ayuntamiento* is to present a request or complaint in writing which will be stamped *recibido* (received) on presentation and must be acted upon in a reasonable period of time. The greater the number of people registered on the *padron*, then the greater the funds received from regional government.

Collecting taxes

One role of the town hall is to collect local taxes. *IBI* is a local tax, rather like rates/poll tax/council tax in the UK, but at a fraction of the cost. The services offered by a municipality are considerably less than in the UK. Home owners may have to take their rubbish to a central collection point. Street cleaners are rarely evident. Social services exist but only to a limited degree. An *IBI* bill for a town house may only be 100€ per year reflecting a level of service, a degree of central funding ... and more importantly an artificially low level of property valuation. However this has to be balanced against Community Charges for a private development which can be as high as 1500€ per annum reflecting shared costs for roads, pools, gardens and lifts.

EDUCATION

Introduction

The state funded school system is co-educational, highly structured, lengthy, free and has been overhauled in the last decade. The state education system runs alongside private, foreign and international schools. It is compulsory between ages 6 to 16. Learning is a serious matter, with both students and parents committed to education as a gateway to a good career. The stages and levels are:

- Pre School Education: Voluntary;
- Primary Education: Compulsory;
- Secondary Education: Compulsory;
- *Bachillerato*: Voluntary;
- Vocational Training: Voluntary;
- University: Voluntary.

The academic year runs from September until June. Children start compulsory schooling in the September of the calendar year in which they are 6 years old. In order to progress from one cycle of education to the next, students in state schools have to meet teaching and learning objectives. Compulsory schooling could last longer than in the UK where students progress from one year to the next automatically.

The language of instruction is Spanish or a combination of Spanish and a regional language. Teachers employed in the state sector do not necessarily speak English, and in any event lessons are not taught in English. If English is taught as a foreign language, which is mostly the case, then there is a teacher at the school whose main job is to teach English.

Parents must pay for books, materials and any extracurricular activities. Low income families may be able to get a grant for these items. School uniform is not always a pre-requisite.

For a foreign child to apply for a place at a Spanish state school which is publicly funded the parents' passports, the child's full birth certificate, marriage papers and documentary evidence of domicile in Spain are required. For older children, age 14 upwards, it may be necessary to have results of their studies in the UK officially validated.

Pre school education

Pre school education is divided into two parts. The first part is for ages one to three and the second part ages four to six. Attendance is both voluntary and free, with nearly all children aged between four and six attending for some time before starting primary education. Free state pre schools are supplemented by private fee-paying nursery schools. Introducing children to the school environment, coordination skills, self-awareness and group activities are objectives of pre school education.

Primary school

Compulsory primary education begins at six years of age for a period of six years, ending at age 12. There are three cycles, each of two years, during which the student is continuously evaluated. In addition to standard subjects the curriculum includes, where appropriate, an autonomous local language, music, physical education and a foreign language, which is usually English. Students who pass this stage go on to secondary education but those who do not have to repeat the final year.

Secondary school

Compulsory secondary education covers ages 12 to 16 years. It completes the compulsory part of education and successful pupils enter *bachillerato* or vocational training. The four years of secondary school are divided into two, two-year cycles, with the curriculum containing both compulsory and optional subjects. The curriculum is not all academic, and technical subjects, part of the vocational training, are introduced.

A pupil who does not pass the first cycle is required to repeat a year. Successful students at the end of the second cycle are awarded a 'Graduate in Secondary Education'. Those not successful receive a certificate stating the school years completed and the qualifications obtained in each subject. About 50% of pupils drop out of the full time educational system at this point.

The Certificate of Secondary Education is similar to GCSE and the *Bachillerato* is similar to 'A' levels. Therefore Spanish qualifications are acceptable for entrance to universities in the UK.

Bachillerato

Bachillerato Unificado y Polivalente or *BUP* simply means 'a pupil who has passed his graduation exam'. It is a non-compulsory part of secondary education providing pupils with two, free, academic courses each of one year's duration. It is a gateway to the university entrance exam or advanced vocational training, and a bridge between school and the mature world outside. In addition to the core subjects four modes exist in the arts, health and environment, technology and social sciences. Some modes are obligatory in order to follow certain university courses. The *bachillerato* is recognised as an entrance qualification by universities worldwide.

Vocational training

The first part of free vocational training provides a general introduction to a practical, technical career such as clerical work, electronics, graphics, design or hairdressing. The second part provides specialised training with pupils dividing their time between studies and on-the-job experience.

Given a choice between *Bachillerato* and vocational training, the trend is towards vocational training. Why? A job and earnings are close to hand. The thought of a long education through university is daunting. It is also easier for the less academically gifted. However there is flexibility between educational establishments, the labour market and vocational training which enables successful pupils to take additional specialist *bachillerato* courses and then proceed to a higher education.

University

There are four different types of university:

- University schools where a three-year vocational diploma is offered in a subject like teaching or nursing;
- University colleges where a three-year course of study leading to a *licenciado* is completed;
- Faculties where five-year courses are offered in all academic disciplines leading to the equivalent of MSc with further studies the equivalent of PhD;
- Advanced Technical Engineering or Architecture where five-year technical courses are undertaken.

About a quarter of all pupils go to university. The education standards are comparable with the best in Europe. Foreign universities, where courses are shorter and more flexible, attract wealthy Spanish students.

Private schools

Around a quarter of all Spain's schoolchildren attend private schools. They have small classes, are more relaxed and have a less rigid regime than state schools. Spanish schools can be state- or privately-owned. Fees are payable in some private schools, but not all. Some private schools are subsidised by the Spanish government and therefore tuition is provided free.

There is a wide range of private co-educational schooling including Spanish, bilingual and international schools which follow a variety of syllabuses including British and Spanish. However most Spanish private schools teach wholly in Spanish, are state-subsidised and follow the Spanish state-school curriculum. Some international schools follow the Spanish curriculum, but bilingually in English and Spanish.

This provides language skills to their pupils and attracts a state subsidy.

Foreign children

English speaking parents with young children will be aware that the sooner a child is exposed to a multi lingual situation the better. Conversely an older child will have more problems in adjusting. Foreign parents often prefer to educate younger children in Spanish nursery and primary schools, where they quickly learn Spanish, and then send children of secondary school age to a private school.

As with any state system, Spanish schooling is not without criticism – some complaining it is weighed down with traditional and unimaginative teaching methods, poorly paid and poorly motivated teachers. But this view is not universal. Some have nothing but praise for the Spanish school system, delighted their children are doing so well and more importantly, are happy and well adjusted.

The younger a child when entering the Spanish school system, the easier they cope. The language is assimilated quickly and although the first month can be traumatic, it isn't long before young children are speaking Spanish well. It is also the case that the older child has greater problems. Teenagers find it much more difficult learning the language, integrating socially and dealing with a demanding school curriculum. The result is often an unhappy child, at a difficult time in life and poor school results. It is understandable that so many older foreign children coming to live in Spain are sent to private, English-run schools. Here they can continue in the education system they know, and at the same time learn Spanish.

Most foreign children cope well with being educated in Spain be it private or state education. Living in a foreign land is an adventure which offers both change and challenge and most rise to the occasion. In no time at all their thinking becomes international, allowing their behaviour to become the same in later life. Spanish children are aware that the EU is made up of many different nationalities as most attend schools with pupils from different countries.

International schools

There is a growing number of international schools in Spain which follow a British curriculum. Fees for day students are usually lower than school fees in the UK, but demand for places can be high. Some English-speaking, private, international schools follow the American curriculum. Whichever style is chosen, most international schools are required to teach a small part of the Spanish curriculum in addition to the international one.

Bilingual schools

There are a few private schools in Spain with bilingual programmes. These are different to most international schools because children will be taught in more than one language. Many bilingual schools are private schools in that they do not receive any funding from the Spanish government, but some grant maintained private schools offer a bilingual education too. Some state schools are introducing a bilingual system with half of the school day following the curriculum in English.

Statistics

Thirty per cent of Spanish schoolchildren are currently being educated in private schools, most of which are co-educational day schools. Ninety per cent of all children between the age of four and five attend nursery school and over 55% of students remain at school until their 18th birthday. Of these, a further 25% go on to vocational training and 30% to university.

HEALTH SYSTEM

The Spanish are healthy people. Their diet of fish, fresh fruit and vegetables, olive oil instead of unsaturated fats, plus a glass of red wine per day contributes to this. For sufferers of rheumatism, arthritis and bronchitis, Spain's climate is therapeutic. A relaxed lifestyle can have a positive effect on mental health since it is a well-known fact that people who live in sunnier climates are generally happier than those who live in cold, wet climates.

Spain has no special health risks apart from over indulgence. Tap water is in the main drinkable although during periods of shortage the quality may suffer and people revert to bottled spring water. Red wine is plentiful, cheap and beneficial when consumed in moderation.

Complaints associated with smoking-related ailments are high. Smoking is the leading cause of death among adults, with cheap cigarettes causing 55,000 deaths per year: Spain has the second highest number of smokers in the EU.

Health care facilities are good. Medical staff are highly trained and hospitals equipped with the latest technology. The public and private systems live happily together. The Red Cross also makes an important contribution. Spain's health system is very different from the UK.

Visitors

EU residents visiting Spain can take advantage of health care agreements providing their home country has a reciprocal agreement with Spain. The UK does. EU residents should apply for a European Health Insurance Certificate (EHIC) three weeks before planning to travel. The EHIC card is used for valid emergency or urgent medical treatment. If payment is required, obtain a receipt and apply for reimbursement back home.

A person under retiring age who has paid regular social security contributions in another EU country for two full years prior to coming to Spain is entitled to public health cover for a period of six months by passing on cost of treatment to their former social security system. For ex-UK residents, this benefit is approved in advance by the Social Security office in Newcastle.

New permanent residents

Temporary health cover administered through EHIC is not an acceptable solution for Spain's new permanent residents. It is of course possible to take out medical insurance, which is one way of dealing with this issue.

Emergencies, visits to the doctor and hospital are normally covered by such a policy but medicines and dental treatment are usually not.

Public health benefits under the Spanish state health scheme called *INSALUD* (*Instituto Nacional de la Salud*), include general and specialist medical care, hospitalisation, laboratory services, medicines, maternity and some dental care. Anyone who pays regular social security contributions to *INSALUD* by virtue of their employment is entitled, for themselves and family, to free medical treatment.

Free entry into the scheme is allowed for:

- EU residents holding a *residencia* who are in receipt of a state pension and are over 60 (female) or 65 (male);

- A dependant of someone (wife or husband) can also enter the scheme provided they are both residents of Spain. For example, a man not yet 65 who is married to a wife who is 60, is regarded as a dependent and both are entitled to enter the scheme;

- EU nationals, resident in Spain, who are disabled or receive invalidity benefit;

- EU nationals of retirement age, but not in receipt of a pension, may be entitled to health benefits.

Here is the procedure to obtain a *Tarjeta de Sanitaria* (Health Card):

- Obtain form E121 from the Social Security Office back home;

- Assemble a *residencia* (or proof of application), a passport and a copy and *NIE*;

- Go to the appropriate Social Security office to complete some paperwork;

- Follow directions to a nominated Medical Centre who will allocate a doctor.

What to do in an emergency

In a life-threatening emergency call for an ambulance and mention the nature of the emergency. Telephone numbers, which can vary from province to province, are in the phone book, near the start, under the heading *Servicios de Urgencia*. Ambulances come under the umbrella of social security ambulances, Red Cross ambulances or 24-hour private medical centre ambulances. They are equipped for emergencies with staff trained to provide first-aid. The ambulance service is usually free.

Taxis must transport medical emergencies to hospital when requested to do so. A private car can claim priority by switching on its hazard warning lights and waving a piece of white material from the window.

In an emergency go to a hospital casualty department or a 24-hour public health clinic. It may be important to check which local hospitals are equipped to deal with the situation. In an emergency a hospital must treat you regardless of ability to pay.

Doctors

Finding a doctor who speaks English can be a problem. In the public sector the doctors are Spanish and are unlikely to speak English. In the private sector, particularly in cities and resort areas, there are many English-speaking German and Scandinavian doctors. Private-sector doctors advertise their services in the expatriate press.

Private health insurance gives a choice of doctor from a list provided. Within the public sector the choice is nil – the patient is allocated a doctor. Within the private sector, specialists do not require patients to have a doctor's referral although this is necessary in the public sector.

Chemists

A chemist (*farmacia*) is recognised by a green-cross sign. The address of the nearest 24-hour chemist and list of duty chemists is posted outside and published in local newspapers. A pharmacist in Spain owns and runs his own business. Chains of chemist shops are illegal.

Prescriptions under the public health scheme are charged at 40% of the cost of the medicine (or nothing at all if a pensioner or disabled). Basic medication, such as aspirin or cough medicine purchased in supermarkets in some countries, can only be purchased from a *farmacia* in Spain. Chemists are highly trained and provide free medical advice for minor ailments. They are able to sell remedies without recourse to a doctor, and can supply a wide range of medicines without prescription.

Chemists sell prescription drugs, non-prescription medicines, cosmetics, diet foods and toiletries. A *drogueria* sells non-medical items such as toiletries, cosmetics and household cleaning items, but not medicines. A *herboristeria* sells health foods, diet foods and herbal remedies.

Hospitals

Hospitales de la seguridad social (public hospitals) and *hospitales privados* (private hospitals) are the core of the health system, together with other establishments such as nursing homes, emergency clinics and analysis laboratories. Admittance or referral to a hospital or clinic for treatment is by a doctor or a specialist. Conversely it is possible to leave hospital at any time by signing a release form.

For private patients it is essential to provide evidence of health insurance or the ability to pay. If a private insurance company does not have an arrangement with a hospital to pay direct, then the bill has to be paid by the individual and the cost reclaimed later.

Spanish families are accustomed to looking after their relatives while in hospital and even after they return home. Patients are expected to convalesce at home, not in hospital and they are often discharged earlier than would be the case in many other countries.

Most foreigners are very satisfied with treatment in Spanish hospitals.

The difference in treatment varies little between the best public and private hospitals. It stands comparison with the best the UK can offer.

Dentists

There are many private English-speaking dentists. They are permitted to advertise their services and do so freely. Dentists expect to be paid immediately after treatment is completed.

Opticians

Although the optical business is highly competitive (simply count the number of shops in a main street) and prices for spectacles are not controlled, it is surprising to find glasses are more expensive in Spain than in other European countries. An ophthalmologist in Spain is the same as anywhere else – a specialist doctor trained in diagnosing and treating disorders of the eye, performing sight tests and prescribing spectacles and contact lenses.

BEGINNING ... AND THE END

Birth

Registration of a birth must be made within eight days at the local civil registry at the town hall or the hospital or clinic where the child was born. Registration applies to everyone irrespective of his or her nationality or residential status. There are two forms of birth certificate, a short certificate and a full certificate.

Unusually a birth certificate must state whether a child is legitimate or illegitimate (an illegitimate child is born less than 180 days after its parents' marriage or within 300 days of a divorce, annulment of a marriage or the death of the father).

Abortion is legal, tolerated in a liberal society and by the Catholic Church.

It is currently available during the first 12 weeks of pregnancy in certain circumstances, e.g. when a pregnancy threatens the mother's life, the foetus is severely deformed or the pregnancy was the result of rape.

Marriage

To be married in a Roman Catholic Church in Spain at least one partner must be a Roman Catholic. A divorcee is not permitted to marry in a Spanish church if the previous marriage was solemnised in church.

In order for non-Catholic foreigners to marry, one must have lived in Spain for at least two years. Marriages are held at Spanish civil registry offices and are presided over by a judge, as church weddings for non-Catholics are not legally recognised.

Many British people find it easier to get married in Gibraltar where the ceremony takes place in a registry office in front of two witnesses. The colony has special regulations which allow 'quickie marriages' by the Governor's Special Licence for non-residents. All you have to do is to prove you are not married to someone else, swear an affidavit at the Registry Office, pay about 100€ and attend the wedding ceremony.

Divorce

A couple must be married for one year before they can file for separation and divorce by mutual consent. The separation must be legalised before a notary. After two years of legal separation the divorce is automatically granted.

The normal grounds for divorce are adultery, cruelty, desertion, mental disorders, alcohol or drug addiction. In these cases where the separation is not by mutual consent, the period of legal separation is five years before a divorce is granted.

Foreigners who were married abroad can be divorced in Spain provided one of the partners is resident.

Death

In the event of death, a certificate must be prepared and signed by the doctor who attended the death and legally certified by a judge. Death, like birth must be registered at the town hall of the district where it took place. If the deceased was a foreigner, the town hall will need a passport or *residencia* card. An international death certificate will then be issued. The death also needs to be notified to the deceased's local consulate or embassy in Spain. When a person dies, several copies of the death certificate will be required for banks and the execution of any will.

A body can be buried or cremated or flown to another country for burial. A body cannot be interred sooner than 24 hours after death, but this usually takes place within 48 hours or if refrigeration is available, within 72 hours. Internment is above ground and bodies are placed in niches set into walls, which are rented for a number of years. After the rental period has expired bodies are interred in a common burial ground within the consecrated cemetery grounds.

Many towns with a high proportion of retired foreign residents now have a crematorium. They operate in exactly the same way those in the UK.

KEEPING WITHIN THE LAW

Spain has three main police forces, often with overlapping roles. They are the local municipal police, the national police and the civil guard. Some regions, including the Basque area and Catalonia, have their own police forces. An elite, special operations group is responsible for combating terrorism and guarding Spanish ambassadors and embassies abroad. Other forces include the port police and armed guards employed by banks and security companies.

Municipal police

The municipal police are attached to local town halls in small towns. They wear blue uniforms with white chequered bands on their hats and sleeves and patrol in white or blue cars. Municipal police deal with minor crime such as traffic control, protection of property, civil disturbances and the enforcement of local laws.

National police

Stationed in large towns they deal with serious crime such as robbery, murder and muggings. Other duties include guarding embassies, railway stations, post offices, army barracks and controlling demonstrations. They are housed in a conventional police station some of which have an *extranjeros* (foreigners) department dealing with *residencia* cards and other matters relating to foreigners.

Civil guard

The *Guardia Civil* patrol Spain's highways in cars or motorcycles. They mainly deal with traffic offences and road accidents, but also act as immigration officers and frontier guards. In villages too small for the national police the *Guardia Civil* stand in for all duties.

Denuncia

If you have a complaint against someone (for example a neighbour encroaching on your land, making too much noise, or creating smells) you can make an official complaint. It is called a *denuncia* and is made to the *Guardia Civil*. The form, called the *Certificate de Denuncia*, is completed with an official stamp. It may take time but the complaint will be investigated. The *denuncia* is a good Spanish custom.

In the event of theft or loss of property a police report is required within 24 hours in order to reclaim this loss from an insurance company. The report is again the *denuncia*. In large cities and tourist areas where theft is common, or pickpockets operate; it seems standard practice to have a translator on hand to help.

CONSUMER PROTECTION

Shopping

All products sold must be suitable for the use for which they are intended. Faulty goods can be exchanged or fully refunded irrespective of whether goods were purchased at full or discounted price. Always keep a receipt (*recibo*), as a complaint will not be entertained without one. Make a complaint within 14 days or it can be dismissed. In addition normal consumer protection laws exist for products and services where complaints should be made directly to a supplier or manufacturer.

Oficina Municipal de Informacion al Consumidor

The Ministry of Health and Consumer Affairs (*Ministerio de Sanidad y Consumo*) have local offices called *Oficina Municipal de Informacion al Consumidor* or *OMIC*. *OMIC* offices are established jointly with town halls. *OMIC* is not limited to basic consumer problems such as defective goods or incorrect prices. They can deal with much broader issues too. *OMIC* offices are helpful and make an effort to see action is taken. A serious complaint may be referred to an *OMIC* regional office in a regional capital. A business can be fined a substantial amount if a complaint is upheld.

Asociaciones de Amas de Casa

Housewife associations have both a watchdog and an educational role. These organisations generally require membership in order to benefit from their services. The main consumer organisation in Spain is the *Organizacion de Consumidores y Usuarios* (www.ocu.org). *OCU* runs a programme to inform tourists of their rights, and publishes a magazine called *Compra Maestra*.

Serious complaints

A serious complaint concerning weights and measures can be directed to the *Jefatura Provincial de Comercio Interior* (Provincial Department of Internal Commerce). This office is responsible for ensuring that weights are correct, prices are within limits on controlled items, and products are up to standard.

Exhausted all administrative channels? The ombudsman or Defender of the People is the last resort when justice has not been done. If going to the *OMIC* fails to bring the desired result, or if unjustly treated by any government agency, then try the *Defensor del Pueblo*, the regional ombudsman.

Other procedures

There are special complaints procedures for many organisations including utility companies, the post office, public transport companies, insurance companies and the public health service. Professional associations covering *abogados*, doctors and such like have their own complaint procedures. The best known is banking. Every Spanish bank has its own central *Defensor del Cliente* (Defender of the Customer), who will hear a complaint when satisfaction has not been obtained from a branch office.

Hoja de reclamacion

All businesses are required by law to keep a complaints book or complaints forms (*libros/hojas de reclamaciones*), which must be produced on demand. Requesting a complaints form often results in a speedy and satisfactory outcome to a dispute, as copies of all complaints must be forwarded to the authorities within 48 hours. The *hoja de reclamacion* comes in three copies. The business keeps one copy and the customer takes the other two, one to keep and the other to present at the local *OMIC* office if necessary. A business must respond to a client's complaint within 10 days. If it does not, the consumer can take his case to *OMIC* and the business can be fined.

12
BUYING A PROPERTY

PEOPLE INVOLVED IN BUYING

Agent

- A good agent is one who can offer a wide variety of properties for sale.

- Greater security is offered by dealing with an agent who is professionally qualified or belongs to a professional organisation.

- For first time buyers, uncertain of the laws and customs of the country, a good agent will give additional assistance during the difficult moving-in stage.

Agents dealing in Spanish property do take a high commission. The lowest start at around 3% but the average is 10%. When selling a *finca* it can be 25%. How do they justify such exorbitant charges? Their answer is ambiguous, making reference to high advertising costs, commissions due in two countries and complex transactions involving different nationalities.

The commission rate for selling a new house on behalf of a builder is usually fixed at around 10%. If a number of agents are selling the same property they may compete with each other, discounting their commission by offering furniture packages to prospective purchasers.

A different commission structure operates for the sale of a second-hand property, commonly termed a resale property. In some cases the agent operates on a fixed commission, but more customary is the following arrangement:

- The agent asks the seller the price he wishes for the property.

- The agent advertises and negotiates the sale of the property at another, higher price.

- The difference between the two prices is the agent's commission, which is rarely less than 10%, can be up to 15% and can in special cases reaches 25%.

- This pricing structure gives rise to considerably animosity. It is compounded when buyer and seller seldom meet, creating an atmosphere of mistrust in relation to the commercial motives of the agent.

Abogado (solicitor)

It is important to remember the appointment of a legal representative is principally to protect the buyer. The agent is working for the seller. Rather like many other aspects of daily life, it is a system of checks and balances. But let us be clear at the outset. The Spanish system of house conveyancing is different. You are not dealing with solicitors who draw up and exchange contracts on completion.

So what does the *abogado* do?

- Draws up a contract if asked to do so.

- Helps complete the conveyance of the property.

- Provides help and guidance on legal matters, principally the content of the contract and payment methods.

- Makes arrangements to obtain and receive a power of attorney should this be necessary if the parties will not be available to sign the *escritura*.

- Obtains an *NIE* number so that a client's personal identification is by name and also number.

- Makes arrangements for signing the *escritura* and final property payments.

Bank

A bank may be recommended by a friend, an agent, an *abogado* or be linked with a bank back home. Here are some recommended criteria for selecting a bank:

- Some staff, preferably the manager, should speak English.

- In order to have access to major services such as mortgages and investments, the bank should be a major player in the Spanish marketplace.

- Money transferred into Spain for the purchase of a property will come through the clearing bank system. The bank back home and the Spanish bank should both be main branches to prevent delays in money transfer.

Need a mortgage? The Spanish bank is a provider. Need a short term bridging loan? Forget it. These two statements demonstrate a difference in attitude towards borrowing money. A loan is for business, a mortgage is for home finance and the two are kept strictly separate.

Notario

In Spain all deeds for a property are drawn up by public notaries who are appointed by the government. They are qualified lawyers who have studied to become notaries. They are very important people in the Spanish community, responsible for legalising many documents including the power of attorney, drawing up wills, certifying copies of passports, and most importantly approving the deed of a property, known in Spain as the *escritura*.

The *escritura* is signed and witnessed by the *notario* in the presence of the seller(s) and the purchaser(s) unless any party has utilised a power of attorney. The *notario*'s duty is to:

- Check the name of the titleholder and whether there are any charges or encumbrances against the property;
- Check the contents of the *escritura*;
- Ensure the *escritura* is read to the purchaser(s) prior to signing;
- Check that both parties have been advised of their legal obligations;
- Certify the *escritura* has been signed and the money paid.

The *notario* represents the state and does not guarantee or verify statements, or check the contractual terms. The *notario* protects the interests of the buyer or seller by pointing out any pitfalls, by offering advice on legal points and volunteering information.

The end product of a visit to the *notario* is the *escritura*. It is a hard backed copy of the deed, which is covered in official stamps, signatures and writing. It is typed on thick, numbered paper and is an impressive document produced to a standard format.

Avoiding problems

Problems associated with purchasing a property abroad have been highlighted many times in the popular press. From a legal viewpoint, Spain has not always been the safest place to buy. Most horror stories come at the start of the buying process. It is at the contract and deposit stage where things go wrong, where insufficient checks have been made, or inadequate procedures followed.

It cannot be emphasised too strongly that anyone planning to buy a property in Spain must take independent legal advice (in a language in which they are fluent) from a lawyer experienced in Spanish property law. Always deal with professionals and do not assume that because you may be dealing with a fellow countryman that the advice is better, cheaper or even unbiased.

Do not sign anything, or pay a deposit, until you have sought legal advice. One of the most common phrases heard in Spain is about buyers 'leaving their brains behind at the airport'. It is true! The rush to buy a dream home, or a pressurised selling trip, or even the euphoria of the moment often makes people do incredibly stupid things – including literally handing over cash deposits to agents or owners with little or no security.

UNDERSTANDING LEGAL DOCUMENTS

New property

Many people choose to buy a new property that has yet to be built. It may be identical to a show house or built to an individual design to be constructed from a builder's plans. The documentary procedure below should be followed.

- A plan of the house: a three dimensional line drawing, or an architect's plan which shows the dimensions of each floor and each room in square metres.

- Locating the plot: a line drawing locating the plot which is called *plan parcial*, a Spanish term meaning a plan of parcels, or plots of land.

- The *nota simple*: this document, which translated means a simple note, is issued by the Land Registry Office which is a copy of the property registration details. It will show proof that the person selling the land or property is the registered owner and that there are no debts.

- The agent's agreement sometimes known as a pre contract: this document represents the first step in the buying process. It is an outline agreement to reserve the property.

- The contract signifies that the plan of the house and the location of the plot are satisfactory; the *nota simple* has been checked and is in order; the contract has been read and understood. It releases a non-returnable deposit and signifies the purchaser has the necessary monies to complete the transaction.

- Details of the community charge: buying a property in Spain on an urbanisation invariably means becoming a member of a community of property owners. The annual payment and communal facilities should be stated.

- The *Certificado Final de la Direccion de la Obra*: translated this simply means 'Certificate of the Termination of the Building'. It is a certificate produced by the architect when the house is completed and enables declaration of a new building to be made at the notary's office.

- The *Licencia de Primera Ocupacion* is obtained from the town hall on production of the *Cerificado Final de la Direcion de la Obra*. It is a licence to inhabit the property, registers it for the purpose of local taxes and the connection of services.

- The *escritura* is the deed for the property. The *copia simple* (not to be confused with the *nota simple*) is a simple copy of the *escritura*, less the signatures, which is sufficient to prove ownership. It is available on the day of signing at the notary and recognised as suitable for most legal purposes. It is normal for the purchaser to hold a copy of this document. *Escritura de Compraventa* is the document signed in the notary's office. *Escritura Publica* is the *Escritura de Compraventa*, complete with many official stamps from the Property Register, converting it into a public document.

- *Registro de la Propiedad* is the last piece of paper in the buying cycle. The *Escritura de Compraventa* has to be registered with the Property Register making it an *Escritura Publica* and being over-stamped *Registro de la Propiedad*. This simple, one page document simply closes the loop to the *nota simple* that was considered at the commencement of the buying cycle.

Resale property

Documentation for a resale property is slightly different.

- Obtain a copy of the seller's *escritura*.

- Obtain a copy of the *nota simple*.

- Obtain a copy of the seller's passport or *residencia*.

- Obtain a copy of the seller's *empadronamiento* certificate, which will have been issued by the town hall, which simply states the names of those residing at the address.

- Although not always possible, try to obtain a copy of a scale drawing of the property.

- If sold furnished, obtain a signed copy of the furniture inventory.

- Obtain the last copy of the paid bills for utilities such as water, electricity, and telephone, together with rates and community charges.

- Sign the contract and pay the deposit.

- Sign the *escritura*. Make the final payment. Obtain the *copia simple*.

- Arrange insurances.

- Ensure service and utility supply accounts are changed into the new owner's name.

- Obtain a final copy of the *escritura* and the *registro de la propiedad*.

The first four steps are simply to ensure the person who is selling the house has the right to do so. The name(s) on all the documents should be the same. If not, it is important to find out why. The dimensions of the property in the *escritura* should agree with the dimensions in a scale drawing. If not, this requires investigating as building alteration may have taken place. The seller's *escritura*, the *nota simple* and the financial checks will give details of mortgages and encumbrances on the property. The *copia simple* is the necessary identification required by utility suppliers in order to change the ownership.

MONEY MATTERS

Stage payments

Stage payments vary with the type of property being bought.

New property	10% on signing the contract
	40% stage payment
	25% stage payment
	25% on completion
Resale property	10% on signing the contract
	90% on completion
A partly-built property	50% on signing the contract (walls, roof, windows and doors completed)
	25% stage payment
	25% on completion

The basic rules

- A deposit of 10% or less is normal for a new or resale property. For a partly-built property it will vary according to the amount of work completed. It is payable by cash or banker's draft to the agent or to the seller.

- The deposit is non-returnable if the buyer fails to complete, unless there is a clause in the contract to the contrary.

- If the builder fails to deliver a new property on time penalty charges accrue. Again these should be stated in the contract. In practice the contract will always state a flexible date of completion.

- If a seller fails to complete the transaction, the buyer is recompensed to a value twice the amount of the deposit unless the contract states otherwise.

- Final and stage payments should be paid by banker's draft in euros.

Allowing for additional buying costs

It is normal to allow 10% of the property value declared in the *escritura* for the additional costs in buying, this covers three taxes, two fees and charges from the *abogado*. A breakdown of these costs is as follows:

Transfer Tax or *IVA* (Value Added Tax)	7%
Stamp Duty on a new property only	1%
Plus Valia Tax	0.5%
Notary Fees	0.5%
Property Register Fees	0.5%
Charges from the *abogado*	1%

Black money

It is quite common in Spain to have two purchase prices for a property. One price is the actual price paid, exclusive of any fees or taxes. The other is a lower price declared in the *escritura*. As a guideline, the difference between the two prices should be less than 15% to 20%. The difference between the two prices is normally paid to the vendor in cash.

Agents, buyers and sellers, builders and developers, the *abogado*, the bank manager and the notary are aware of what goes on. The tax authorities know it. In fact everyone knows it. It is a mechanism of tax evasion, which if not radically abused, is tolerated by the Spanish taxman. Many people are now seeing the folly of this practice, but once started it is difficult to stop. The saving on initial taxes when purchasing can easily be outweighed by a greater loss in capital gains when re-selling.

INHERITANCE

A person with British nationality at birth will find that Spanish authorities permit an estate to be bequeathed to whoever they choose, so long as this is allowed by their own national law. But a Spanish estate is subject to Spanish inheritance tax. Anyone with assets in Spain should make a

Spanish will disposing of their Spanish assets in order to avoid time-consuming and expensive legal problems for heirs. A separate will should be made for disposing of assets located in the UK. Make sure a UK will states clearly that it disposes only of assets in the UK and make sure a Spanish will disposes only of assets in Spain.

Inheritance tax is regarded by many as the cruellest of taxes. Having spent a lifetime paying income tax yet another lump of assets amassed over the years will be claimed back by the tax authorities. With careful planning people need pay little or nothing in inheritance tax. It has been described as a 'voluntary levy paid by those who distrust their heirs more than they dislike the *Hacienda* (Spanish Tax Office)'.

Spanish inheritance tax is payable when an inheritor is a resident of Spain, or the asset inherited is property in Spain. Spanish inheritance tax is not payable if the asset is outside Spain and the recipient is not a resident in Spain. Inheritance tax is the liability of each beneficiary and not the deceased's estate.

There is no exemption between a husband and wife where each holds joint ownership of a property. In many countries a property can be held in joint names. If one person dies the property passes automatically to the other person. This is not the case in Spain where each person holds an equal share. Upon the death of one person, the other is subject to inheritance tax when inheriting the other half.

Spanish inheritance taxation law does not recognise a common law spouse. The relationship has no legal standing. They have no inheritance tax exemptions. They are also taxed at a premium rate being treated as non-relatives.

Note

This is only a summary of the property buying process. A full explanation is given in the author's companion book *Buying a Home in Spain* and the complexities of inheritance are explained in *Knowing the Law in Spain* both published by How to Books.

13

FOOD AND DRINK

KEEPING IT SIMPLE

Spain has the Romans to thank for the foundation of its cuisine. Then the Moors arrived and to the fields they brought almonds, oranges, other fruits and sophisticated agricultural techniques. They brought artichokes, eggplants, spinach, rice and the reintroduction of saffron. To the kitchen they brought the characteristic combination of finely chopped ingredients that eventually led to dishes like *paella*. They also introduced spiced casseroles, stews, sauces and fruit syrups.

It was Rome that gave Spain wheat, the olive and the vine. When sitting down at any table the cornerstone of Spain's culinary history – bread, oil and wine – will be present. These are not sufficient in themselves, but when all are present we move on from simple sustenance to the art of fine food. To all this add garlic. Indeed garlic is included in many dishes – garlic soup, bread rubbed with raw garlic and garlic sauces such as *alioli* (garlic mayonnaise).

Spanish cookery is unpretentious. Food will never be tarted up and made to look grand, rare, costly, or more colourful. There is no over-reliance on sauces. There is no confusion of tastes. Simplicity is prized, but simplicity can be a very difficult thing to achieve. The greatest effort in the Spanish kitchen goes into raw materials: correctly cured meats, carefully made cheese, correct types of rice, and how a fish is taken – by net or hook.

In recent years Spanish food has made great strides forward. In the most surprising places, sometimes hidden away in villages of the interior, or next door to a tourist resort along the coast, one can find restaurants with a style of their own, offering quality products, practising modern cuisine, sometimes delving into the *avant-garde*, but always faithful to their roots.

CLASSIC FOOD

Gazpacho

Gazpacho is a chilled raw soup originating in Andalusia made by pounding bread and garlic with tomatoes, cucumber and peppers. Olive oil and vinegar gives it a refreshing tang. It is usually garnished with diced salad vegetables and croutons.

Paella

Is this the national dish of Spain? Consisting mainly of rice seasoned with saffron, it can be a combination of chicken, vegetables and seafood, or a combination of sausages, rabbit and other meats with chickpeas. Each region will have its own variation. The combinations are practically limitless – ranging from meatless 'Lent' *paella* containing only salted codfish and cauliflower, to *paella* made using small game fresh from the hunt. Although many people consider *paella* the most typical of Spanish dishes, its origins are fairly recent. The first *paella* was prepared in Valencia in the late 19th century. *Paella* is cooked in a flat metal pan with two handles riveted to the sides.

It is a popular dish at fiesta time and curiously enough often made by men. The Valencian phrase 'to go *paella*-eating' is used throughout the region, which may involve outings, parties, picnics and such like.

The genuine Valencian *paella* always has a good helping of wide-pod green beans and giant dried butter beans. As for meats, chicken, pork and rabbit are used and exceptionally wild duck. To add extra flavour white-shelled mountain snails provide what some call an exquisite taste. There are also seafood and shellfish *paellas* which in recent years have become increasingly popular, particularly the high-priced, mouth-watering, lobster *paella*.

Whatever the ingredients may be, when an orthodox *paella* reaches the table, grains of rice should be dry, loose and golden, never mushy or sticky or leaving a trace of oil if served on the plate. When a *paella* has been cooked over an outdoor wood fire, the *paella*-eating ritual calls for diners to sit in a circle, to eat from the communal pan and to scrape the nearly burnt rice from the bottom. Some say this is the best part.

Cocido

Many consider the traditional meal of Spain to be a meat stew called *cocido*. It is a slow-simmered stew of beef, chicken, ham and pork belly with chickpeas, cabbage, *chorizo* (red sausage) and *morcilla* (black sausage) producing a dish usually served in three courses. The broth is served first, then the vegetables, and then the meats.

In Madrid it is called *cocido a la madrilena*. It is a stew of chicken, chorizo sausage, maybe some ham or other cured meat, potatoes, cabbage, chickpeas and macaroni. Again it is eaten 'from front to back'. But this is a dull dish. There are so many good things to eat in Spain why bother with *cocido*? Yet the people of Madrid love, dream about and sing about it.

Flan

For an after dinner sweet have a custard dessert such as *crema catalana* (*creme brulee*), a very rich, sweet custard usually flavoured with lemon zest or cinnamon or both. A top coating of sugar is caramelised before serving. There are many similar desserts, some incorporating rice, such as *arroz con leche* (rice pudding) and others simply labeled 'flan'.

Sweets of Moorish origin

Sweet floury breads halfway between normal bread and confectionery are zealously eaten, together with pastries and confectionery. To this list should be added *leche merengada* (ice cream made from milk, egg whites and flavourings) and crisp almond cookies called *avellana*. Top of the list for sweet-toothed performers in Spanish gastronomy is the nougat-like *turrones* from *Xixona*, made from an abundance of almonds and honey produced in various districts of the province.

Hot chocolate

From a nation that wrested chocolate from the New World and carried it back to the old, chocolate is often a disappointment, especially if you have just come from Switzerland or Austria. Hot chocolate that people drink from early morning to midday in *chocolaterlas* is good, although it's not what you would expect. It's thick, more of a chocolate porridge than a drink. It is good with *churros* or other not-too-sweet pastries.

REGIONAL CHOICE

Green Spain

Some of the most delicious seafood comes from the Atlantic coast with specialities including mussels, scallops, lobsters and octopus. The north coast also supplies crabs, anchovies and tuna. Soft, blue cheese comes from the mountains of Cantabria. Later in this chapter it will be seen that it is wine that gives this region its fame. Spain's most prestigious red wine, Rioja, is matured to a distinctive vanilla mellowness; its grapes influenced during growth on hilly, stony soil by both the Mediterranean and Atlantic weather systems.

Eastern Spain

Catalonia too is known for good food. *Amanida* is a salad with vegetables, cured meat, cheese, and fish. *Sequet* a fish and shellfish stew. Sausages come in all shapes, sizes and colours. But the most famous dish is a pudding called *crema catalan*: a rich egg custard with a golden brown layer of grilled sugar on top, served very cold.

Andalusia

Its historic Arab inhabitants have heavily influenced food from this area. Traditionally almonds, rice, lemons, oranges, grapes and olives were grown. Today's crops now include strawberries, apples, melons, cherries and pears. Barbecued meats, sauces flavoured with cumin or saffron and sweets made from crushed almonds, are all typical dishes of today. Grilled fish, especially sardines and *calamares* (squid), and whole fish baked in a crust of salt, are popular dishes.

Central Spain

Game such as wild boar, pheasant and partridge is plentiful in Central Spain. La Mancha maintains a tradition of robust cooking with a variety of one-pot pulse stews. Castilla y Leon is known for its suckling pig and milk-fed lamb roasted whole in enormous bread ovens. Many convents and shops in Toledo continue to make popular little marzipan cakes.

The region is well known for *cocido* and *patatas a la importancia* that are egg coated potatoes fried and then simmered in wine and *Manchego* cheese.

Islands

Regional food is gradually being squeezed out, but traditional egg dishes still remain to be eaten in good Mallorcan restaurants. In the Canary Islands however, regional food does not exist, forgotten in the commercial need to provide international blandness. Bananas are grown here, a small, sweet variety, often used in fritters and tarts.

EATING WELL

Cutting the ham

In town and country no bar, or supermarket will be without a festoon of *jamons* hanging from the ceiling. It seems an unnatural thing to do, hanging meat in a warm place with lots of people around and in some cases lots of tobacco smoke too. But it tastes good.

The English words ham and gammon and the Spanish words *jamon york* all mean much the same thing. The leg joint of the pig is processed containing water, salt and preservatives. Parma ham and the Spanish variety, *jamon serrano* are simply hung and cured on the bone for a long period of time in carefully controlled conditions of temperature and humidity.

Mountain ham from white pigs fed on acorns gives almost the best *serrano*, but the premier product is the *pata negra* from Huelva which is produced from brown pigs with black feet and cured for 12 to 18 months. How do you get the wafer thin slices of tender ham? The leg is clamped onto a wooden rack while a long sharp knife shaves the thin strips.

The bigger cities have places that specialise in offering ham for sale. Customers stand around bars eating plates of ham cut off the bone, *Manchego* cheese, crusty bread with loads of olives and drinking glasses of red wine. It is the food of the gods!

Slicing the sausage

Dry, long life, colourful sausages in different shapes and sizes hang in the supermarket next to hams. To understand sausages let us consider the raw and the smoked. Under raw we have the red, black and white. Under smoked we have black and white.

Chorizo is the most common cured, red sausage. The colouring is achieved by paprika, the ground powder of the dried sweet red capsicum. This along with salt, garlic and black pepper, is used to season a ground mixture of pork and pork fat. It is smoked or hung to dry like ham. It has a bright red colour, a chewy texture and a spicy taste.

Salchichon and *longaniza* are cured white sausages. They are similar to *chorizo* but made without paprika. Some variations are spiced with oregano or nutmeg. Others are more delicate. They are round and can be very long and thin.

Morcilla is a cooked Spanish black pudding. In the *morcilla* recipe is pork fat, salt, and spices, onion or chopped nuts. A very common addition is cooked rice. Some *morcillas* are made sweet. Its soft texture does not need chewing.

Lastly are the white cooked sausages called *butifarras*. Like *morcillas* they are made straight after slaughtering the pig, cooked with spices and other ingredients.

Food from the sea

The Spanish have always ventured seaward in search of food, adventure and trade. While each region has its traditional specialities there is hardly a fish you cannot find in any major city. Like the Italians, the Spanish will eat any creature that emerges from the depths. When it comes to fish their favourites are *bonito* (tuna), *bacalao* (cod), *sardinas* (sardines), *anchoas* (anchovies) and *pulpo* (octopus). Shellfish such as *gambas* (prawns) and mussels are eaten as part of normal life.

Lovers of fish will drool at the sight of masses of different fish species on offer in supermarkets, although some sizes are ridiculously small and should never have been caught. Some of the other typical fish from which delicious dishes are made include hake, red mullet, sole, swordfish, gray mullet, narrow-mouthed cat shark, cuttlefish, redfish, mackerel, blue-mouth rockfish, wreck-fish, and rays. Fantastic salmon is imported from Norway.

Wisdom is often to be found in simplicity. Fish and shellfish in Spain are usually prepared in uncomplicated yet mouth-watering ways; baked in the oven, hot from the grill, done over charcoal, lightly fried, or cooked in succulent yet simple stews.

Two delicacies from the sea must be mentioned here. The first is the *anguila* and the second the *percebes*; both almost unheard of outside Spain.

The life of *anguilas* (eels) is just as astonishing as the life of the salmon, but in reverse. The adult lives in the river then goes to the ocean to spawn and die. When spawning time arrives, they descend the northern Spanish rivers in great shoals heading out to the Atlantic Ocean and to the Sargasso Sea on the edge of the Bermudas.

They spawn and the females die leaving their fertilised eggs behind. When they hatch, the elvers are no bigger than a few inches. They begin the long journey home to the rivers of northern Spain. It is an arduous journey. Those that do survive and escape the fishermen's nets will reach up to a metre in length. However, millions are scooped up into gossamer nets, parboiled, put into vacuum packed bags, frozen, or rushed off to Spanish restaurants where diners enjoy the catch.

It was the Spanish fish-addicted nation who first proposed eating *percebes* – a repulsive-looking crustacean known as a gooseneck barnacle. They can be seen displayed in the windows of up market seafood restaurants. *Percebes* are the most expensive protein source to be found in Iberia. Even those who routinely call for a lobster for lunch are inclined to think twice about ordering these delicacies.

Percebes should be boiled in a few cupfuls of Atlantic sea water for a couple of minutes. The initial incision is made in the tough neck, juice and sea water sucked out, then the soft stem devoured. Prise away a stone, the weather beaten skin and a sliver of flesh is left. The meat is chewy, a little like octopus in texture and flavour, albeit soaked in the fresh salt of the Atlantic. Skills verging on those of a micro-surgeon are required.

The jagged coastline of rocky inlets around Coruna to Finisterre is the most exposed stretch of the Spanish coastline. *Percebes* thrive there in conditions that make their harvesting particularly awkward. They prefer wild seas or at least strong tides, growing on the rocks at tide line where the mighty Atlantic breakers crash. Removing them from their rocks requires a fine sense of timing, as fisherman risk being swept off the polished rock faces by freak waves. *Percebes* must be harvested from land and not sea. Gathering involves one fisherman being lowered down a steep cliff-face on a rope to prise off a handful of *percebes* and being lifted above the highest waves.

Cheese

Spain's geographic diversity and extensive herds of cows, sheep and goats, combined with traditions developed by generations of artisans in thousands of villages have resulted in an enormous variety of cheeses.

Several hundred types, varying in taste, size, shape, fat content, freshness, methods of maturing and texture, bear a *Denominacion de Origen* label and meet exacting quality standards and specification. Making fine cheeses is no longer simply a village industry. Continued improvements in technology and transportation and a much greater commercial awareness in both the public and the food industry, led to the introduction of the *Denominacion de Origen*. As with wine it identifies type and quality.

Just as wine is dependent on the type of grape, the quality and characteristic of cheese ultimately depends on the quality and nutritional value of the pasture consumed by cows, sheep and goats in their different habitats, which vary according to soil type, climate, altitude and water. Cheeses also vary according to methods and maturing time.

More than half the cheeses produced in Spain are mixtures that combine three animal types. In such mixtures, the cow gives acidity, the sheep high fat content and goats the white colour. The mixtures are classified into three groups called *Queso Hispanico*, *Iberico* and *Mesta*.

Although the range of Spanish cheeses is impressive, they cannot compare with the variety available in either France or the UK. A good hard *Manchego* cheese made under government regulation will give a consistent and reliable product. Hard sheep's milk cheeses from the heart of Spain's La Mancha are delightful when well matured. *Cabrales*, a sheep's cheese rather like blue Roquefort from Asturias is also worth trying.

Fruit and vegetables

Spain is the market garden of Europe. It produces and exports more fruit and vegetables than most other nations of the EU and has almost every climate and microclimate. The range of fruit and vegetables available to a Spanish cook is enviable.

Strangely, Spanish fresh fruit and vegetables have to be purchased with care. Locally grown produce in season is cheap and available all year long, but of course, like all European countries, Spain exports most of its Class I produce. Quality produce is better purchased from the *fruteria* at the *mercado central* than from the supermarket.

EATING OUT

Food is important. Spaniards enjoy café life. Like the French they live to eat.

Breakfast is a coffee with bread or a croissant. *Cafe solo* is a small cup of strong coffee not for the thirsty. *Cafe con leche* is coffee with milk. *Cafe americano* is a large cup without milk. *Churos* – a doughnut-style fried pastry with hot chocolate, forms a traditional breakfast of mega calories.

Lunch takes place between 14.00 and 16.00 and if taken outside the home will consist of *tapas* or, alternatively, a light three course meal with wine and bread.

Dinner is late – 20.00 to 22.00. The Spanish are famous for eating at, what to some, is a ludicrously late hour. Who in most countries would think of sitting down to a full meal at nine o'clock in the evening? This late night eating is all to do with the Spanish siesta-adjusted body clock, with most people not finishing work until half past seven or eight o'clock. It is usually a reversal of lunch, with a bit more wine and a bit less food. No one wants to go to bed on an over-full stomach.

Restaurant meals usually consist of three courses. Many restaurants in Spain offer a luncheon known as the *Menu del Dia*. The choices for *Menu del Dia* are chalked up on a blackboard outside the restaurant. It must consist of three courses plus bread, water or wine. The third course is always dessert. The price is always less than if you were to order the same items *a la carte*. It is one of the best deals in Spain. There may be only two or three choices per course or as many as a dozen.

With a bottle of table wine and fine food at prices that compare very favourably with that paid for a meal in northern Europe, eating out can cost next to nothing. It is a constant source of amazement that restaurants can produce a three-course meal with wine, for as little as 10€. A service charge is included in some restaurant and hotel bills, but waiters will appreciate an additional five to ten per cent tip.

But beware! Among the basic intake of food and drink should be included tobacco. Men smoke, women smoke and teenagers smoke. Whenever you go into a Spanish establishment you will soon be enveloped in a thick blue haze of cigarette smoke and the Spanish do not have the faintest idea this could be uncomfortable to anyone.

TAPAS

In addition to restaurants there are many attractive *tapas* bars offering freshly-made snacks and appetisers. The *tapas* bar is unique to Spain. Alicante is known as one of the best *tapas* areas where the ritual of *tapa* eating has reached sublime levels.

Tapas come in all sorts of delicious forms and are readily available in most bars. Rows of dishes are arranged in a chilled cabinet in front of the customer. They comprise tortilla, spicy meat balls, big plump olives, sausages, fried aubergines, egg salad, courgettes, spicy potatoes, liver, cheese, *serrano* ham, sardines and prawns in garlic, anchovies, mussels, fried squid, *calamares*, *sepia*, and small fish in olive oil.

Nibbling at small amounts of food is popular, but of equal importance is that the *tapas* bar is an essential part of life, a place where people meet to eat and drink, to gossip, to carry out business and generally pass the time of day.

BAR OR CAFÉ?

A bar is mainly a male-dominated environment serving beer, wine and *tapas*. They may specialise, creating an individual image through music, cocktails, cabaret or beer. Picture a popular bar situated in a tiny street of a small village anywhere in Spain about 10.00. Dark, with basic tables and chairs, walls painted some time ago in a murky yellow colour or any colour provided it is murky. A stuffed boar's head adorns the wall, the shelves contain a variety of silver cups for football behind which are pictures of the teams. There is also a large picture of grandfather looking starched and bemused, of grandmother starched and not amused, a proud man holding a horse, of pretty granddaughters and daughters in their national costumes taken during one of the many fiestas. Also dotted around are gaming machines, dart boards, posters displaying ice creams, boxes of crisps, wines, beer and spirits. That's just the wall.

Along the base of the bar, especially first thing in the morning, are cigarette ends. They do get brushed up but are soon replaced as older Spaniards don't bother with an ashtray. The top of the bar will be littered with plates, cups and saucers, glasses, bottles and the remains of food.

The noise of people will be deafening as they all talk at the same time. Later on in the morning, when everything has been brushed up and the bar surface cleared, the older retired men will take up positions at the tables and either play cards or dominoes. Bars in villages and towns are social clubs where people meet and keep abreast of what is happening, aided by watching the inevitable television set high up in a corner that can be showing anything from football to bullfighting to pornographic films. As very few watch, it leaves one wondering why the TV is on in the first place! No one needs to be alone at home because bars exist and are open sometimes seven days a week from early morning till late at night.

A café, on the other hand is where you partake of a coffee and a pastry or, when it's hot, a large ice cream. It is where you have a work break, read a newspaper, take shelter from the sun or rain, watch the world go by, or even nip inside to use the toilet. In the city it is a haunt for all ages and sexes, but in the country, segregation takes place, with the ladies visiting the café and the men the bar.

WHERE TO DRINK

In Spain eating and drinking are things done together. The notion of going to a bar where only alcohol is served is foreign to the Spanish. Pubs, saloons, cocktail lounges, bars, and *cervecerias* (beer bars), all watering holes that are taken for granted in the UK, are rare in Spain. Many places called a bar are really *tapas* bars, although it is possible to stumble into a small, dark establishment serving little more than beer or sherry to a subdued audience of elderly men.

The best way to enjoy cider is in a *sidreria*, an establishment where cider is made, served, or both. *Sidrerias* are common in the Atlantic region and in the Basque Country. They are usually rustic places, with plain wooden benches and long tables. Huge wooden vats line the walls, with each vat named after a patron saint, or a sports hero, or a movie star.

Cider must be poured with ceremony and enjoyed in a prescribed fashion. If poured from the vat, a tube about the size of a cigarette is pounded into the vessel's side at about shoulder height to act as a tap. The drinker, stands at the ready with a wide glass in hand. When the tap is opened it shoots a thin stream of golden cider out a distance of about five feet. This draught cider also comes in green bottles. In order to achieve the same aeration that the vat method provides, the cider server takes the bottle and holds it up as high as possible while holding the glass in the other hand as low as possible. In experienced hands, no cider ends on the floor.

If a tipple isn't on the agenda, try establishments dedicated to the drinking of non-alcoholic beverages. *Horchaterias* serve *horchata* and little else, although the grander ones also offer *horchata* ice cream, coffee and soft drinks. The *chocolateria* is an institution in Spain, though at first glance it looks hardly any different from a café. You might think it's something like a coffee shop, but the sign over the door says *chocolateria*. They usually stop serving chocolate by lunch time, but you can always get a soda or a snack. Except in Barcelona and parts of Madrid you won't see much in the way of dedicated coffee or tea houses. Virtually every eating and drinking establishment in the nation serves coffee with few people drinking tea.

INTRODUCING WINE

Spaniards drink a lot. It is part of everyday life where most people consume alcohol every day. They may start the day having a coffee laced with brandy, take a bottle of red wine for lunch and sit in a bar all evening. But you only rarely see a drunken Spaniard. The prices of local wine, sherries and brandies are very cheap and, while whiskey, gin or rum may be expensive in comparison, the measures are extremely generous.

The Spanish are casual in their attitude to wine. They do not take it seriously, drinking mostly young table wines. At the same price as a bottle of water, a carton of milk, or a soft drink it is something that can be taken or left with a meal. In a restaurant frequented by workers having their lunch, half a bottle of unwanted red wine is frequently discarded. Wine is cheaper in Spain than in many other countries. A good quality Rioja costs 4€ only and it has not increased greatly over the years.

Spain has a long history of wine production with old stone wine presses still evident in the mountains. Storage in oak casks followed in the 15th century. In the 1960s Miguel Torres established the first stainless steel wine making equipment in his Catalan winery, maintaining precise control over the fermentation procedures. Most producers followed suit and now Barcelona is a world centre for the manufacture of wine making equipment. This forward-looking attitude has given rise to a new approach to Spanish wine making. After almost 2,500 years, we can now enjoy the best of Spanish wines.

The extraordinary diversity of wines produced in Spain is not only due to the skill of the winemaker, but also to the different climatic and soil conditions. There are three main soil types. Chalk, a bedrock called schist, and clay. Chalk and schist provide water retention during the driest part of the year, while clay is rich in trace elements such as iron.

There is a downside to Spanish wine. A lot of mediocre 'plonk' is still produced and it suffers from a poor international reputation. This has much to do with worldwide marketing skills as the quality of Spanish wines has improved enormously over the last few decades with the introduction of new grape varieties and more consistency in processing. International varieties of grape are now grown such as Chardonnay, Cabernet Sauvignon, Merlot, Malbec, Pinot Noir and Riesling. They have joined the native varieties of Garnacha Tina, Graciano, Tempranillo, Albarino, Moscatel, Parallada, Pedro Ximenez, Verdejo and Xarel-lo.

CLASSIFYING WINE

Wine is classifed by law and the classification is shown on the label. It makes it easier for customers to know what they are buying. There are three broad classifications covering Table Wine, Quality Wine and Ageing Wine. Table Wine is a European classification of basic quality of which there are four types.

- *Vino de Mesa* (*VdM*): a table wine blended from various regions. The label will state '*Vino de Mesa*, Produce of Spain' and carry a brand name, but no regional name and no date.

- *'Vino de Mesa ... '* a table wine with the regional name inserted on the label, e.g.: *Vino de Mesa de Toledo.*

- *Vino Comarcal (VC* or *CV):* a regional wine. There are 21 such classified areas. The label states *'Vino Comarcal ... '* followed by the regional name.

- *Vino de la Tierra (VdlT):* Translated this is 'Wine of the Land', meaning country wine that is likely to apply for Quality Wine status in the near future. The label will say *'Vino de la Tierra de ... '* followed by the district name.

Quality Wines meet European standards of quality control with each wine-producing zone made up of a council of growers, winemakers, biochemists and government representatives. When a new Quality Wine is promoted from *VdlT* standard, regulations are established, approved by the regional government, followed by Madrid and finally Brussels. There are two levels of classification.

- *Denominacion de Origen (DO):* this is the main quality wine classification in Spain. There are 54 *DO* zones all tightly controlled. Regulations relating to a *DO* region include the type of grape that can be used, yield per hectare, minimum alcohol strength, permissible amount of natural sugar, the maturity process and period, bottling and labelling. The classification also has two labels. On the front is a label stating the name of the wine zone with the additional words *'Denominacion de Origen'* On a small back label is the official seal, a small map and the serial number of the bottle.

- *Donominacion de Calificada (DOCa):* this is a higher quality of wine applicable from 1991 to the Rioja region. It guarantees wines that have performed to a high quality over a number of years through lower yields and grape selection. Labelling is the same as the *DO* category.

In addition to the classifications of brand name, producer's name, *DO* zone and the official seal, Spain has its own system of classifying wines by age. The definition of age is time in an oak barrel plus time in the bottle before being released for sale. There are five classifications.

- *Joven*: young wine – harvested one year and on sale the next – light and fruity.

- *Crianza*: six months (at least) in the cask and two years maturing.

- *Reserva*: three years maturing – with a minimum of one in oak and one in the bottle.

- *Gran Reserva*: from finest vintages – five years in cellar of which two years are in the cask and three in the bottle.

- It should be noted that the time for age classification differs from red to white and rosé. White and *Rosado* require six months in oak and can be released a year earlier than the red.

Spanish wine regions fall into four main areas. The north, where the best Spanish wines are produced, contains the regions of Galicia, Castile y Leon, Navarra, Aragon, Rioja, Catalonia and the Balearics. The central zone includes La Mancha and Extremadura. Andalusia, the birthplace of Spanish wine, and the Canaries. The coastal region of Valencia and Murcia, containing almost half of Spain's total vineyards. Spain has three climatic systems. Green Spain to the north, the climate of the Meseta and the Mediterranean coast. The best vineyards however are situated in microclimates, mixed soils or well-drained sheltered slopes.

The most famous Spanish red wine is *Rioja*, a strong wine with a distinctive oaky flavour gained from the time it spends maturing in an oak barrel. Few international wines can match *Rioja*, or its near neighbour *Navarra*, for price and quality. Pick up a wine list with offerings from all over the world and the name *Rioja* will appear.

The words 'Catalonia', 'Penedes region', 'microclimate', 'the Torres family', 'outstanding commercial success' and 'good young wines at sensible prices', say it all. Penedes is renowned for its white wines, although it also produces fine reds and much of Spain's premier sparkling wine.

Spanish sparkling wine is called *cava*. It is said that it is as good as

French champagne, but much cheaper. But more correctly it is a quality, young sparkling wine in its own right. *Cava* is classified by sweetness or dryness and all *cavas* come under the same *DO* irrespective of where they are produced.

SANGRIA, SHERRY, BRANDY AND OTHERS

Sangria is a summer drink. It is a fruit and wine punch diluted with lemonade. On occasions it may have the addition of some brandy to give it an extra kick. Care has to be exercised in buying *sangria* for it can be a way to use up poor quality red wine. There is no way of knowing this, but exercise care by always buying a branded product or drinking it at a reputable restaurant.

Sherries have always been popular. The English dominate the sherry trade in Jerez de la Frontera in Andalusia where it is produced. Many of the brands, such as *Harvey's* and *Sandeman*, are foreign. Sherry is matured in oak barrels and produced from a variety of vintages by progressively blending young and old wines. There are various types of sherry to suit most tastes and occasions. Classic sherry is *fino* (dry) or *seco* (sweet). *Amontillado* is deeper in colour and taste and usually drunk chilled as an aperitif. The very dry *manzanilla* is a fortified wine which has a slightly salty after taste, attributed to the salty soil of the area where it is produced.

Brandies make a perfect end to a meal. Some prefer *anis*, which is a Spanish aniseed drink rather like *Pernod*. But many more prefer the popular after dinner drink called *sol y sombre* (sun and shade) a combination of brandy and anis. It is not for the faint-hearted.

Beer is not generally what people think of when they think of Spain. They think of wine, sherry and *sangria*. Get ready for a shock. Spain's sales of beer surpassed sales of wine in the early 1990s. The most famous branded beer is *San Miguel*. It is quite strong (5.4%) and has a light, slightly sweet fruity taste to it. *Cruzcampo* is the closest you'll get to light beer without asking for it. It is a light and dry brew with a somewhat sour flavour.

Atlantic Spain grows a great quantity of apples that are fermented in chestnut barrels to produce a tangy, light, and mildly effervescent cider. Mass-produced, it is available in dry and semi-dry varieties but natural cider, more like a 'home brew' is cloudier, fruitier and drunk young.

VISITING A *BODEGA*

Many people buy wine from the supermarket and hypermarket. The quality and range is good and, after all, there is always a 'special offer'. Supermarkets stock few imported wines. A *bodega*, which is a store selling only wine and drinks, usually has as large selection. Look for a string of parked cars outside *bodegas* attached to a wine-producing unit. Large quantities of wine are sold straight from the barrel at ridiculously low prices.

CORK

Where does cork come from? Answer, from the evergreen cork oak tree which grows in the south of Spain. Cork is used as a stopper in wine bottles. Growing to a height of 15 metres the cork oak lives for 600 years. It takes 20 years for the first bark to appear and when cut a further seven years to regenerate. When the cylinders of cork are removed by axes the tree immediately starts to bleed resin, protecting it until a new bark grows. The cut cork bark is left in the sun for a year, then boiled to soften it prior to processing at a factory.

14

TRADITIONAL CULTURE OF OLD SPAIN

FLAMENCO

Flamenco is a form of song, dance and guitar music commonly associated with the Andalusian Gypsies of southern Spain. The roots of *flamenco*, though somewhat mysterious, seem to lie in the Roman migration from Rajasthan (in northwest India) to Spain between the 9th and 14th centuries. These migrants brought with them musical instruments, such as tambourines, bells, and wooden castanets and an extensive repertoire of songs and dances. In Spain they encountered the rich cultures of the Jews and the Moors. Centuries of cultural intermingling produced the unique art form known as *flamenco*.

Today the popular, romantic image of singing and dancing gypsies, together with swaggering bullfighters is unreal. But *flamenco* does occupy an important place in Spanish culture, particularly in the culture of Andalusia: not simply preserved folklore, but rather a vibrant and important art of song and dance. It is certainly true that some *flamenco* has been commercialised and turned into a sanitised spectacle that sometimes bears little relation to the raw vigour of the real thing.

The problem for the spectator is where to see and hear the real thing. To find *cante jondo* (deep song), which is the authentic, heart-rending sound of flamenco or its other pure forms, there is a need to enquire if there is a *pena flamenca* (a *flamenco* club) or *un bar donde se canta flamenco* (a bar where flamenco is sung). More commercial *tablao flamenco* (*flamenco* show) is available in many of the larger Andalusian cities such as Seville, Cordoba, Granada and coastal tourist resorts.

In the south during the late spring and summer there are local *ferias* (festivals) where it is possible to experience a version of *flamenco* called the *sevillana*. Even in the smallest villages groups of people can be found, many in costume, singing and clapping to the rhythm, while the dancers wind themselves around each other in what can only be described as a controlled and highly stylised dance.

Gypsy women also practise fortune telling and reading Tarot cards. Tarot cards are popular in Spain with card readers advertising in newspapers and on notices in shop windows in many Spanish towns. Several TV stations feature women spreading out a Tarot deck on a table covered with an elaborate cloth and speaking to callers who have problems with their life, families, children, neighbours, business or career. The aura of mystery and power may be one reason why fortune telling has always appealed to gypsy women but more likely it is a relatively simple way of earning money that does not require literacy or formal education.

FIESTAS

Fiestas celebrate a national religious occasion or a local thanksgiving where towns and cities come to a stop as men, women and children dress up to enjoy themselves, aided by a plentiful supply of food, wine and laughter. Processions with music start the evening; dancing and singing follow. Fireworks close the evening with a loud colourful bang. Each *fiesta* has its own distinctive character – sounds, colours, flavours, smells, costumes, rituals and a typical dish. There are celebrations for the dead and the living. Some *fiestas* appease the forces of nature. Others drive out evil spirits. Often they are based on historical events or include medieval or ancient customs. There is always a *fiesta* somewhere. They can last for a day, a week or a fortnight.

Perhaps the best-known *fiesta* is the one in celebration of the re-conquest of the Moors by the Christians held at Alcoy near Alicante, but also replicated in many other Spanish towns in that region. Throughout the world there are many colourful processions, but few can compare with the medieval pageantry which is accompanied by the music of brass instruments and loud kettle drums, as the marchers slowly sway rhythmically in the early darkness of a summer's evening.

Light, fire and gunpowder are key elements in *fiestas*. *Las Fallas* in Valencia are unparalleled *fiestas* of fire signifying renovation, spring-cleaning and a change in season. Huge caricatures of politicians, film stars, comic strip personalities, full of satire and humour, are erected in the streets and then, to the accompaniment of a firework display, at midnight they are set on fire. The following day plans are made for next year's figures. For one week in March the province of Valencia turns into a giant carnival giving in to its most primal urges and celebrating the secret of fire. As a pagan ritual originating in ancient Mediterranean culture and brought to Spain in remote times, this is arguably one of the most colourful and exciting festivals.

La desperta occurs every morning during *Fallas* week and consists of hand-thrown bangers and rockets. Just when you think that particular bit of morning madness has died down, the first of hundreds of bands start parading through the streets playing their hearts out in a repertoire of *pasodoble* and marches.

The noisiest part of *Fallas* week by far is the *mascieta*; a pyrotechnical display of sound beyond comparison. Most neighbourhoods set off a *mascieta* around midday but just once in a lifetime one should experience the 2 o'clock *mascieta* set off in Valencia in the Town Hall Square. Every day during the *Fallas*, nearby offices are temporarily deserted, birds disappear and thousands of people jam tightly into the streets near the town hall so that movement is impossible. Then, in a matter of minutes up to one hundred kilos of gunpowder are exploded.

The *mascieta* is only a prelude to further fireworks displays that are staged at every conceivable opportunity. Each individual town competes in the grand fireworks stakes and many are spectacular. However, the most famous night of fireworks, *Nit De Foc* is held along the ancient riverbed of Valencia's Tuna River. On that night an extraordinary display called a *castillo* (castle) is performed in which 2,500 kilos of pyrotechnical material are ignited. This produces not only a lot of sound, but also carefully choreographed flashing lights that explode in the shapes of sparkling flowers, enormous palm trees and dozens of other colourful contrivances that shimmer and glisten across the black March sky.

The culmination of the *Fallas* celebration is difficult to understand. An entire year's work, for thousands of people, costing hundreds of thousands of euros is deliberately devoured by flames in one evening. But that is missing the point. The *Fallas* were created to be burned this way, to wash away winter worries in a tribute to spring. When the effigies begin to disappear in flames all the satirical meaning they represent are purged.

FIREWORKS

The following statement encapsulates a common problem.

> *'The council has issued a new by-law banning unlicensed firework displays and imposing strict guidelines which private companies must adhere to in order to safeguard the public. The new by-law was pushed through after last year's* fiesta *season saw deaths and serious injuries caused by lax regulations.'*

Fireworks are still a way of life in Spain. Factories still make them. Shops import 'bangers' from China. Children are brought up to the noise of fireworks and crackers. It's big business with complex computer-controlled displays. Children's pocket money is spent on making a noise irrespective of the time, place or occasion. Pets huddle in corners, frightened. The tolerant adult smiles: after all they are children, they can do no wrong.

BULLFIGHTING

The sun poured onto the saffron sand, picking out crimson. A hush had descended on the 19th century auditorium as the man in the sparkling suit, head held low, eyes intent, drew out a sword from behind his cape, gaze fixed on the huge creature in front of him: a panting, angry bull, pawing the ground and snorting while the blood splashed down from the web of muscles encircling its massive neck. Six hundred kilos of testosterone concentrated into two frighteningly large, wide horns, with points as sharp as sabers, facing a lithe slip of a man squeezed into a tight suit, his only defence a red cape, and the sword. He held the bull motionless in front of him by the sheer force of his stare. Slowly the matador raised his weapon, turning his body so that his whole energy was directed through it in an arc. As the audience hushed he surged forward and in one movement sank the sword into the bull's neck, to its hilt. The animal danced in a confused circle while the man stood motionless, holding its gaze. As the bull's knees started to buckle, the creature suddenly burst forward with its last gasp of life, but the matador did not flinch. He raised a hand and, the tenacious look still pinning the bull, slowly lowered his outstretched arm, inches away from the top of the bull's head. With this movement, almost at the matador's command, the bull sank at his feet. For a split second before it died, before the thunderous applause and waving of white handkerchiefs erupted, the bull and the man were held in a perfect moment, the fight over, strange comrades in the curious ballet that is bullfighting.

Blood and Sand by Kamin Mohammadi

Bullfighting is big business in Spain today. It is estimated that 150,000 people are in some way involved in the industry. Despite the condemnation of international animal welfare groups, shifts in attitude have been slow in coming. The owners of the 300 bull breeding farms represent a powerful lobby group, receiving subsides from the EU and exemption from the 1998 amendment to the Treaty of Rome which covers animal welfare. In 1996 the Ministry of Culture provided nearly 40 million pesetas to support the *corrida* (bullfight). This does not include the subsidies given to individual bullrings by local and regional councils. The reasons are legion. The young people of Spain are becoming impressed with bullfighting again. Television pays big money for major bullfighting events; indeed it is hard to escape the *corrida* during the season which runs from April to October. Matadors, revered as rock stars, mobbed at every turn, followed around by groupies are comfortable showing off their homes in the glossy pages of *Hola!*

This is not the place to discuss the morality of a bullfight, but it is worth making one important point. Most foreigners are aware that in the bullfight several bulls are going to be hurt and then killed. They will be lanced, they will have sharp barbs stuck in them and in the end they will be killed, more or less efficiently, with a sword. There will be blood and there will be death. If a foreigner does not want to see this, or may be upset by it, or if they think it is barbaric and cruel, then it is really not worth going because they will certainly not enjoy it.

Posters

Bullfights are always advertised on posters in bars or on the street. The posters will announce whether it is to be a *corrida de toros* – a bullfight with four to six-year-old bulls and with senior *matadores* or a *corrida de novillos* – with younger bulls and junior *matadores*. Posters will give the place, date and time of the bullfight. The bullring is called *la plaza de toros*.

Seating

The major distinction between the seats at a bullfight is between those in the *sol* (sun) and those in the *sombra* (shade). There are also tickets called *sol y sombra* (sun and shade), which are for seats that start in the sun but are in the shade by the middle of the event. *Sol* tickets are much cheaper than *sombra* and most of the activity takes place on the *sombra* side of the arena. As you go in, people will probably be renting cushions. Since the seats will be stone, brick or concrete, it is a good investment.

The format

Six bulls are fought during a normal bullfight. They are not domestic animals that have been maltreated to make them aggressive. They are a breed of bull raised on specialist ranches. In a herd in the field they are tranquil but once isolated and in a closed space they are fearsome. They are fast, deadly accurate with their horns and have so much strength that they can lift a man as though he were a rag doll.

Three teams perform during the afternoon. Each of them consists of:

- A *matador*, who is the main performer and who will kill two bulls;
- Three *banderilleros*, foot assistants who help him with their cape work and who also stick the *banderillas* (coloured sticks) into the bulls;
- Two *picadors*, who are mounted on heavily padded horses and armed with a metal-tipped lance, which they use to stab the bull.

The *matadors* perform in order of seniority determined by the date on which they were registered and not in order of fame or popularity. Each *matador* will fight two bulls. The senior man will take the first and fourth, the next most senior the second and fifth, and the last the third and sixth.

The entry of the bull

When the arena is clear the president will signal with the use of a white handkerchief for the first bull to be released; trumpets sound and the door to the bull pen is opened. Above the door will be shown the weight of the bull. A good bull will charge into the arena and attack anything that moves. It is not a good sign if a bull looks back towards the pens or is unwilling to come out. Contrary to the popular image, a bull which paws the ground before attacking, is not particularly ferocious. It is, in fact, slightly cowardly because it is threatening without wanting to charge.

The first passes

The *matador*, or more usually one of his assistants, will make a few passes with the large, pink-and-yellow cape to try to work out the quality of the bull. The *matador* needs to know whether it will charge, whether it can see properly, and whether it attacks better with its left or right horn. After a few passes the president will signal for the next part to begin. When the *matador* takes over is he calm and still? Ideally he should have his hands held low and move the cape slowly and gracefully. He should be able to slow down the bull's charge in this way. He should step into the bull's path and at the moment the bull reaches him he should be still. A step backwards is not a good sign. The correct impression is that he is the one in control.

The *picador*

The *picador* on a well-padded horse is led into the arena and the bull is encouraged to the opposite side. Once the first *picador* is in position, which usually takes place on the shady side, the *matador* or one of his assistants goads the bull into charging the horse. The *picador* then plunges the metal-spiked tip of his lance into the large hump on the bull's shoulders. The bull receives two lance thrusts, the object being to reduce the strength of the bull and to break down the strong neck muscles so that the bull charges with its head down thus allowing the *matador* to work closer.

The *banderilleros*

Once again the president signals for the act to be changed. The trumpets sound and the *picadores* leave the arena. The *matadors* who are not performing come into the arena to help the *banderilleros*. Two of the three *banderilleros* perform at this point. The first holds a *banderilla* in each hand and once he has the bull's attention, runs in a curving path towards the bull which is now running towards him. When they meet he thrusts the *banderillas* into the hump on the neck of the bull and turns around its flank to escape. The second *banderillero* repeats the process. The careful placing of the *banderillas* can alter the way a bull charges.

The *banderilleros* are judged by elegance of movement and control. At the moment of placing the *banderillas*, the man should ideally have his feet together with both off the ground. The *banderillas* should be placed close together in the hump. As he turns away from the bull he only needs to run a few steps and then walk away calmly to indicate he is well in control and the bull is truly dominated.

The final stage

Once the *banderilleros* have finished their work, the final act begins. With his first bull of the afternoon the *matador* will take his sword, the *muleta* – a small, red, cape-like cloth – and approach the presidential box. He will salute the president with hat in hand and formally ask permission to perform and kill the bull.

The *matador* has a whole repertoire to select from for this part of his performance, which will last about ten minutes. When he judges that it is time to kill the bull he uses his *muleta* to encourage the bull to charge and when the two are almost in contact, leans over the horns and thrusts the sword in between its shoulder blades.

The kill itself is rarely achieved with one thrust of the sword. Usually a dagger is subsequently used to sever the bull's spinal chord, causing instant death. If a bull has been especially brave, the spectators will applaud it heartily at its death. The bull's body is then dragged out by a team of mules. Should a *matador* have impressed the audience they will wave white handkerchiefs and demand an award of either one ear, two ears or the tail. The *matador* will walk around the ring, displaying the trophy to the audience, whose cheers are only matched by their eagerness to shower him with gifts: a variety of objects that range from the customary flowers to wineskins, hats and handbags. The highest accolade a *matador* can receive is to be carried out, shoulder-high, from the ring's main gate by an excited crowd.

On some occasions *matadors* are caught by bulls and badly gored. Some foreigners have been known to stand and loudly applaud the bull. But this is one piece of visitor behaviour that does upset Spaniards. It provokes a horrified and indignant response, as they are unable to understand how the suffering and possible death of a human being could be greeted with such applause. One of the most famous Spanish poems is an elegy, written by Lorca, a lament for the bullfighter Ignacio Sanchez Mejias who was gored to death at five in the afternoon.

At five in the afternoon
It was five in the afternoon exactly
A child brought the white sheet
At five in the afternoon
The rest was death and death only
At five in the afternoon
A coffin on wheels was his bed
At five in the afternoon
Bones and flutes echo in his ear
At five in the afternoon
How terrible this five in the afternoon

Mention cruelty to an *aficionado* (a supporter) and he will talk of the shoddy practices that in the last few decades have haunted the *corrida*. Allegations of foul play include shaving of a bull's horns – not only incredibly painful but also disturbing to its sense of balance – to lessen the risk for the *matador*, the drugging of bulls with sulphates to induce severe pain and further lack of coordination in the ring, or the injection of sedatives.

BULL RUNNING

Pamplona's chief tourist attraction is the Fiesta de San Fermin (honouring St. Fermin, its first bishop), described in Ernest Hemingway's novel *The*

Sun Also Rises. Starting on July 6, the eve of the saint's festival, the *fiesta* lasts until the 14th, with daily bullfights preceded each morning by the famous *encierro* (enclosing) of the bulls, when they are driven through the streets behind crowds of frantically running men and boys.

There are many other *fiestas* in Spanish towns and villages where young and frisky, lean and mean bulls are turned loose in closed-off central squares. Bulls are not injured in these events but the only real defence against them are good strong legs.

It is important to stress that there is nothing fake about these events. The bulls are real and extremely dangerous. People, even experienced runners, have been badly injured or killed. If you enjoy raw excitement and the thrill of adrenalin pumping through your system then you will certainly find it running the bulls.

PELOTA (BALL)

Pelota comprises any of a number of glove, racket or bat court games requiring a rubber-cored ball. Variations of *pelota* can be classified as either direct (where the players face each other and the *pelota* is hit freely between opponents) or indirect (where the ball is hit off a wall). The second class has many variations, including bare-hand. *Pelota* courts include the two- or three-walled *fronton*, and a small, covered court, called the *trinquet*.

Outside the Basque country and at the northern end of the Costa Blanca, people are likely to miss out on what has to be the most exciting and certainly the fastest ball game in the world. Playing handball as a teenager against a single wall in the school yard is the most rudimentary Spanish version. Those memories are light years behind the game the Basques invented and have perfected wherever they are in the world.

The game is very much part of Basque identity as every village worthy of its name has its own *fronton,* the building that houses the *pelota* court. The Basque version of the game known as *pelota vasca* is a unique national sport. *Jai-alai* (happy game) is also a Basque term for the game. Originally played on stone courtyards and against walls, it is still played this way in many Basque villages today.

The Basques originally played *pelota* with their bare hands, then with leather gloves, wooden paddles and primitive rackets. The curved woven basket known as a *cesta*, that is able to propel the ball much faster, came into use in the mid 19th century. Another major innovation was the use of rubber balls, a development that made the sport even faster. Several players have been timed hurling the ball with a *cesta* at speeds of over 180 miles per hour. It is not only the speed of the ball that makes the game exciting, but also an incredible test of eye and hand coordination.

It was gambling more than the spectacle that brought *pelota* to the notice of the world. In Spain, *pelota* and gambling have always been insepa-rable. While the current crop of village athletes thrash it out against the church wall, an older group nearby will be yelling and groaning, tapping their wine-reddened cheeks to signal whether their money was riding on the red or blue team.

Navarra hosted the 2002 *Pelota* World Championships, a far cry from the village courts where most of the players honed their skills. While two teams smashed a ball around the court, teams of blazer-clad touts posted betting slips into slotted tennis balls and threw them to punters in the stands.

Today, matches of both *pelota* (without the *cesta)* and *Jai-alai* (with the *cesta*) are shown regularly on several local Spanish television stations in the Basque country and Valencia.

SIESTA

A *siesta* is a wonderful Spanish institution traditionally intended to protect people from the heat of the midday sun. It has been carried forward to today. There is something wonderful, particularly in the summer months, about drawing the curtains and lying down for a couple of hours in the afternoon. Many quickly learn to appreciate a *siesta*, even stray cats and dogs.

European business in the cities is reducing the importance of the *siesta* but in many parts of Spain it is still common practice. It is best to expect very little activity between 13.30 and about 16.30, when offices, public buildings and shops tend to be closed. A *siesta* is however particularly significant during the summer when many parts of Spain are blisteringly hot and the only sensible thing to do is to rest behind closed shutters. A *siesta* also allows the body to deal with late Spanish nightlife.

SOCIAL STRUCTURE

It may be surprising to know that Spain has a traditional social structure. It is a cultural legacy from its historic past. Let's look at some of the levels.

- The Royal family – top of the pile.

- Grandees – the leading nobility having a gateway to all the correct social circles.

- Nobles – with an assortment of various titles.

- Politicians – suitably despised.

- Professionals – working directors or business owners.

- White-collar workers and blue-collar workers.

- New resident foreigners – wealthier than gypsies and Moroccans.

15

CULTURE OF NEW SPAIN

RELIGION

Catholicism is still an influence over Spanish society. Although church attendance is falling, on a Sunday, around midday, families can be seen dressed in their best attire strolling home from their place of worship. Images of saints watch over shops, bars and drivers' cabs. Traditional *fiestas* mark church feasts. Whilst these are the simple facts, the attitude of the modern Spaniard towards the church needs to be examined more closely, for change over the last 40 years has been dramatic.

The pre-1975 image abroad was that of a reactionary, deeply repressive Catholic Church hostile towards any other religion, women's rights, abortion, homosexuality, divorce, and any open expression of eroticism. It represented a country out of step with the rest of Europe, with a very high birth rate, massive unemployment and a constant flow of emigrants seeking a better life abroad.

The Church had been an ally of the Franco regime with Pope Pius XII sending Franco a telegram of congratulations at the end of the war which read 'Lifting up our hearts to the Lord, we rejoice with your Excellency in the victory so greatly to be desired, of Catholic Spain'. For almost four decades, from the end of the Civil War to Franco's death in 1975, the Spanish Catholic Church had supported a dictatorship, standing for opposition to liberal and democratic ideas.

Church and State, unfortunately, were joined as one. The Church was exempt from taxation and was offered grants to construct churches and other religious buildings. It acquired the right to ask for published material it found offensive to be withdrawn from sale. The Church was given the opportunity to found universities, run radio stations, own newspapers and magazines. Police were forbidden to enter churches and the clergy could not be charged with criminal offences.

Things had to change. It was the Second Vatican Council which first brought this cosy relationship into question. Church and state had to separate. Over the years tolerance to other religions, particularly Islam has grown. European liberalism and female equality have played its part. But the Catholic Church has paid a price for its association with Franco, for today it is but a shadow of its former self. 80% of the population identify themselves as Catholics. Only 18% of Spaniards go to Mass once a month and about 50% never go at all. There is a major shortage of priests. Moreover, the Spanish birth rate has fallen to one of the lowest in the world.

FOOTBALL

On a Sunday evening Spain's bars are crowded. Huge screens show football. Football is Spain's national sport and the country's most important spectator sport. Spanish soccer fans are among the most dedicated in Europe, matched in their fanaticism only by the Italians. Every town in Spain has a football pitch and a team … and lots of TV screens. A number of La Liga matches are shown live on TV each week, invariably involving either Real Madrid or Barcelona and other top teams such as Deportivo La Coruna, Real Sociedad and Valencia.

The Spanish league is one of the most competitive in Europe with teams enjoying considerable success in European competitions, although the glory days of Real Madrid and Barcelona are long gone, and the successes of Spanish clubs have been overshadowed in recent years by the Italians. Spain has never been able to repeat its clubs' successes at international level.

There's a huge gulf between the top Spanish clubs and the rest. Real Madrid and Barcelona stand head and shoulders above the rest. Real Madrid play at the imposing 130,000 seat Bernabeu stadium, while Barcelona's home is the equally impressive 120,000 seat Nou Camp stadium. Outside the top clubs, attendances at most first division matches are low.

Like the British Premiership and Italian clubs, the finances of Spanish clubs have been rescued by revenue from televised football matches over the last few years. Top clubs demand instant success and tend to swap their coaches almost as often as players change their shirts. Real Madrid had three coaches alone in the 2004/5 season.

NIGHTLIFE

Spain is famous for its vibrant nightlife, which extends until dawn and beyond in major cities and resort areas. There is a wide choice of night life for all ages including jazz clubs, cabarets, discos, sex shows, flamenco clubs, music clubs and bars, nightclubs, music halls and restaurants with floor shows.

For many Spaniards the day doesn't begin until nightfall and most clubs and discotheques start to warm up around midnight. Young Spaniards dance around the clock with discotheques closing at daybreak.

Ibiza is home to the northern European raver. It's the place to be in summer when it boasts Europe's most vibrant nightlife and biggest and boldest dance clubs. The authorities in Madrid, Barcelona and other cities have been forced to restrict Spain's incessant day and nightlife in an attempt to reduce drug abuse and the resulting high number of fatal car accidents.

Bars in these cities must now close at 02.30 and discos at 04.30.

Along busy main roads or in cities, flashing neon lights beckon the unwary into a nightclub. These are not disco, cabaret, musical or dancing extravaganzas. If not eating, drinking red wine, or singing, the Spanish male has a reputation of being a great lover. That may, or may not be the case, and for all we know a nightclub may be the place to learn, for they are essentially registered or unregistered brothels. It is certainly not a place to take your mother or sister!

Apparently fewer Spanish women are selling themselves nowadays. Increasingly, Spain's prostitutes are foreigners. A lot come from eastern Europe, Africa and Latin America. Yet another outstanding example of the live-and-let-live atmosphere of contemporary Spain is the space taken up by prostitutes' advertisements in the daily and weekly newspapers.

Barcelona has long been liberal or degenerate, depending on your point of view. It is the Hamburg or Amsterdam of southern Europe. You can buy hard porn off news-stands or watch live sex at nightclubs. But in this respect, Barcelona differs from the rest of Spain only in degree, for it probably has something to do with the fact that Barcelona is a port.

GAMBLING AND LOTTERY

Like people in all Mediterranean countries, the Spaniard loves to gamble. They will bet on almost anything including the lottery, football pools, bingo, slot machines, casinos, and *jai-alai* games. Many things have changed in today's get-rich society and it's hard to believe that gambling was actually banned under Franco who only approved of the state lottery.

The *Organizacion Nacional de Ciegos Espanoles (ONCE)* was created by General Franco's Nationalist government in 1938 to provide employment for the blind, whose numbers had been swollen by the civil war. As a way of financing it, Franco agreed to an idea that had first been tried out previously, when blind people had banded together to organise local raffles. A blind man or woman, standing on a corner, draped with strips of lottery tickets soon became an integral part of Spanish street life. It is a sight which surprises many foreign visitors, but one which successive governments have defended on the grounds that the blind in Spain thereby have the opportunity for more regular and normal contact with the rest of society.

Roughly half the proceeds from a *ONCE* draw are returned in the form of prize money. The balance goes towards operating costs, *ONCE*'s schools, other institutions and profit. *ONCE* is big business taking about 60€ per year from every Spaniard, having a massive turnover and investment portfolio of which many public companies would be proud. It owns companies, arguing the presence of *ONCE* directors on boards of many organisations in which it has invested creates employment for its members, and its presence in the media helps change public attitudes towards the disabled.

The world's biggest lottery takes place each Christmas (*El Gordo*). Ticket prices are high and therefore mainly sold to syndicates with winners arguing over the spoils. *El Nino* (The Kid) the second biggest lottery takes place in early January. Winning the lottery isn't a guarantee of a happy life when disputes arise over ownership of tickets. Campello was torn apart when 5,000 of its inhabitants shared 126 million euros, setting neighbour against neighbour, friend against friend, and even splitting families.

In addition to the *ONCE* lottery, many regulated casinos operate in resort areas, with well dressed, well heeled clientel, playing roulette, blackjack and *chemin de fer*, offering another more sophisticated method of loosing money.

PERSONALITY

Conversation

One important characteristic to be relied upon is Spaniards' readiness to communicate. Compare the discreet silence of a group of English people who do not know each other with the friendly chatter which quickly develops among a similar group of Spanish people. A good deal of social life is maintained *en la calle* (in the street) or any public place. Bars are particularly important. Spaniards generally enjoy conversation, invariably loud, where everyone seems to talk at once.

One thing Spaniards don't discuss openly is the Franco years. Many people are alive today who have memories of that era. A successful soap opera dared to look back at Spain's most sensitive years. The groundbreaking series *Cuentame Como Paso* was a story of a family living through the Franco regime at the end of the 1960s. Most people thought Spain's skeletons were best left in the cupboard, but the success of the show proved that Spain had grown up enough to look back at its painful times.

Pride

In Chapter 6 it was stated that familiarity is a hallmark of Spanish life. Handshaking and kissing on the cheek the usual form of greeting. Old-fashioned courtesy and formal manners are however still a custom in rural areas. Great store is set by personal loyalty and friendship, but it is also very important to take account of a Spaniard's personal sense of honour and pride, which is easily offended.

A second source of pride exists – civic pride, occurring even in the smallest town and village. Streets are clean and free of litter. Householders sweep the street outside their property. Houses are well painted on the outside and the owners fill their terraces and window boxes with a riot of brightly-coloured flowers. Seafront promenades are restored. Roundabouts are elegant by design, and in towns which are not really tourist resorts there is ample and ornate street lighting. One other thing is the almost total absence of graffiti, except for some inexplicable reason, on the sides of railway carriages.

INTERACTING WITH OTHERS

The family group

The family group is strong with sometimes two or three generations living within one house. Spaniards' love of children is well known. Children will be beautifully dressed with a confidence that befits offspring in the new millennium. Mother and father will be proud parents with a deep sense of honour. Grandparents will be friendly, courteous, generous, not fully comprehending the staggering changes that have taken place since their own childhood.

The young handsome male will study in the evening for personal advancement, will watch football and own a fast scooter. The beautiful dark haired *senorita* will be of slim build and somehow be one foot taller and one foot narrower than her mother. Young Spaniards are the same as the young of any European country, seeking freedom, equality and enjoyment alongside their worldly brothers and sisters.

Nowhere is the strength of family group better demonstrated than on Sunday afternoon when they congregate together for lunch. It may be in a restaurant or at home. It is a ritual not to be missed without good reason, as grandparents and grandchildren meet at the home of proud parents.

The *paseo*

Outside the restaurant, in the main square or along the promenade, the evening *paseo* will commence with young girls and boys, parents and grandparents strolling in a leisurely manner. For some it is gentle exercise in the cool of the evening, for others a prelude to a good night out; for the spectators, it is an entertainment.

In villages chairs are placed in the narrow streets, as occupants emerge from the dark interior of their houses to talk and gossip about the day's events.

Getting things done

Spanish bureaucrats, in common with those of other nations, when asked to render a service often find it easier to say 'no' than to say 'yes'. Spaniards are in general insistent in their demands, whether this be in a market, bar or government office. They most certainly do not easily accept 'no' for an answer, and new residents should not either.

When something, which is being refused, really needs to be done, it is best to remain patient but persistent. Losing your temper or becoming angry in such circumstances is counterproductive. The trick is to maintain a conversation, keep the bureaucrat's attention and get them to respond to you as a person and not simply a problem.

So much in Spain is achieved through a network of contacts and friends of friends that many problems can be resolved through these channels. It is not always possible to buy your way out of problems or difficulties, but things do get done for friends.

To keep abreast of bureaucrats, always insist on a receipt, keep it and file it away as a complaint will not be entertained without a receipt. Keep records of taxes paid, bank statements, bills paid, guarantees and such like. They may never be required, but in view of the Spanish love of paper, without documentary proof, there is little possibility of an issue being resolved. All payments to the town hall, all motoring taxes and all utility bill receipts should be kept. You never know when they will be required, but when they are it will invariably be to your benefit.

How not to be an *Inglés/Inglesa*

Inglés is a word sometime used disparagingly about tourists or foreigners living in rural Spain. It is about their colour, their dress and sense of humour. It is not doing things the Spanish way! So, how do you avoid being treated as *Inglés*? The answer is actually quite simple. Be sensitive to Spanish codes of behaviour.

Beachwear is not an appropriate dress for urban areas, whether this is a city, town or village. It is not that Spaniards are particularly prudish about the sight of bare flesh, for they too will wear skimpy bikinis and shorts on the beach. The concern is *where* flesh is revealed.

MUSEUMS

In addition to visiting blanket, wickerwork, guitar and craft factories, *bodegas*, vineyards, distilleries, breweries, mineral water springs, farms and dairies, Spaniards have an appetite for going to museums. There are over 800 which says a lot about successive invaders and Spain's inglorious history.

Important national collections exist in Madrid and Barcelona, but surprisingly there are a large number of small local museums. A local artist is revered, with paintings accorded display rights at cultural centres.

TOILETS

Try to find a public toilet in Spain – it's easier to find a needle in a haystack. Except in railway stations, shopping centres and places of public interest, they don't exist. What do you do? Go to a bar, café, hotel or restaurant nearby. In thanks, it is normal to buy a drink on the way out – which rather defeats the object of the visit in the first place. Owners of food establishments are well accustomed to this behaviour, granting a request to use their facilities with a smile or a wave of the hand. Here are a few essential words.

Damas	– ladies
Caballeros	– men
Senoras	– women
Senores	– men
Toilet	– *servicios* or, *aseos*
Where is the toilet?	– *Donde estan los servicios por favor?*
Are there toilets here?	– *Hay servicios por favor?*

SCOOTERS

No reference to new Spanish culture can be made without reference to this little, brightly coloured, buzzing and swarming machine otherwise known as a motor scooter. Invented in Italy, now made in the Far East, scooters have made their home in new Spain. They can be seen massed outside schools and colleges, at sports centres, at vantage points for consuming Big Macs and at any other point where teenagers converge. They are noisy two wheeled cycles for annoying adults and impressing girl friends. They can be fun too!

AMERICANISATION OF CULTURE

In the 1960s Spain opened up foreign investment and tourism, and also encouraged Spaniards to emigrate to other European countries in search of work. Both these developments brought increased foreign influences, which undermined the government's desire to keep the country relatively isolated. Since the 1960s Spanish culture, and particularly that of its youth, has increasingly become part of a homogeneous, heavily American-influenced international culture.

For young people the most significant aspect of the international culture is rock music. There are many Spanish rock musicians, but few of these have achieved much recognition outside the country. The most successful of Spain's popular singers is undoubtedly Julio Iglesias, but his appeal is to an older audience.

The internationalisation of culture can also be seen in a variety of other ways. American fast-food chains such as *McDonald's* and *Burger King* can be found in the major cities. The 24-hour-a-day convenience store *7–11* opened in Madrid in the late 1980s. Much of the television programming is foreign and especially American.

16

GETTING OUT AND ABOUT

BE POSITIVE

Going to live in Spain is not just about a physical change. A few weeks after landing in a new country the shock of a different culture, changes in attitude and frequent frustration can have an adverse effect on one's well-being. Isolation, feeling powerless and finding fault with everything are classic symptoms. The blow can be cushioned if an understanding has been reached beforehand about Spanish ways. Understanding the symptoms, too, can also help. The first stage is a honeymoon period, which everyone experiences. It can be followed by a period of feeling inadequate, lonely, withdrawn and wanting to go back home. By being positive, becoming more assertive, you will soon find you can deal with situations and start to feel more relaxed. The final stage is feeling at home, embracing the new culture, enjoying a social life, getting out and about.

Of course there is the sun worshiping and the *cerveza* drinking but that novelty soon wears off. With time one needs to develop a more positive attitude to life, an attitude that says, 'Get out, learn about the country, develop new interests and meet new people'.

LEARN ABOUT THE COUNTRY

Learn more about Spain. It's different! The real way to learn is to travel. There are other methods, such as reading books and tourist guides, which are colourful and informative. Watching travel films, too, have their place. But it is only by going to see somewhere that a true appreciation can be obtained. There are places where you can enjoy the sun, the sea and the mountains. Places where you can benefit from the climate and keep in shape with your favourite all year round sport. Where you can discover local history and monuments, travel down hidden byways and forest tracks, participate in local *fiestas*, meet local people … and much more.

Learning about the country falls into a few predictable steps. Firstly explore the surrounding area by going inland and developing a deeper understanding of its history, culture and ambience. Secondly, as a minimum, visit the two major cities of Barcelona and Madrid. Thirdly, do what many residents of the Costas do – get away from it all by going to northern Spain, preferably in the summer to get away from the searing heat.

Travel inland

Jump into a car and go! On minor country roads the traffic is amazingly light, even in the height of the holiday season. Go 20 kilometres inland and there is virtually no traffic on the roads throughout the year. Go inland and experience the real Spain.

Driving a few miles inland; the buzz of the coast disappears. Park the car and just walk in the countryside and you are immediately struck by how calm everything is. Of course you hear the sounds of nature: birds singing, strange rustlings in the long grass made by some unseen creatures, the breeze in the trees overhead, but at other times there is almost complete silence. Go higher into the mountains, stop for a few minutes and just listen to … nothing.

The further inland, the more unspoilt it will be. Some of villages have hardly changed for centuries, inhabited by families who have always lived there, the properties being handed down from generation to generation. Their way of life is very different from that on the coast. Herdsmen still lead their flocks out to the grazing grounds; farmers gather their crops of olives and almonds. Life stands still! Use trips inland as a learning experience.

Neveras

High in the mountains of the Costa Blanca can be found well preserved snow wells called *neveras*. They were built in strategic locations to catch the snow as it drifted into dips or hollows. Dug deep into the ground, and lined with stone, they had an access door and a conical roof to keep out sunlight. Stone steps or iron rungs enabled the pressers and block cutters to reach the bottom. The size and solid construction of *neveras* are truly amazing. Snow was commercially harvested, compacted in the *nevera* and left until summer, when it was cut into blocks of ice. In the cool of the night the ice was carried down the mountains by mule, donkey and cart to distant villages and towns.

Era

Where there is a large old farmhouse, there will always be a well, an oven and a threshing area known as an *era*. Threshing and crushing of cereals was achieved by means of a metre-long, tapered stone pulled over grain on a flat surface. Some farmhouses had separate accommodation for workers, a small church and a place for children. The animals were held in an open area attached to the house that faced south with a windowless north wall. The key however was a well with water, for without it no one survived.

Legacy of the Moors

Mozarabic is a term used to describe narrow stepped trails which cross over mountains from valley to valley. They are true marvels of engineering zigzagging down into the depths of the deepest ravines and up the other side. The trails are characterised by thousands of steps with supporting walls in tricky places. Many have withstood the ravages of time and lack of maintenance. They are best seen in the Val de Laguart south of Valencia.

Watch towers

The authorities built round lookout towers along the coast in the 16th century to provide early warning of pirate raids. Raids by ships from Africa were quite common. After the final expulsion of the Moors in 1609, the raids became so frequent that the authorities had to take steps to combat them by building towers and by providing a fleet of defensive ships. In 1636, the pirates, after pillaging Calpe, took nearly all the population back to Algiers. They were released many years later when a ransom was paid.

Windmills

The windmill is one of the images of Spain made famous by the story of Don Quixote. Windmills need the best possible location to utilise their power source. Remains can normally be found on high ground near villages on the coast or on top of cliffs. Near the coastal town of Javea, there are remains of over ten on the cliff edge. Many windmills date from pre-Moorish times. The wind caught sails which were made of canvas, and turned wooden shafts with gears attached to flat stones for grinding wheat.

There are 150 windmills, or remains of windmills around Cartagena. Many can be seen from the motorway. Some have been restored to full working order, but others are no more than circles of stones where once the wind turned sails. They were used for grinding grain or for raising water from underground to irrigate the fields. During the latter part of the 19th century windmills were increasingly built to raise water for crop irrigation.

Today a new type of windmill dots the Spanish landscape. Thousands of tall, elegant, white windmills used for power generation: more than in any other country in Europe. The amount of energy from Spain's wind-powered generators exceeds the amount of energy supplied by its seven nuclear power stations: 7,681 megawatts of power are supplied by wind power compared to 7,606 megawatts supplied by nuclear power. The majority of Spanish electricity comes from water power (16,731 MW), followed by coal-powered generators (11,425MW). The capacity of wind-powered generators depends on weather conditions. Periods of peak demand, usually when it is either very hot or very cold, often coincide with periods of low winds.

All creatures great and small

In the country, strolling among pine trees, walkers should watch out for the Processionary Caterpillar Moth known in Spain as the *Orugas*. The moths lay their eggs in white cotton wool like nests in pine trees easily visible from paths in the countryside. On hatching, the caterpillars make their way to the ground in a nose to tail chain in search for the next place in their life cycle. Don't touch them or poke at the nests or let animals near them. They cause a nasty rash and give off a dust which causes respiratory problems for adults. Children can become ill, cats and dogs have been known to die. The traditional natural antidote for the rash is vinegar, although olive oil and lemon juice are also recommended.

The only poisonous snakes found in Spain are vipers. They are very easy to recognise with a triangular head, brown-yellow in colour, with a wavy black line down the spine and dots on the side. They measure 60cm and avoid people. Snakes are very active in warm weather, especially in the middle of the day and may be found basking on a rock. Be careful when you sit down! Do not move rocks and remember that snakes live in walls. The bite of a viper needs urgent medical attention.

Spain has a plentiful supply of honey. Indeed exclusive shops sell many varieties. In the country, bee hives are best avoided. Small wooden hives, well signposted, located in sheltered warm places in the mountains are home to the honey makers. Keep moving, leave the bees well alone.

Mosquito bites leave painful, red, itchy blotches. Although in our latitudes any subsequent illness is moderate, the bite of the mosquito can cause problems for animals as well as humans. The females need to take blood to mature and lay 200 to 400 eggs in stagnant water. Therefore avoid abandoned containers, flooded gutters, puddles, and water troughs that contain tepid water. On the other hand clean ponds with fish will eat the larva of the mosquito. Eliminate stagnant water for it is indispensable to their reproduction.

VISIT PREMIER CITIES

Madrid

Situated in the centre of the country the capital, Madrid, is a city of over three million people and a crossroad for rail, road and air travel. Its altitude of 660 metres gives rise to a temperature profile of cold winters and hot summers, making spring and autumn the best times to visit. Those who can escape from Madrid during August make for the cooler north or go south to the Mediterranean.

Despite the climate, the capital city has developed its own unique personality. It boasts the *Parque del Retiro*, a world famous area of leafy paths and avenues, a royal palace and grand public squares. Its museums are filled with Spain's historic treasures. The *Museo del Prado* contains the world's greatest assembly of Spanish painting, particularly the works of Velazquez and Goya. It also houses impressive foreign collections.

Madrid is a city that offers the best in shopping facilities including availability of the latest designer clothes sold in elegant up-market stores. There are food markets throughout the city. The centuries-old *Rastro*, open every Sunday, is one of the world's greatest flea markets.

There is a good choice of music; classical, jazz and rock competing with Madrid's own comic style opera known as *zarzuela*. Saturday night starts in the cafés, moves to the *tapas* bars, restaurants or clubs, and continues throughout the night, adding to the city's high level of traffic noise.

Barcelona

Looking for premier city life? Then this unquestionably is the place. One of the Mediterranean's busiest ports, it is much more than the capital of Catalonia. Culturally, commercially and in sport it not only rivals Madrid, but also, rightfully, considers itself on a par with the greatest European cities. The success of the Olympic Games confirmed this to the world. It is always open to outside influences because of its location on the coast and its proximity to the French border.

Barcelona is a city with impeccable style and vitality, demonstrated by the very best of Catalan, Spanish and International fashion design and complemented by a stunning live arts scene: Barcelona regularly plays host to some of the world's best musicians. Las Ramblas is the most famous street in Spain. It is busy round the clock, especially in the evenings and at weekends. News stands, caged birds, flower stalls, tarot readers, musicians and mime artists throng the wide, tree shaded, central walkway.

GO NORTH

The concrete chain from Catalonia to Gibraltar is all but complete, with barely a missing link. In places it is low-rise and low-key, backed by orange groves and as distinctly Spanish as it was before the builders arrived. But in general, in summer, the beaches are packed, the sun is merciless and night-time heat makes an insomniac of even the deepest sleeper. The answer is to head north. A trip to forgotten Asturias brings immeasurable relief. It is a land straight from the pages of a fairy tale. The mountains are fierce, sitting close to the coast; perhaps put there by some imaginative storyteller. The foothills behind the cliffs are so green, the cows that graze in them so picture-perfect, the woodlands and vegetable patches so ornate.

Most Spaniards, long term visitors and nearly all of Spain's new residents go north at some time to the Costa Verde – Green Spain. 'Get away from the Costas' is the cry. Increasing numbers of people are discovering the deep green landscapes, the solitude of the mountains and the quiet sandy beaches of northern Spain. The grass really is greener on Spain's Costa

Verde, where the lush scenery, quiet beaches and delicous local cider provide an escape from the summer madness for people in the know.

The most obvious attraction is a group of mountains called the Picos de Europa that straddles two communities of Austurias and Cantabria. A vast fortress of rock and snow, these mountains, set in a national park, offer excellent rock climbing and good hiking, but in winter, when covered in snow, they are extremely dangerous.

The Asturians eat extraordinary bowls of rich bean and sausage stews, and drink cider for breakfast, lunch and supper. The cider is poured from bottles held high above the head in one hand, into a glass held well below the waist in the other, eyes looking neither up nor down, but strictly dead ahead.

Trawlers anchored in harbours leave no doubt that many locals still look to the sea for their livelihood. Likewise, menus pinned outside the many eateries list shrimps, giant marine crabs, clams and octopus as local delicacies. Other dishes such as *Merluza a la sidra* (hake in cider) combine the best that land and sea have to offer. Here, too, well-fed dairy cattle grazing in green pastures make it easy to see why Asturias has a reputation for quality milk and cheeses such as the famous *Cabrales Blue* and *Queso Gamoneu*.

Old roads provide an unhurried journey through quiet villages where vestiges of a more traditional way of life remain. Women gather-in freshly-cut hay from the fields by horse and cart, and cattle are kept alongside farmhouses. Everywhere there are onions, or washing, hanging on covered balconies attached to traditional, wooden Asturian granaries built on raised stone piles.

The Costa Verde may not have wall to wall sunshine, but it does have an un spoilt landscape, friendly people and it is not overcrowded like much of the Mediterranean coast. The weather is variable because of the Atlantic influence but it's very mild in winter. Europeans are now discovering what Spaniards have long known, in summer the rich go south, the wise go north.

ENJOY SPORTING ACTIVITIES

The diverse geographical nature of Spain with its mountains, woodlands, beaches and sea gives a wonderful backdrop for sporting activities. Golf clubs, sports centres, bowling greens, gymnasiums, swimming pools, marinas and tennis clubs are all striving to make better use of leisure time. The newcomer faces a bewildering choice of activities – only handicapped by an ageing process, which probably rules out bull fighting, bungee jumping and hang gliding. Football, rugby, running and hockey are now passive spectator sports, as a battle with the waistline is probably lost too. A short cycle ride to the supermarket seems to be more appropriate than dressing up each Sunday in matching bright lycra outfits, ripping calf muscles to shreds, ascending narrow mountain roads, astride the latest 21-gear machine.

No! It is time to put the more active stuff on the back burner. Slow down. Remember, this is Spain – where time is not important. Consider the less athletic pursuits where skill, knowledge and abilities can be honed to perfection with practice, practice and more practice. Golf and bowls perhaps! Tennis or maybe hiking! Tone up at a gym. Take up fishing.

Golf

Golf in Spain is booming, driven by tourism and the climate. The worldwide success of Ballesteros, Olazabal, Jimenez and Garcia has contributed to this success. Ballesteros is a star in Spain and an icon in Britain.

The Costa del Sol is often referred to as Costa del Golf; such is the profusion of new courses. They are carved out of barren landscapes, pampered and watered to produce lush green fairways. Consequently golf is not cheap: 60€ for a round is common. In Scotland, the home of golf, it is a game for the working man. In Spain, it is a game for the tourist or wealthy resident.

Hiking

Walking or hiking clubs exist in all the main areas. For the adventurous, the best places to go are the Picos de Europe in northern Spain, the Pyrenees near the French border, the Costa Blanca inland from Benidorm and around the Sierra Nevada near Granada. Strangely, hiking is not very popular with Spaniards, but it is hugely popular with foreign residents.

Many holiday companies offer Spanish walking tours. This has given rise to some excellent English language publications describing good detailed routes with clear concise maps. Trails are way-marked and the only hazards encountered are dogs and the unhygienic nature of some refuge huts. It is important not to underestimate some of these rugged trails with snow on high ground, rapidly changing weather and exposure on steep paths.

Bowling

The capital cost to establish a bowling green is low. Demand is high. It is one of the few competitive sports for those of advancing years, which combines well with social activities. Such is its popularity on the Costa Blanca that a winter league of nine clubs has a full page devoted to its activities in the local weekly paper.

Sailing

Adapting to the demands of a thriving tourist industry has led to the growth of pleasure craft harbours of which there are now hundreds stretched along the Mediterranean coastline. They range from small harbours that cater for a fishing fleet and dinghies to large, glitzy harbours – such as Puerto Banus close to Marbella – which can cope with a thousand boats, many being no more than a display of wealth, or floating gin palaces. It is hardly surprising that marinas are full to capacity, but they do offer a full selection of services at a reasonable price. The Customs authorities allow foreign-registered boats to be used for six months of the year and to remain in the country for the rest of the year, during which time the boat may be used for habitation.

The development of marinas and new harbours has spin-offs such as ships chandler's, restaurants and bars and up-market apartments. Yachting is for the rich: it is dinghy sailing for the rest of us. The Med can be choppy. Unfortunately there are not too many totally sheltered bays and, regrettably, even fewer supervised dinghy sailing clubs.

Fishing

So popular is fishing that the basic equipment is sold in supermarkets or newspaper shops. Sea fishing from the shore is still a sport for the youngster with only the smaller species being caught. River or lake fishing in northern Spain is a far more serious matter altogether, with trout and salmon, pike and carp available. The local tourist office is the place to enquire about licences, season tickets and such like.

Tennis

Tennis is practised everywhere. It has been made popular by the many Spanish superstars. It is a low capital cost, highly popular activity. Every small town, hotel and club has its tennis courts utilised all year around. Many urbanisations, in addition to having a swimming pool, have a tennis court maintained through their community charge.

Running

It is not too hot to run! Spain, like all countries, has its runners and joggers. It has superstars too. It has often been host to international athletics meetings. Each town has its own sports ground complete with a running track. Marathons and half marathons are commonplace – but not in summer.

Gyms

Many privately-run gymnasiums tend to be devoted to muscle building. But northern Europeans much prefer the weight reduction clubs of bright lycra, cardio-vascular training, running and cycling machines, sauna and steam bath. Modern gymnasiums exist, located in new building complexes.

Baring all on the beach

While France accepted nudism, it was not until the early 1970s that topless sunbathing first appeared in Spain, although the patrolling *Guardia Civil* advised people to 'cover up'. Today it has changed with the practice common and nudism allowed in certain designated areas.

The first nudist resort appeared in 1979 near Estepona on the Costa del Sol but other beaches, about 60 in number officially designated and additionally others not, are widely accepted as locations for naturism.

Irrespective of what is worn, Spain now boasts the highest number of Blue Flag beaches and marinas in Europe. The Blue Flags are awarded where a high standard of water quality, environmental management, education, safety and the provision of services have been achieved. Keep updated on www.blueflag.org.

Skiing

Ever heard of the Costa Blanca Ski Club? It sounds unreal. The Costa Blanca is sun, sea and sand! Literally hundreds of skiers travel from the Costa Blanca and all parts of Spain to the Sierra Nevada each year. It has several unique features as it is the most southerly ski centre in mainland Europe and is also one of the highest giving a long season with good sunshine, lasting until May. It is only 150 kilometres from the Costa del Sol and 400 kilometres from the Costa Blanca.

Just outside Granada, the resort is well developed with parking for thousands of cars and buses, 19 ski lifts capable of carrying 30,000 people per hour, 54 kilometres of marked slopes and 3.5 kilometres floodlit for night-time skiing at weekends. There are17 hotels. Equipment hire and lessons present no problems.

The area is well named. It is called Solynieve (sun and snow).

Sports federations

There are many other sports available – squash, beach and water sports, horse riding, mountaineering, gliding, cycling and, of course, football, football and more football. Each sport has its own federation, which is always a good starting point for information.

MIXING SOCIALLY

Foreigners seek their own wherever they go, but perhaps the English-speaking do so with more enthusiasm than other nationalities. Some pursue intensely social lives within the community, while others deliberately shun the company of their compatriots. In the early stages the support received from other expatriates is often important in cementing friendships and forming social networks. The newcomer is typically ascribed a subordinate or dependent role, seniority among expatriates being mainly determined by their length of residence. A second influence is the degree of permanent or seasonal residence: long-term residents tend to look down on tourists, even those of their own nationality.

In 1992 the BBC filmed Eldorado, an ill-fated soap drama near Mijas, creating an image that the British expatriate community in the Costa del Sol lived in an artificial world. The programme was based on a conceived stereotype of 'Brits in Spain' presenting them as living an idle existence in the sun, drinking too much alcohol, behaving like old colonials, and certainly not integrating into the Spanish way of life. Sometimes the ex-pats were portrayed as having a wonderful time, on other occasions as being poor and isolated, while the presence of a few exiled criminals was turned into all manner of stories.

Of course it is not true! While British residents rarely integrate effectively with local Spaniards, they enjoy a well-structured lifestyle which on the whole keeps them busy, happy and healthy. They also join the many expatriate clubs, which cater for a wide range of activities and interests. Many people join these clubs to meet people of similar background and interests and to widen social circles. Social clubs are a method of meeting people, of sharing a common interest, past or present. They are meeting places to deal with problems or to seek information, and are an aid to settling into a new country. Golf and hiking may be the top sports but a meal, a drink or a visit to a club are the main social activities.

RELAXING

Spain's *manana* attitude can help people to relax and become more philosophical. Does it really matter if there is a delay, so long as emergencies are dealt with as they happen? Does it matter if there are queues; it does not seem to bother the locals, and what's the point of getting upset?

Simply rising late or early, every morning to blue skies, looking towards a green golf course, mountains or sea and thinking, 'Am I lucky or not?' is enough in itself. At the end of the day when skies are clear and a brilliant canopy of stars cover the heavens, a similar thought occurs.

17

ARTS, LITERATURE, MUSIC AND ARCHITECTURE

Spain has a long, varied, and distinguished artistic heritage, which includes some of the most important figures in Western culture. The period from about 1500 to 1681, known as the Golden Age, is considered the most brilliant era of Spain's artistic history. Still, at no time has Spain ceased to be a culturally vital country, and the 20th century in particular has been a highly productive and creative one; indeed its first few decades came to be called the Silver Age. The Spanish Civil War of 1936–39 marked a break in the development of arts. Many leading artists and intellectuals went into exile at the end of the war. Within Spain the Franco regime practised sweeping censorship which limited the form artistic expression could take. Some major 20th-century artists have now sought inspiration in the country's history and folk traditions, while others have joined the most modern developments in their field.

ARTISTS – MORE THAN JUST DALI

El Greco

El Greco was born in 1541 on the island of Crete and died on April 7, 1614 in Toledo, Spain. He had a highly individual dramatic and expressionistic style, met with the puzzlement of his contemporaries, but gained newfound appreciation in the 20th century. He was also a sculptor and architect.

Diego Velazquez

Diego Rodriguez de Silva Velazquez, who died on August 6, 1660, was the most important Spanish painter of the 17th century; a giant of Western art, Velazquez is universally acknowledged as one of the world's greatest artists. The naturalistic style in which he was trained provided a language for the expression of his remarkable power of observation in portraying both the living model and still life. Stimulated by the study of 16th-century Venetian painting, he grew from a master of faithful likeness and characterisation into the creator of masterpieces of visual impression unique in his time. With brilliant diversity of brushstrokes and subtle harmonies of colour, he achieved effects of form and texture, space, light, and atmosphere, which make him the chief forerunner of 19th-century French Impressionism.

The number of personal documents remaining is very small, and official documentation relating to his paintings is relatively rare. Since he seldom signed or dated his works, their identification and chronology has often to be based on stylistic evidence alone. Though many copies of his portraits were evidently made in his studio by assistants, his own production was not large and his surviving autographed works number fewer than 150. He is known to have worked slowly, and during his later years much of his time was occupied by his duties as a court official in Madrid.

Francisco de Goya

Francisco de Goya was born on March 30, 1746, at Fuendetodos, Spain and died on April 16, 1828, in Bordeaux, France. He was an artist whose multifarious paintings, drawings, and engravings reflected contemporary historical upheavals and influenced important 19th and 20th-century painters. The series of etchings entitled *The Disasters of War*, 1810–14 records the horrors of the Napoleonic invasion. His masterpieces include *The Naked Maja* and *The Clothed Maja.*

Pablo Picasso

Picasso was born on October 25, 1881 in Malaga, Spain and died on April 8, 1973 in Mougins, France. Classified as a Spanish expatriate painter, sculptor, printmaker, ceramicist and stage designer, he was one of the greatest and most influential artists of the 20th century and the creator of Cubism.

An enormous body of Picasso's work remains, and the legend lives on, a tribute to the vitality of the disquieting Spaniard with the 'sombre piercing' eyes who superstitiously believed that work would keep him alive. For nearly 80 of his 91 years Picasso devoted himself to an artistic production that contributed significantly to, and paralleled the whole development of, modern art in the 20th century.

On 27 April 1937, Guernica, a little Basque village in northern Spain and the historical site of the Basques' traditional rights guaranteed to them by Spanish monarchs, was mercilessly bombed by the German volunteer air-force in the service of General Franco's nationalist forces (greater detail was provided in Chapter 2). At that time it was the worst bombing from the air of a civilian population in history. Sixteen hundred civilians were killed or wounded and the town burned for three days. News of the massacre reached Paris immediately and by May 1st more than a million protesters flooded the streets to express outrage in the largest May Day demonstration in the city's history.

Picasso was shocked and outraged by the still photographs and the newsreels and immediately rushed home to sketch the first images of his mural that would become the 20th century's most powerful statement on canvas of the horrors of war, and his personal statement of the obscenity. The central figures are a woman with outstretched arms, a bull, and a horse in agony. The painting *Guernica* was delivered to the Spanish Pavilion at an Exhibition already in progress. It soon became the most visited attraction and in the course of a few years, a constant reminder of what had engulfed Spain.

On the centenary of Picasso's birth and after Franco's death, Spain's new King and government celebrated the event by transferring the painting to Spain. It is now housed in the Reina Sofia, Spain's national museum of modern art in Madrid and has long been acclaimed as a masterpiece. For many years it has represented artistic and intellectual opposition to the Franco regime.

Salvador Dali

Dali was born on May 11, 1904 in Figueres, Spain and died there on January 23, 1989. He was famous as a surrealist painter and printmaker, influential for his explorations of subconscious imagery. As an art student in Madrid and Barcelona, Dali assimilated a vast number of artistic styles and displayed unusual technical prowess as a painter. It was not until the late 1920s, however, that two events brought about the development of his mature artistic style: his discovery of Sigmund Freud's writings on the erotic significance of subconscious imagery, and his affiliation with the Paris Surrealists, a group of artists and writers who sought to establish the 'greater reality' of man's subconscious over reason. To bring up images from his subconscious mind, Dali began to induce hallucinatory states in himself by a process he described as 'paranoiac critical'.

Once Dali hit on this method, his painting style matured with extraordinary rapidity, and from 1929 to 1937 he produced the paintings which made him the world's best-known Surrealist artist. He depicted a dream world in which commonplace objects are juxtaposed, deformed, or otherwise metamorphosed in a bizarre and irrational fashion. Dali portrayed these objects in meticulous, almost painfully realistic detail and usually placed them within bleak, sunlit landscapes that were reminiscent of his Catalonian homeland. Perhaps the most famous of these enigmatic images is *The Persistence of Memory* (1931), in which limp, melting watches rest in an eerily calm landscape.

In the late 1930s Dali switched to painting in a more academic style under the influence of the Renaissance painter Raphael, and as a consequence he was expelled from the Surrealist movement. Thereafter he spent much of his time designing theatre sets, interiors of fashionable shops, and jewellery, as well as exhibiting his genius for flamboyant self-promotional stunts in the United States, where he lived from 1940 to 1955. In the period from 1950 to 1970, Dali painted many works with religious themes, though he continued to explore erotic subjects, to represent childhood memories and themes centering on his wife. Notwithstanding their technical accomplishments, these later paintings are not as highly regarded as the artist's earlier works.

WRITERS – MORE THAN JUST LORCA

Many of Spain's 20th-century authors have achieved international recognition, including five who won the Nobel Prize for Literature: dramatists Jose Echegaray (1904) and Jacinto Benavente (1922), poets Juan Ramon Jimenez (1956) and Vicente Aleixandre (1977), and novelist Camilo Jose Cela (1989). The most famous writer of the century, however, was poet and playwright Federico Garcia Lorca.

Federico Garcia Lorca

Federico Garcia Lorca was born on June 5, 1898 at Fuente Vaqueros in Granada province and died August 18 or 19, 1936, between Víznar and Alfacar, Granada province. He was a Spanish poet and playwright who, in a career that spanned just 19 years, resurrected and revitalised the most basic strains of Spanish poetry and theatre.

Garcia Lorca's poetry and plays drew heavily on the folklore of his native Andalusia, and especially on that of the Gypsies. The symbolism of his poetry is often elusive and difficult to interpret. Major themes of his plays are the suppression of instinct by social convention and the suppression of women. His works include the poetry collections *Gypsy Ballads*, *Lament for a Bullfighter*, *Blood Wedding*, *Yerma* and *The House of*

Bernarda Alba. In the early 1930s Lorca helped inaugurate a second Golden Age of the Spanish theatre. He was executed by a Nationalist firing squad in the first months of the Spanish Civil War and became a symbol of art perishing at the hands of fascism.

Miguel de Cervantes

Miguel de Cervantes was born on September 29, 1547 in Alcalá de Henares, Spain and died on April 22, 1616 in Madrid. He was a Spanish novelist, playwright, and poet, the creator of *Don Quixote* (1605, 1615) and the most important and celebrated figure in Spanish literature. His novel *Don Quixote* has been translated, in full or in part, into more than 60 languages. Editions continue regularly to be printed, and critical discussion of the work has continued unabated since the 18th century. At the same time, owing to their widespread representation in art, drama and film, the figures of Don Quixote and Sancho Panza are probably familiar to more people than any other imaginary characters in world literature.

Miguel de Cervantes was Spain's greatest literary figure. Held captive by the Turks for five years, he was almost 60 when he wrote the comic masterpiece *Don Quixote*, La Mancha's favourite son. Many iron figures in today's La Mancha are testament to this popular figure and his creator. Statues of Don Quixote and Sancho Panza are landmarks that abound in Spanish towns. Their portrait and pose are likely to stare from tiled murals on the walls of schools, museums and cultural centres. The familiar figures of the tall, lanky, and gaunt knight-errant with his rusty sword, crooked lance and broken helmet, perched on his emaciated old plough horse turned charger, towers over the stocky peasant Sancho Panza sitting astride his mule.

> *Don Quixote sees only what he believes to be there. His reading of stories about knights and damsels in distress shape his imagination. Windmills are giants waving their arms in mock defiance. Wine barrels are insolent enemies. He takes them all on, to the amusement of all those who watch and mock.* (Cervantes)

Gabriel Miro

Gabriel Miro was born on July 28, 1879, Alicante, Spain and died on died on May 27, 1930 in Madrid. He was a Spanish writer distinguished by the finely-wrought rich, imaginative vocabulary contained in his essays, stories, and novels. Miro studied law at the universities of Granada and Valencia. His many novels include *Our Father Saint Daniel* and *The Leprous Bishop*, both of which are critical of religious customs. Among his non-fiction works are *Figures of the Passion of Our Lord* and a series of books describing life in the Alicante region.

Ernest Hemingway

Ernest Hemingway was born on July 21, 1899 in Oak Park, Illinois, USA and died on July 2, 1961, in Ketchum, Idaho. An American novelist and short-story writer, he was awarded the Nobel Prize for Literature in 1954. He was noted both for the intense masculinity of his writing and for his adventurous and widely publicised life. His succinct and lucid prose style exerted a powerful influence on American and British fiction in the 20th century.

He worked at odd jobs in Chicago before sailing for France as a foreign correspondent of the *Toronto Star*. Advised and encouraged by other writers in Paris – Scott Fitzgerald, Gertrude Stein, Ezra Pound – he began to see his non-journalistic work appear in print. In 1926 he published *The Sun Also Rises*, a novel with which he scored his first solid success.

The writing of books occupied Hemingway for most of the post war years. He remained based in Paris, but he travelled widely for skiing, bullfighting, fishing, and hunting that by then had become part of his life, and formed the background for much of his writing. His position as a master of short stories had been advanced by *Men without Women* in 1927 and thoroughly established him with stories in *Winner Take Nothing* in 1933. Among his finest stories are *The Killers, The Short Happy Life of Francis Macomber*, and *The Snows of Kilimanjaro*. To the public however, the novel *A Farewell to Arms* (1929) overshadowed such works.

Hemingway's love of Spain and his passion for bullfighting resulted in *Death in the Afternoon* (1932), a learned study of a spectacle he saw more as tragic ceremony than as sport. Soon after this, Spain was in the midst of a war. Still deeply attached to that country, Hemingway made four trips there as a war correspondent.

The harvest of Hemingway's considerable experience of Spain in war and peace was the novel *For Whom the Bell Tolls* (1940), a substantial and impressive work that some critics consider his finest novel in preference to *A Farewell to Arms*. It was also the most successful of all his books measured in sales. Set during the Spanish Civil War, it tells of Robert Jordan, an American volunteer who is sent to join a guerrilla band behind the Nationalist lines in the Guadarrama hills.

All of his life, Hemingway was fascinated by war. As World War II progressed, he made his way to London as a journalist. He flew several missions with the Royal Air Force and crossed the English Channel with American troops on D-Day. Attaching himself to the 22nd Regiment of the 4th Infantry Division, he saw a good deal of action in Normandy and in the Battle of the Bulge. He also participated in the liberation of Paris and, although ostensibly a journalist, he impressed professional soldiers, not only as a man of courage in battle, but also as an expert in military matters, guerrilla activities, and intelligence collection.

In 1953 he received the Pulitzer Prize in fiction for *The Old Man and the Sea*, a short heroic novel about an old Cuban fisherman who, after an extended struggle, hooks and pulls on board a giant marlin, only to have it eaten by voracious sharks during the long voyage home.

MUSIC – DOMINGO TO IGLESIAS

The influence of the past has been particularly strong in the field of music. Composers such as Isaac Albeniz (1860–1909), Enrique Granados (1867–1916), Manuel de Falla (1876–1946), and Joaquin Rodrigo (b. 1901) drew heavily on popular and regional music for their inspiration. One by-product of this was the creation of a serious musical repertoire for the guitar. The instrument gained additional stature from the performances of the great guitarist Andres Segovia (1893–1987). A number of Spanish composers, however, worked in more modern idioms, the most important being Roberto Gerhard, Cristobal Halffter, and Luis de Pablo.

Spain has produced some of the world's leading opera performers including Victoria de los Angeles, Teresa Berganza, Montserrat Caballe, Jose Carreras, Placido Domingo and Alfredo Kraus. Regular performances are held in Madrid, Barcelona, Oviedo, Bilbao and other cities. Barcelona has a recognised opera house, the Gran Teatro del Liceu, considered second only to La Scala in Milan. An opera house was opened in Seville in 1992.

Spaniards hold a wealth of excellent music festivals including a festival of religious music in Cuenca; the international festival of music and dance in Granada which is Spain's most important musical event; the Santander international festival of music, dance and drama; an international music festival in Barcelona and an autumn festival in Madrid. A wealth of traditional folk music is played on the classical guitar. An international festival of the guitar is held in Cordoba.

Placido Domingo

Placido Domingo was born on January 21, 1941 in Madrid, an operatic tenor whose resonant, powerful voice, imposing physical stature, good looks, and dramatic ability made him one of the most popular tenors of the second half of the 20th century. Domingo's parents were noted performers in *Zarzuela*, a form of Spanish light opera. He grew up in Mexico, where he studied piano at the National Conservatory of Music. In 1961 he made his operatic debut in Mexico City and then went to Dallas, Texas, to perform in its opera company. From 1962 to 1965 he was a resident performer at Tel Aviv's Hebrew National Opera. He made his debut at the New York City Opera in 1965, at the Metropolitan Opera House in New York City in 1968 and at La Scala in Milan in 1969. A prolific and versatile performer, Domingo has made numerous recordings and several film versions of operas venturing into popular music as well.

Julio Iglesias

Born in 1943, the popular Spanish singer has a huge international following. He has reputedly sold more records, in more languages than any other recording artist.

A possible career as a goalkeeper with Real Madrid was finished when a serious car crash injured the 18-year-old Iglesias so badly that he was in a wheelchair for almost two years. In hospital, a doctor's assistant gave him a guitar and his interest in music began. He trained as a lawyer in Spain and at Cambridge University before winning the 1968 Spanish Song Festival in Benidorm with his own composition *Life Goes on Just the Same*. That success secured him his first recording contract. He represented Spain in the 1970 Eurovision Song Contest with the song *Guendoline* which he later recorded in English, French, and Italian.

Through the 1970s he toured and built an international following through hit songs such as *Manuela* (1975) and *Hey* (1979). In 1981 he broke into the English language charts with *Begin the Beguine*, following this up with the million selling album *Julio*. This featured duets with well-established American stars such as Willie Nelson and Diana Ross. *My Love*, recorded with Stevie Wonder, was a massive international hit in 1988, and he has also worked with singers such as Dolly Parton, Art Garfunkel, and Sting.

Iglesias's style is relaxed and intimate; his phrasing conversational. He is a successful songwriter and thoughtful interpreter of other people's music. Those qualities, combined with considerable charm, good looks, and shrewd management have made him one of the most popular recording artists in the world, with hundreds of gold and platinum recordings worldwide. In 1989 he was appointed Special Representative for the Performing Arts by UNICEF.

ZARZUELA

Zarzuela is a Spanish musical stage piece which mixes music, songs, and dialogue. The *zarzuela* derives from the 17th century when the Spanish court would visit the royal residence of La Zarzuela to see entertainment based on stories usually concentrating on myths and heroes. However, the form is constantly evolving and today a *zarzuela* might use jazz elements in the music, for example. This is in keeping with the general style of entertainment, which often deals with current issues.

There are two types of *zarzuela*: *zarzuela grande*, which has a number of acts, is dramatic in intention and the *zarzuelita*, which is shorter and comic. They are intended to have immediate impact and often play up the absurd, fantastic, or melodramatic aspects of a story. Adding to this immediacy is the easy style of singing, improvisation, and back-chat between stage and audience.

While many *zarzuelas* are performed only once, others go on to have long runs in theatres.

ARCHITECTURE

Spain has always imported its major cultural architecture: Moorish from North Africa, Romanesque and Gothic from France, Renaissance from Italy. Each style, however, has been interpreted in a Spanish way, with contrasts between light and shady areas, façades alternating between the austere and the extravagant, thick walls pierced by few windows to lessen the impact of the sunlight.

As well as its cathedrals and palaces, local craftsmen have met the needs of local communities. They take account of the climate, with little reference to formal architectural styles, and have constructed buildings of clay, stone or timber. A variety of distinctive buildings cover the countryside. Where the rock is soft, subterranean cave houses have been excavated. Granaries raised on stone stilts to prevent rats climbing up into the grain are a common sight in northern Spain.

Almost every town in Spain has its main square, the *plaza mayor.* It acts as a focus for local life. A church, the town hall, shops and bars usually overlook it. Seats are placed around the edges. In addition almost everywhere there exist white painted *ermitas,* isolated chapels or shrines dedicated to the local saint. In villages and towns they will be a focal point for religious events and processions throughout the year. They are situated on high ground overlooking the town, surrounded by tall elegant fir trees and are reached by a long winding path each having 12 religious stations.

Antonio Gaudi y Cornet (1852–1926) was the most famous, as well as the most unusual architect of the early 20th century. Through an eclectic approach he created a unique style reminiscent of the *Mudejar*, an architectural style blending Muslim and Christian design. During his life he had no influence outside of Spain as most of Gaudi's work was done in Barcelona. His most famous building is the unfinished Expiatory Temple of the Holy Family. Spain's leading architect of the late 20th century was Ricardo Bofill, who worked both in Spain and many other countries.

18

SHOPPING EXPERIENCE

Spain's shopping experience is absolutely different from the UK, with specialist family-run outlets forming the bulk of sales activity. This is, however, changing fast, with out of town shopping centres springing up everywhere, but in the cool of the evening, with a stop for a *cafe con leche* or a *tapas*, indulging in a multilingual conversation with the occupants at the next table, shopping can still be a pleasurable activity.

CONSUMER CHOICE

Tiendas

The smaller *tiendas* (shops) are cheerful, friendly, helpful places where the owners and assistants are anxious to please. This is also where the annoying Spanish characteristic of 'not forming queues' is seen at its worst. People push and shove to the front to be served. This is best borne with patience as the perpetrators of this behaviour are often elderly and seem to think that their advanced years entitle them to non-queuing privileges. Alternatively say '*perdone*' and address the sales assistant who usually knows what is happening.

Opening hours for *tiendas* vary between summer and winter, but normally are 09.30 to 13.30 and 16.30 to 19.30 Monday to Friday, plus a Saturday morning. The afternoon siesta seems inappropriate in winter but essential in summer when the shops open later, as no one wishes to go shopping during the intense heat. There is, however, pressure to change this custom from businesses and other Europeans. Banks and some organisations open at 08.00 and close at 14.30. Holiday resorts, restaurants and hypermarkets open 7 days a week, 12 hours a day, having already squeezed the siesta out of existence.

The *tienda* retailing backbone is highly specialised.

Bread shop	– *La panaderia*
Butcher	– *La carniceria*
Cake shop	– *La pasteleria*
Chemist	– *La farmacia*
Clothes shop	– *La tienda de ropa*
Delicatessen	– *La charcuteria*
Fruit shop	– *La fruteria*
Fishmonger	– *La pescaderia*
Grocer	– *La tienda de comestibles*
Hairdresser	– *La peluqueria*
Ironmonger	– *La ferreteria*
Launderette	– *Lavanderia*
Newspaper stand	– *El quiosco*
Shoe shop	– *La zapateria*
Travel agent	– *Agency de viajes*
Tobacconist	– *El tabac*

Hypermarkets

French owned hypermarkets such as *Carrefour* and *Intermarche* dominate food retailing. Smaller German supermarkets such as *Lidl* and *Aldi* compete on price but not on product range. Spanish companies such as *Mercadona* are now gaining a firm foothold. Hypermarket shopping is an experience not to be missed, with everything possible being sold under one roof: clothes, footwear, garden plants and equipment, sports goods, bicycles, electrical goods, hi-fi, furniture, DIY, motoring accessories, kitchenware, toys and books. The food hall has a massive product range. The fruit and vegetables are highly colourful. The delicatessen counter is staggering, with a huge variety of sausages and cheeses. The fish counter is laden down with salmon, trout, mussels, skate, mackerel and a whole range of unrecognisable species. The wine, spirit, soft drink and bottled water section stretches for miles. These hypermarkets have 40 to 60 checkouts. Staff are equipped with roller skates to get from point to point. Franchised within the same building are restaurants, banks, jewellers, newsagents and the National Lottery.

Clothing

There is one major, famous chain store in Spain – *El Corte Inglés*. It has a similar marketing strategy to other European retailers, selling mainly male and female clothing together with books, CDs, electrical goods, computers, kitchenware and sports equipment. Price points are similar to, or higher than, the rest of Europe with occasional cut-price sales (*rebajas*).

With the exception of a large number of international sports brands, clothing is not yet a fashion statement outside big cities. It is conservative in taste, for Spain is not yet a fashion centre; its citizens sticking to fairly traditional styles.

European chain stores, like European banks, have only a few outlets in major cities. The marketplace may be penetrated by individual foreign brands, but not by foreign retailers. Where they do exist they tend to be a poor relation of their national counterparts.

Out of town shopping

It is here where change is occurring. Electrical chains, computer stores, sports clothing and equipment shops, fast food chains, cinema complexes … the lot, are being built everywhere. They are not like British style shopping malls, but based more on the outdoor USA experience.

Open air markets

There is a profusion of open-air markets which stop normal activity in a town for one day each week. *Mercadillo* is a term used to denote a weekly outdoor market, which has a special attraction for those who enjoy the more leisurely stroll and social atmosphere of shopping outdoors. People flock from kilometres around to buy hams, dried fish, fresh fruit and vegetables. Clothing too is sold, together with some ceramics and leather goods. Beware of designer items, watches and jewellery as they may well be fakes.

A *mercadillo* is a recognised form of retail business regulated by municipal and national Spanish law. Although merchants pay a fee to the municipality for the use of public space according to the area of their stall, there is still a certain amount of unregistered or illegal goods, even though all merchants are required to display their licences prominently to carry on trade. Many of the stalls have been owned by the same family for generations.

The statistics are impressive. There are 8,000 outdoor markets on a weekly or less frequent basis. More than one-quarter of the Spanish population regularly do part of their shopping in a weekly *mercadillo*, accounting for 2,000 million euros in sales. Seasonal products are at least 20% cheaper than in supermarkets or *tiendas*.

A *mercadillo* is a fun place to shop, with lots of shouting and good-humoured banter, with people seeking strange, exotic bargains within a rainbow of colours and fragrances, free from scooters and cars. Bargaining takes place, but it is an unnatural custom for northern Europeans. Want to bargain? Express an interest in an item. Haggle on price. Say 'no' and walk away. The stall owner comes after you. That's when you get the low price, not before.

The hustle and bustle can be of some interest, but be cautious. Pickpockets, operating in gangs of two or three, are often present at open-air markets. They don't have to worry about store alarms.

Mercado central

An indoor central market (*mercado*) is run by the local council. Most towns have one. They are efficient, clean, hygienic purveyors of fish, meat, pastries, fruit and vegetables, and a traditional alternative to supermarket shopping. Little English is spoken but a smile accompanies each purchase.

Anything else?	– *Algo mas?*
That's all.	– *Eso es todo.*
Thank you.	– *Gracias.*

Spain exports most of its Class I fruit and vegetables. Quality produce is better purchased from the *fruteria* at the *mercado central* than from a supermarket.

Older indoor markets are distinguished by their imposing architecture, often with classical iron work. They are open every weekday and Saturday morning. Some of them go back many centuries and originally incorporated warehouses and wholesalers. This type of market existed for centuries in Covent Garden and Billingsgate and can be seen in almost replica form in Valencia, with other towns having smaller versions.

Tabac

One other national institution has to be mentioned – the *tabac, a* state owned tobacco shop selling all brands of cigarettes, cigars and tobacco at very low prices: 20 euros for 200 cigarettes is quite normal. It is fairly obvious from these prices many people still smoke. In bars and restaurants, shops and public places, the cigarette is still part of the Spanish way of life. The *tabac* has other functions. It provides government forms for taxation and sells postage stamps. Never stand in a long queue at the main post office for stamps when a *tabac* is nearby.

Have you ever been stopped by someone offering to sell you a carton of cigarettes at a ridiculously low price? They are cigarettes made in the USA, imported into Gibraltar and then smuggled illegally into Europe through Spain. It is no secret. The imported price is about 10€ for a carton of 200 cigarettes.

Food from home?

Bread can come in all its various guises. A fresh Spanish 'barra.' A French baguette. Bread from the UK, Germany and Holland is also available. The traditional English loaf is made under licence. Spanish cheese is good and supplemented by popular cheeses from the rest of Europe. Lovers of cheese soon branch out and try these different Spanish chesses. They find they can survive without Cheddar, though this is readily available.

Any conurbation of northern Europeans of one nationality will invariably have supermarkets meeting demand for well known food products they apparently cannot live without. Freezers contain gammon steaks, bacon, English sausages, steak and kidney pies and so on ... and German products too. Imported, long life, tinned or dry products are freely available ... soups, pastas and such like. They come in a branded wrap, such as *Baxter's*, *John West* or even from *Tesco* or *Waitrose*. We are all grateful.

BEST BUYS

Wine

The best buy in Spain is undoubtedly wine from a tightly regulated industry. It is cheap and the quality good. As we have seen earlier, Spain produces excellent wines, but their product marketing has been poor, leaving France holding the premium market and Spain operating at the bottom end. Tighter government regulations have seen a continuous rise in wine quality but not in the marketing strategy.

At an identical cost to a soft drink or a bottle of water, it is natural accompaniment to a meal. Branded wine, with an individual number on the back of the bottle, blended house wines, *vino de mesa* (table wines), young wines or supermarket brands at up to 3€ per bottle are all exceptional value for money.

Olive oil

There are 400 million olive trees in Spain and 80% are grown in Andalusia. Driving around Cordoba and Granada it is possible to see fields and fields, acres and acres of olive trees. The experts in Brussels say there are too many; olive oil production is too high. *Aceite de Oliva* (olive oil) is used in cooking, as a salad dressing and as a substitute for butter and margarine.

It is a sad fact that olive oil consumption in Spain has dropped in recent years. Compared to other forms of oil such as corn and sunflower it is expensive to produce, as it is labour intensive. Picking olives by hand compares unfavourably with mechanised farming methods employed elsewhere. It has been said that olive oil contributes to a good complexion, efficient digestion and strong hearts. It is probably true, as olive oil contains little cholesterol.

The Romans first introduced olive trees to Spain, and the best olive oil is still sent back to Italy and then re-exported. However the 1,000-year-old, drought and fire resistant trees remain. So too, do the harvesting methods which consist of shaking the tree and picking up the olives from a net on the ground. Green olives are harvested in September and black ones in December.

Most of the olives picked are pressed for oil. The label on the bottle should be examined for the acidity and the number of pressings. Extra virgin is from olives picked ripe and pressed immediately; it contains a maximum of 1% acidity. Virgin *fino* is up to 1.5% acidity and virgin *corriente* up to 3.3%. Virgin *lampante* is strong oil with little taste and acidity level above 3.3%. The higher the acidity, the lower the price and stronger the flavour. *Aceite de Oliva Refinado* is an oil with an unsatisfactory taste, but once refined it becomes a healthy, usable product. *Aceite de Oliva* is a blend of both refined and virgin oils, this being the overall market standard.

It is a tightly regulated industry giving a consistent quality product and follows practices similar to the wine industry by issuing *denominacion de origen* labels.

Saffron

Saffron is one of the best buys in Spain. Look to see that all the threads are of uniform length, are a deep burnt orange colour and the aroma is genuine. Because of its extremely high market value, saffron has always tempted fraud. Ground saffron is easy to replicate with turmeric or saffron simulators.

Spain once held a virtual monopoly on saffron and still accounts for more than 40% of the world's trade. Crops from Iran and Turkey have begun to outstrip those of La Mancha and Albacete in quantity, though there is no disputing the difference in quality. Spanish saffron is the best there is. Its aroma is stronger, its filaments are longer and its red is less deep than that grown in the Middle East. Because of these distinctions, the remaining crocus farmers of Spain have grouped together to protect their product by introducing a system of *denominacion de origen*.

At 2,500€ a kilo, saffron is in a league of its own. No other spice comes close in terms of price, but then no other spice demands so much of those who produce it. Crocus flowers are sterile, so reproduction is through the corms, which are planted in June and July under a hot, baking sun.

Harvesting the crocuses is even harder, back-breaking work. Pickers spend the mornings of late October and early November crouching over the rows of flowers, baskets hanging from their waists or dragging behind them as they gather the crop. It takes more than 60,000 crocus flowers to produce one kilo of saffron, and years of experience to be able to pick swiftly enough to beat the rising sun and wind on the plains.

Once the flowers are gathered, the orange-red stigmas of saffron are separated from the blooms. Families and neighbours share the task, sitting at long tables laden with lilac-coloured crocus flowers. Each bloom is taken and squeezed gently to open the bud and then the three stigmas are gently plucked and placed in dishes.

Once separated, the stigmas are completely dried. A hint of moisture will spoil the filament and with it, the crop. So the next step is to sieve them over the embers of a charcoal fire, taking care not to burn them. This process reduces the weight of the filaments by up to 80%, and leaves the stigmas bright red, rigid and without wrinkles. The dried and weighed saffron is stored in large, antique, wooden trunks lined with metal plate to protect the precious crop from heat, cold, and above all, moisture.

Ceramics

A *regalo* is a gift or a present. They are sold in tourist souvenir shops of the same name and in household furnishing shops. Spanish *regalos* are ornate rather than simple; decorative rather than functional. Ceramics, lighting and ornaments are often used to decorate a traditional home. Ceramics in particular are decorative, bright and colourful.

Leather goods

They may be made in Mallorca or mainland Spain or imported from Morocco, but all are high quality. Handbags, travel cases, belts or clothing all represent good value for money.

SHOPPING ABROAD

If you live in Spain, why not shop in Andorra, France, Portugal, Morocco or Gibraltar? Disadvantages may be that these countries are some distance away, and if the goods are faulty they may have to be returned to the place of purchase. The euro and credit card has assisted cross-border spending.

The tax-free shopping havens are Gibraltar and Andorra.

Andorra is close to France, attracting visitors of many nationalities. Electrical items are the most popular, but do not expect the sales assistant to explain the product, just to take the money. Cheeses and other foodstuffs are good buys. It can be a long way to go for a bargain, but not so onerous if combined with a skiing trip. Gibraltar, too, is the home of tax-free electrical and liquor stores.

People do not visit Morocco, Gibraltar or Andorra solely for shopping. Morocco has an exotic taste of Africa, Gibraltar a taste of the old country and Andorra … what can be said about a small town where terrifying mountains encroach on pavements and where nobody, but nobody ever smiles, where shops offer luxury goods at a only a small discount compared with any normal shopping centre in Europe, where the barman of a fancy café looks with enquiring eyes and never says a word of welcome? Perhaps Andorra is best seen covered in snow.

19
TRAVEL

TRAVELLING BY TRAIN

History of rail transport

During the 19th century Spain was one of the poorest and least economically developed countries in western Europe and politically unstable. Railways were therefore relatively late to appear. The first line to be built was a short link from Barcelona to Mataro which was opened in 1848, although by that date a line was already working in Cuba – then part of the Spanish empire. It was not until laws were passed in the 1850s making railway investment more attractive to foreign investment that railway building on a large scale began.

One major misfortune was a decision taken at an early stage, that Spain's railways should be built to an unusual, broad track gauge of 1674 mm (roughly 5ft 6in, or six Castilian feet). The choice of gauge was influenced by Spain's hostility to neighbouring France during the 1850s: it was believed that making the Spanish railway network incompatible with that of France would hinder any French invasion. As a result, Portuguese railways were also built to a broad gauge.

This unfortunate political decision would be regretted by future generations, as it hindered international trade and also made railway construction more expensive. As a result of the cost of building broad-gauge lines, a large system of narrow-gauge railways was also built in the poorer parts of Spain, especially in the north-west of the country.

The main-line network was roughly complete by the 1870s. Because of Spain's (until recently) relative lack of economic development, the Spanish railway network never became as extensive as those of most other European countries.

During the Spanish Civil War the railway network was extensively damaged. Immediately after the war the Franco regime nationalised the broad-gauge network, and in 1941 *Red Nacional de los Ferrocarriles Espanoles RENFE* was formed. Narrow-gauge lines were nationalised in the 1950s, later being grouped to form *FEVE*. It took many years for the railway system to recover from the war; during the 1950s it was common to see intercity express trains being hauled by 100-year-old steam locomotives on poor, worn-out track.

Following the decentralisation of Spain after 1978, those narrow-gauge lines which did not cross the limits of autonomous communities of Spain were taken out of the control of *FEVE* and transferred to the regional governments, which formed, amongst others, *Eusko Trenbideak* and *Ferrocarrils de la Generalitat de Catalunya*; Madrid, Barcelona, Valencia and Bilbao all have autonomous subway services.

In recent years Spain's railways have received very heavy investment, much of it coming from the EU. Most recently a standard-gauge high-speed rail line (*AVE*) has been built between Madrid and Seville. In 2003 a high-speed service was inaugurated on a new line from Madrid to Lleida, due to be extended to Barcelona by 2007 and eventually onwards, via an international tunnel beneath the Pyrenees, to Perpignan where it will link up with the French *TGV* high-speed system. Delays on the part of the French government in authorising construction on its side of the border have held up Spanish plans to some extent. Further high-speed links are under construction from Madrid to Valladolid and from Cordoba to Malaga, and a new line is planned to Lisbon.

The state-owned *RENFE* operates the Spanish rail network consisting of 15,000 km of track and 2,500 stations. The network covers all major cities and is supplemented by a few suburban networks and private narrow-gauge railways. Compared with the volume of goods shipped by road, little freight is transported by train. *RENFE* operates a service that is continually improving. The fastest services are called the *AVE* and the *TALGO* their names being acronyms for high-speed trains that run along these routes. *Grandes Lineas* (long distance), *Regionales* (regional) and *Cercanias* (local) are other, self explanatory, marketing names.

Madrid and Barcelona stations

The Spanish railway system is centred on Madrid, with three main lines radiating out to other parts of the country. Consequently there are good links between Madrid and other cities. It is however difficult to get from one regional capital to another without going through Madrid.

 Madrid has three main stations.

- **Chamartin** serves Albacete, Alicante, Barcelona, Bilbao, Cadiz, Cartagena, Cordoba, Malaga, Santander, Seville, Zaragossa, and France.

- **Atocha** serves Castilla-La Mancha, Almeria, Andalusia and Extremadura, including Cadiz, Ciudad Real, Cordoba, Cuenca, Granada, Salamanca, Toledo, Valencia and Portugal.

- **Principe Pio** serves Coruna, Leon, Lugo, Ovense, Oviedo, Salamanca and Valladolid.

The main stations in Barcelona are **Franca** and **Sants**. Trains to all major Spanish cities and to France leave from Sants, while Franca has daily international trains, called the *TEE* (*Trans European Express*) to Geneva, Milan, Paris and Zurich. At border stops it may be necessary to change trains due to Spain's wider gauge track.

The *AVE* and *TALGO* high-speed services

The introduction of the *AVE* (*Tren de Alto Velocidad Espanola*) utilises French and German technology by running on special lines and travelling at speeds of up to 250 kph. It has improved rail travel in Spain. Using the same gauge as the rest of Europe, the routes to Seville, Huelva, Cadiz, Malaga and Algecerias from Madrid are now operational. Routes to Portugal, France, Barcelona, Valladolid, Bilbao, and Valencia are planned. The *AVE* and the slightly slower *TALGO* system will eventually comprise part of a European, high-speed rail network. Details of high-speed and international connections are:

- *AVE* connects Madrid and Sevilla in less than three hours;
- *TALGO* 200 connects Madrid and Malaga in four and three-quarter hours;
- The *EUROMED* connects Barcelona, Valencia and Alicante.

Other services

Grandes Lineas are air-conditioned intercity trains of a high standard operating between major cities with services including waiters and airline type meals. *Regionals* are again modern trains. There are suburban services to all large cities. *Interurbano* is the Spanish equivalent of the suburban line. A metro system operates in Madrid. Business people still rarely commute to work by train; the car is still the preferred means of city transport, which helps to explain city traffic jams.

There is also a variety of slow, local and short-distance trains. The *expres* is a slow night train, usually with sleeping cars and the *rapido* is a daytime version of the same. Despite the names, the *expres* and *rapido* are not particularly fast. Night trains (*estrellas*) are slow trains with a choice of *literas* – a mixed compartment with six bunk beds or a *cochecama* (a compartment with two beds).

Tilting trains

1999 marked the introduction of the first tilting trains on the busy route between Madrid and Valencia. This route is central to *RENFE*'s fortunes; with business travellers representing no less than 53% of total revenue, it goes to the front of the queue for service enhancements and investment in the latest rolling stock and technology.

Tickets and fares

AVE, TALGO and *Grandes Lineas* tickets can be booked at the station ticket office or through travel agents. Local and regional tickets are available from the station booking office and ticket machines. *RENFE* operate a variety of trains, all with different speed, service, classification and fare structures. Train travel may be fast or slow, the service good or bad, but Spanish fares are low by European standards.

RENFE's UK representative is the Spanish Rail Service. They are able to deal with information and bookings for all *RENFE* services, including motorail and *AVE*, as well as the tourist trains *Al Andalus Express* and *Transcantabrico*. They may be contacted at the following address:

Spanish Rail
Suite 2
79 Baker St
London WIU 6 RG
Tel: 020 7224 0345
Email: enquiries@spanish-rail.co.uk
www.spanish-rail.co.uk

Tourist trains

The following are special trains following routes of great beauty or cultural value. Several may be enjoyed throughout the year, but most are seasonal.

- **El Transcantabrico**. San Sebastian – Santiago de Compostela. Departures: March to June, October and November. *Transcantabrico* is a 1920s train operating in northern Spain along a long stretch of narrow-gauge railway. It takes in stunning mountain scenery and offers excursions to a number of villages and towns during its week-long journey.

- **Al Andalus Express**. Sevilla – Cordoba – Granada – Jerez – Sevilla. Departures: April to June and September to October. The *Al Andalus Express* is a unique travel experience on a luxuriously converted 1920s train with the six-day round trip commencing in Sevilla and taking in Cordoba, Granada and Jerez. The sleeping cars and suites were built in France in 1929 for the King of England.

- **Tren de la Fresa** (The Strawberry Train). Madrid – Aranjuez – Madrid. Departures: Saturday and Sundays from mid May to mid October approximately.

- **Tren Palma – Soller**. Departures: All year round. In Majorca it is still possible to enjoy a trip on a vintage train running from Palma to Soller, travelling through tunnels and mountains, with some of the best views on the island. From Soller an equally ancient tramcar runs through orange and lemon groves to Puerto de Soller.

- **Azpeitia Railway Museum**. – Azpeitia – Lasao. Departures: Every Saturday, Sunday and public holidays.

- **Limon Express**. Benidorm – Gata. Departures: Tuesday to Saturday throughout the year. Gata is visited for its famous guitar factory and wicker basket shops.

- **Trensnochador**. Alicante – Denia. Departures: Daily between 05.00 and 21.00.

- **Tren Cremallera**. Rives de Freser – Nuria (Gerona). Departures: throughout the year.

- **Tren Turistico del Pirineo**. Lenda – Pobla de Segur. Departures: at specific dates from February to October.

- **Tren Cremallera de Montserrat**. Every day shuttle service between Monistrol-Vila and Montserrat.

- **Tren de Cervantes**. Departures: Madrid Atocha to Alcala de Henares. Dates: From 12 March to 12 June and from 10 September to 11 December. Tourist train with walks around the city.

- **Ferrocarril Turistico Minero**. Minas de Rio Tinto (Huelva). Departures: every day.

TRAVELLING BY ROAD

In recent years major motorway construction covering over 8,000km has been completed. Some are spectacular roads passing through mountains, across valleys, rivers or ravines. Madrid is now connected to all its provincial capitals by fast road communication, and it is also possible to drive from France to Gibraltar by motorway. It fact it will soon be possible to drive by motorway from Perth in Scotland to Lisbon in Portugal through France and Spain. Some of the newer motorways are toll roads (*autopistas de peajes*) which can be expensive.

Driving is still an enjoyable experience in many rural areas (outside the Spanish holiday time of August) when it is possible to drive for hours without seeing another motorist. Driving in Spain's major cities such as Madrid and Barcelona is no different from other major cities in Europe and is not for the faint-hearted.

Unfortunately, Spain has one of the worst accident records in Europe with over 5,500 deaths and over 1.6 million accidents per annum. Around 40% of fatal accidents involve drivers over the alcohol limit. Spanish motorists do drive ridiculously fast.

Roads

Spain's motorways are known as *autopistas* (A roads) or *autovias* (E for European roads). Both are characterised by distinctive blue signposting. *Autopistas* are toll roads found on some short sections of motorway which have been built by commercial contractors or for expensive shortcuts over difficult terrain.

Other major roads in Spain are identified by the sign *Red de Carreteras del Estado* (State Road Network) being *Carreteras Nacionales* and signified by the letter N on maps. These roads tend to be busy, single lane roads, often taking traffic more suited to toll roads. Secondary routes are the narrower *Carreteras Comarcales* (letter C), and minor roads, *Carretera Autonomica* are denoted by the initials of the province followed by a number.

On major roads each kilometre is marked with a number which represents the distance radiating from Madrid or, in the case of provinces, the distance from a provincial capital. These kilometre markers are often used as convenient meeting points or to establish the location of a building or even a postal address.

Speed limits are:

Autopistas	120 km/h
Autovias	120 km/h
Carreteras Nacionales	90 km/h
Carreteras Comarcales	60 km/h
Vias Urbanas	50 km/h, or as signposted.

Driving differences

The most obvious is, of course, driving on the right-hand side of the road. There are other differences:

- Going around roundabouts in an anti-clockwise direction.

- If going in the opposite direction to that desired on a motorway, it is possible to leave the motorway and change direction when the sign *Cambio de Sentido* appears.

- When trying to turn left on a busy road, it may be necessary to turn right first and then cross the carriageway.

- The sequence of traffic lights (*semaforos*) is red, green, amber and back to red.

- Two flashing amber lights means 'slow down, danger ahead'.

- Respect the narrow inside lane, it is for scooters.

- All vehicle documents (or copies) such as insurance details, car registration and technical *ITV* (see page 170) sheets should be kept in the car for inspection by police if so required.

- Motorists must carry two approved red warning triangles, a full set of spare bulbs and fuses and a reflective vest. It is advisable (but not mandatory) to carry a fire extinguisher and a first-aid kit.

One pleasing difference is the cost of fuel. *Gasolina* (petrol), *gasoleo* (diesel), and *gasolina sin plomo* (unleaded petrol) are available everywhere at prices about 35% below the most expensive European prices. The number of filling stations is increasing rapidly. Filling stations also sell newspapers, food and snacks.

Motorway services vary in standard and frequency. On new *autovias* they are of a high quality and are open 24 hours per day. On older roads, the unsuspecting driver will be directed to a town or village where fuel, food, toilets and sometimes beds are available.

Purchasing a new car

The market for purchasing new cars is similar across Europe. Large dealers sell new and some second-hand cars at competitive prices with a good after-sales service. Since all dealerships are monitored by car manufacturers, their service is efficient, well organised and, above all, reputable.

Given Spain's geographical location and the presence of large car manufacturing plants in Valencia, the popular brands are Seat and Ford. French products come next. Quality German cars are always popular and the market penetration of small Far Eastern cars is high. New cars are more expensive in Spain than in many other EU countries, but they depreciate at a slower rate. Spanish-made cars are generally cheaper than imported cars as a result of tax differentials.

Purchasing a used car

Regrettably the second-hand car market does not enjoy a good reputation, with the usual unsavoury dealers in evidence, some of whom are British. Fortunately the quality of a modern second-hand car is high. It is price, poor administration, lack of customer service and dishonesty which gives this market its poor reputation. The Spanish market for second-hand cars is unusual as a large number of one-year-old rental cars, with relatively low mileage, are sold through second-hand outlets. Trade-ins from new sales dealerships are also sold through second-hand outlets.

There is also another source of used cars – the small ads in weekly newspapers. For first-time buyers in Spain the advice is to tread carefully. The risk of a poor product or incorrect paperwork is too great. A simple agreement should be drawn up to sell a car privately. It should contain factual details of the buyer, the seller, and details of the car, the price and form of payment, the date and appropriate signatures. Proof of sale documents should be stamped at *Jefatura Provincial de Trafico* (provincial traffic office) to exempt the seller from future fines, accidents or taxes which the buyer may incur.

Car registration

Spanish registration plates consist of four digits followed by three letters. It is no longer possible to tell where the car is from, or its age, from the number plate. However, there are still many cars on the road with the old style registration plate which consists of one or two letters denoting the province where the vehicle is registered followed by four digits and two more letters indicating the age of the car.

The original registration remains permanently with a car unless it is re-registered. If buying a second-hand car in Spain, it's best to buy one with the new style registration or one registered in the province where you live.

The vehicle registration document is in two parts. One lists details of the car and one details of the owner. The details of the car do not alter whereas, obviously, the section giving details of the owner changes each time there is a change of ownership.

Transfer of ownership

When a second-hand car is purchased from a private individual it will need to be registered within ten days of purchase. When selling a car privately it is important to ensure the transfer is completed correctly by the new owner. Rather like debts on a property, as long as the previous owner is still registered he or she is liable for any parking tickets, road tax and accident claims.

It is a procedure for which many people use a *gestor*, as a visit to a provincial capital and the infamous *Jefatura Provincial de Trafico* office is necessary. This Spanish department has a reputation for being difficult with complex procedures. It is one of the worst examples of Spanish bureaucracy.

Transfer tax

A transfer tax is levied on the sale of a second-hand car, it is called *Impuesto Sobre Transmisiones Patrimoniales y Actos Juridicos Documentados* and is charged at 4% of the fiscal value. The fiscal value of a new car is decided by the tax office. The fiscal value is reduced each year until it is ten years old, when it is reduced to 10% of the new value. The tax is the responsibility of the buyer, but as the seller actually pays it, most sellers include the tax in the sales price. This tax is declared on form *compraventa de vehiculos usados entre particulares* obtained from the *hacienda* and paid to the provincial tax office of the regional government within 30 days of selling.

De-registering

De-registering a car is called *baja de matricula*. This form is again obtained from *trafico* and must have attached a receipt for the current year's municipal vehicle tax. It can be used when scrapping an old vehicle, or if a vehicle is stolen. As an incentive to encourage scrapping an old car, the government will reduce new car registration tax by 480€ to 720€.

Six month temporary stay

Genuine tourists and visitors are permitted to bring to Spain a foreign-registered car, but it is not permitted to stay for longer than six months in any one year. Driving a foreign-registered car temporarily in Spain requires appropriate insurance and a national identity sticker on the back of the car as well as the national requirements listed earlier. The headlights need to be adjusted. In case of an accident, the insurance certificate, the driver's licence and a passport need to be kept handy. Permanently driving a right-hand drive car in Spain is not a good idea, but if kept for more than six months in any year it should be tested and re-registered as a Spanish car.

This six month period is based on the stay of the person rather than the stay of the car. Six months is the length a tourist can stay. A car can remain in Spain more than six months, but it cannot be legally driven. It is of course common knowledge many citizens of other EU countries live full time in Spain without obtaining a residence card and still operate their cars with foreign plates. While the police may turn a blind eye to the movement of EU citizens, foreign-plated cars are viewed as a safety hazard since they may have no roadworthiness certification.

Driving licence

Tourists visiting Spain and driving either their own car or a Spanish rental car can do so with a licence issued in their home country. An international licence issued in the home country would be better as the standard format can be more easily identified by the authorities.

Since 1996 a Spanish resident from another EU country can drive in Spain with the original, home country licence for as long as it is valid, with no obligation to take out a Spanish licence. However if the holder is a resident in Spain and not opting to obtain a Spanish driving licence, it is still legally necessary to present the UK licence to the *Jefatura Provincial de Trafico* where the details are computerised. But the licence will have an old address, and for a new resident of Spain it is better to exchange it for a Spanish one. If anything goes wrong it makes life just that little bit easier. It can reduce problems at roadside checks.

Since 2004 holders of EU photo card driving licences can drive legally in Spain without the need to register or exchange that licence. If the licence bears a previous UK address, drivers should always carry proof of their residence in Spain when they have lived in the country for more than six months.

Road tax

All Spanish registered vehicles are liable for road tax (*impuesto municipal sobre vehiculos de traccion mechanica*). The tax is based on *potencia fiscal* – the horsepower of the car. Tax levels are set by individual municipalities and do vary from place to place, with Barcelona the highest. Budget around 160€ per year for a small family size car. Payment is at the local town hall, or to a sub-contracted collection agency such as *SUMA*, during a published time window after which a surcharge is applied. Unlike many other countries, a tax disk is not placed inside the windscreen. Some people have avoided paying this tax for years but it catches up with them, complete with fines, when a copy of the last receipt is required upon selling or scrapping a car which, incidentally, is an explanation as to why so many abandoned vehicles litter the countryside.

Technical inspection of vehicles

When a car is four years old, a bi-annual vehicle inspection, known as an *ITV* is necessary. Its equivalent in the UK is an MOT. When a car is passed, a sticker is placed inside the windscreen. After ten years an annual inspection is required. If a vehicle fails a test, 15 days are allowed to have it repaired and re-tested.

The *ITV* test is only valid for vehicles registered in Spain. It has no value in other EU countries. A car registered in another EU country must be tested in accordance with the laws of the country where it is registered.

Accidents

Spain has one of the highest road accident rates in Europe. A high volume of foreign drivers is one reason. Speed and alcohol are other major reasons. Spanish drivers are similar to the Italians and French – they often drive in a fast, aggressive manner and frequently take frightening risks. Overtaking, irrespective of speed limits or traffic conditions is a common cause of accidents. Damaged wing mirrors tell of a failure to judge small gaps.

A 'normal' Spanish car has scratched bumpers. Nothing is more frustrating than the constant bumps a car is subjected to in parking lots. There is a total disregard for the wellbeing of someone else's vehicle. For Spanish drivers, it seems bumpers are designed to be scratched.

For new drivers to Spain it is best to regard all drivers as totally unpredictable and drive cautiously. In Madrid, traffic lights are instructions; in Alicante, traffic lights are suggestions; in Pedreguer, they are Christmas decorations!

Drinking and driving

Despite the high accident rate, drunken driving does not create the same social stigma as it does in many other European countries. Random breath tests can be carried out by the police at any time. Motorists who are involved in accidents, or who infringe motoring regulations are routinely given alcohol and drug tests. The limit is low: when blood alcohol concentration exceeds 25mg of alcohol per 100ml of blood (15mg for drivers with less than two years experience or professional drivers) which is about two glasses of wine taken with some food. Drunk driving can result in a fine of up to 602€, suspension of a driving licence and even imprisonment for up to six months. Drivers who refuse to take a breath test are liable to a prison sentence of six months to one year. In either case a period of community service may be an alternative to a jail sentence. An accident while under the influence of alcohol can result in an insurance being immediately suspended meaning the non-payment of repairs, medical expenses and other damages.

Car insurance

Visitors to Spain for a short term tourist stay and driving a foreign-registered car, require insurance. This is a green card, as the international insurance certificate is known. Conversely visitors to the UK, driving a Spanish registered car will also require a green card. In the UK a green card is requested from an insurance company, while in Spain it is automatically issued with the annual certificate. Since there are no longer any border posts, a green card is really a notification to the insurance company of travel abroad rather than a permit to enter a country – many UK insurance companies no longer issue them.

Spanish law, like that in all other EU countries, demands that all vehicles be fully insured for minimum third-party damage. Basic types of car insurance are available similar to those in the UK. There are some notable differences, however, both positive and negative. For example, vehicle recovery in the event of breakdown is normally covered, but protection for passengers may be an extra charge.

Many UK companies operate in the Spanish car insurance market. It is therefore quite easy to obtain car insurance by phone and in English. Understanding the type of cover and possible extras presents little difficulty. Car insurance is relatively cheap. Around 450€ per year for a new car, fully comprehensive, off road parking, four years no claims for a middle-aged driver, a small excess, breakdown cover and any other driver approved by the insured.

Parking fines

No one pays a parking fine. It is a relatively small charge. Pursuing payment results in high municipality costs. People know this and take advantage of the situation. Responsible residents are allowed 15 days to pay or formally protest a fine. A fine may be increased if not paid within a prescribed period.

Random document checks

The police often set up check points stopping motorists randomly to check their identification and car papers. A passport or *residencia*, a driving licence, vehicle registration papers (*permiso de circulacion*) and insurance certificate should be kept with the car. Since this is impracticable, it is better to make a copy of the papers and keep them in the glove box. In law it is no longer necessary to carry originals.

Multas

On-the-spot fines (*multas*) of up to 302€ can be imposed on non-residents for a range of minor traffic offences such as speeding, not being in possession of car papers, and not wearing a seat belt. The list is not exclusive. The police may escort a non-resident to a bank or location where the money can be obtained. A resident is not required to pay on the spot fines, only non-residents who could be untrustworthy, fleeing the country without paying.

GETTING THERE BY AIR

It is possible to fly to 33 Spanish airports from locations in the UK or Ireland. The most popular Spanish airports are Alicante and Malaga, both reachable from 21 UK and Irish regional airports. A list of carriers is given below.

Aer Lingus	www.aerlingus.com	0845 084 4444
AirEuropa	www.aireuropa.co.uk	0034 971 628 900
Air Scotland	www.air-scotland.com	0141 222 2363
Avro	www.avro.co.uk	0870 458 2847
Britannia Direct	www.britanniadirect.com	0800 000 747
British Airways	www.ba.com	0870 850 9850
British Midland	www.flybmi.com	0870 607 0555
BMIbaby	www.bmibaby.com	0870 264 2229
City Jet	www.cityjet.com	0035 318 700 300
easyJet	www.easyjet.com	
Excel	www.excelairways.com	0870 998 9898
Flybe	www.flybe.com	0871 7000535
Globespan	www.flyglobespan.com	08700 566611
Iberia	www.iberiaairlines.co.uk	0845 850 9000
Jet2.com	www.jet2.com	0870 737 8282
Monarch Scheduled	www.flymonarch.com	08700 40 6300
My Travel Lite	www.MyTravelLite.com	08701 564564
Ryanair	www.ryanair.com	0871 246 0000
Tarleton Travel	www.tarletontravel.com	01604 633633
Thomson Flights	www.thomsonflights.com	0800 000 747

GETTING THERE BY FERRY

P&0 Ferries	www.poferries.com	08705 202020
Brittany Ferries	www.brittanyferries.com	08705 360360

ADDITIONAL WEBSITES

British Airports
Authority   www.baa.co.uk

Eurostar   www.eurostar.com

Eurotunnel   www.eurotunnel.com

Foreign Office
Travel Advice   www.fco.gov.uk/travel

20
COMMUNICATIONS

POST

The yellow signs outside each post office best identify *Correos*, the national postal service of Spain. Yellow is also the colour of mail vans, delivery scooters and mailboxes. Normal mail to and from Europe is automatically sent airmail. Heavier packages can be sent by surface mail, which should take around four weeks. Delivery of mail in Spain is within three or four days from the UK. But it can be slow in large cities, rural communities and on urbanisations with only a twice-weekly service.

Try to avoid the inside of some Spanish post offices. They can be small and dark with long, slow-moving queues. Go to the *Tabac* for stamps. The cost of a stamp is the same for all EU countries, although the pricing structure for various envelope sizes seems unnecessarily complex. Spaniards still distrust what was once a diabolical service and send their mail by certified or registered post or seek a receipt for each item sent.

The post office offers a range of services. Registered or express mail, parcel post, redirection, private boxes and banking are all available. Letters are delivered to the door, or to a driveway box. On urbanisations all the post boxes are grouped together besides a focal point such as the swimming pool. It is necessary to go to the post office to collect parcels or registered mail and personal identification may be required.

All is not well with the Spanish postal system. Delays and strikes are common. *Mail Boxes Etc* a USA company has a number of offices in Spain. Although still dependent on the services of *Correos* it operates independently for overnight international parcel delivery through companies such as *UPS* and *FedEx*. It also offers a mailbox service, shipping and packing, fax and photocopying. It sells office supplies and stamps. This enlightened company is refreshing to deal with but its activities are restricted by protectionism offered to the state postal system which is set to be denationalised in a few years.

Name and address

Spanish names are important. A mother's maiden name is added to the end of a full name; women do not change their name when they marry; the formal prefix of Don or Dona is introduced at the start of a name.

Senor Don John Frederick Smith King is simply Mr John Smith with a middle name Frederick and a mother's maiden name King. He is married to Senora Dona Maria Dolores Sanchez Vicario. Got it? Who is Conchita Smith Sanchez? Yes, correct their daughter Conchita. Telephone books can be fun!

An accurate address is also important:

Sr Smith
Calle Madrid 27, 2
03189 Orihuela Costa
Alicante

Translated this means:

Name	Mr Smith
Number, street, floor	27 Madrid St. 2nd Floor
Post code, town	03189 Orihuela Costa
Province	Alicante

The zip code 03189 is made up of 03 as the province number and 189 the post office number.

TELEVISION

This medium is now dominated by digital TV. Most ex-pats want to tune into English language programmes. These can be found on Sky digital systems via a satellite dish. To enjoy the marvels of this technology a set top box is installed, together with an appropriate satellite receiving dish, to have access to hundreds of channels of television and radio. Television companies who supply the cards, such as Sky, cannot legally send cards direct to an address abroad since they have copyright only for a UK audience. However, there are numerous satellite dish installation companies in Spain who can supply cards.

Urbanisations may offer a better selection of English, French, German, Scandinavian and Spanish channels through an underground cable system.

There are several Spanish television stations, but Spanish television is dominated by pay-as-you-view programming of films and football, together with standard news, documentaries, music, soaps and old films.

RADIO

Spanish stations are available by the dozen, all featuring music and chatter. Popular UK-based radio stations are available by satellite or cable. To complement all this activity are a number of new 24-hour English language radio stations giving a unique blend of local news, chat and music.

COMPUTER AND INTERNET

Computer stores are popping up everywhere. A computer bought in Spain will probably come loaded with Spanish software and there are also slight changes to the Spanish keyboard, as the keys have to deal with a language which has accents over some letters.

One accessory worth installing for your computer and television equipment is a surge protector. Spain does experience occasional surges in the electricity supply and this can damage sensitive equipment. Broadband is widely available throughout Spain.

TELEPHONE

Telefonica, the Spanish telecommunications company, has improved its service since it was digitised in 1995, and the state monopoly removed in 1998. It is a well-respected company within the European marketplace in which it operates. Its shares are widely traded in stock exchanges and no portfolio is complete without a holding in this blue chip company.

Dialling

There are no city codes in Spain, each area having its own two- or three-digit code number:

Madrid – 91
Barcelona – 93
Malaga – 95
Valencia – 96
Asturias – 98

followed by a seven or six digit number.

Charges

Charges are among the highest in Europe but have been reducing steadily in recent years. Telephone charges include the cost of the calls, line, telephone and other equipment rental, and the cost of any subscriber discount packages. There are six tariffs, metropolitan (local and internet), provincial, inter provincial, international, mobiles and 90 numbers (*rastro*). Peak tariff hours are from 08.00 to 17.00 from Monday to Friday and 08.00 to 14.00 on Saturdays. Normal tariff hours are from 17.00 to 22.00, Monday to Friday. Reduced tariff hours are from 22.00 to

08.00 Monday to Friday, 14.00 to 24.00 on Saturdays, all day on Sundays and national public holidays. There are numerous discount packages aimed at moving demand from peak periods and, conversely, additional charges for operator-connected calls and other services.

The *factura* (bill) is sent every two months allowing 20 days for payment. It is itemised providing a listing of each number called (except for metropolitan and internet calls) with the date and time, duration, number of units and the charge. Bills can be paid in cash at certain banks, but more usually via a bank account, which is advisable for non-resident homeowners as it ensures the phone line is not disconnected for non-payment.

Directories

Telephone directories are published per province. The first few pages contain useful information.

- Emergency and important local numbers for police, ambulance, fire brigade, etc.
- *Telefonica* numbers and the services offered.
- National and international codes.
- Tariffs and explanation of the *factura* (bill).

The main section is an alphabetical list of subscribers under the town or village name and not alphabetically for the whole of a province. A new subscriber is automatically included in the next edition of the telephone directory unless choosing to have an unlisted number.

Public phones

As well as public telephones (*cabinas*), which allow international direct dialling, there are usually payphones in bars, cafés and restaurants. Phone cards can be bought at news stands and tobacconists (*estancos*). There are also public telephone offices called *locutorios*, containing multiple phone booths and a fax service.

Mobiles

Sales of mobile telephones in Spain have rocketed. They appear everywhere, although sparsely populated areas are not served by either landline or mobile systems. The main players are *Telefonica* (with their brand *Movistar*), *Amena* and *Vodafone*.

NEWSPAPERS

Local, national and international; daily, weekly and monthly; Spanish and English; expensive, cheap and free publications: all clog the news stands. Spanish daily newspapers are mainly middle class. *El Pais* (The Country) and *El Mundo* (The World) have lots of pages aimed at the serious reader and are good value for money. At the bottom end of the Spanish daily press, the content is devoted solely to football.

All the European daily newspapers are available. They are printed in Spain but cost three times more than the national edition. Weekend newspapers also have some sections missing. The best reads for the ex-pat are the locally printed English-language weekly newspapers. They are a good blend of national and local news, gossip, information and advertisements. Indeed some small ads are reminiscent of those in a central London telephone box.

Popular English books are difficult to find, but large and small English bookshops do exist. Second-hand exchange libraries exist too. However a wide choice of books is quickly available via the internet with *Amazon* providing an excellent service from both the UK and USA.

21

WHAT THEY DON'T TELL YOU IN THE GUIDE BOOKS

THE BASICS REPEATED

Anyone moving to Spain to work, rest or play should ask the fundamental question – why? If it is due to an enthusiasm for the country, then whatever the length of stay, great. If the move is based on negative reasons, say because of unhappiness with life in Britain, or working in the wrong job, or in the wrong relationship, or whatever, it may not work out. Transplanting the problem to another country may not be the solution, and the undoubted pressures of moving may make things worse. Don't move because of an enjoyable fortnight's sunbathing in Calpe and thoughts of an extended vacation drinking large gin and tonics. Really ask why. If the good weather and a relaxed time are the reasons, this is not enough, because in Spain the weather is sometimes cold and it is often not relaxed. Spain has disadvantages as well as the advantages, which surprises some people as they think it is all sweetness and light. It isn't – but then nowhere is.

Make sure of something to do – hobbies and interests if retired, or a definite job or business if younger. Many people drift from job to job, spend too much time in bars and drink too much. Do not idealise life in Spain. It isn't perfect and, if employed, it may be necessary to work harder for less money than back home. Do your homework if you have children and think long and hard about how the move will affect them. People considering retirement should do a lot of research before leaving the UK. How much will it cost to live? Don't imagine there will be any state handouts, and be prepared only for lots of self help.

For those taking up permanent residence, try living in coastal, rural and urban environments to see which suits best. Strangely few people try northern Spain as it does not come with wall to wall sunshine, and fewer still try Spain's cities.

Former inhabitants of large built-up areas such as London may miss the buzz of big city living: those accustomed to big-city facilities, attractions and culture will find seaside towns and rural areas dull.

Rent before you buy. Try to rent in the area of Spain you are intending to live in for at least a year before deciding to buy. You need to see it throughout the year, in good weather and bad, when it's full of tourists and when it's not, to decide if it is for you.

It almost goes without saying; foreigners will find it much easier to integrate if they learn the language. You don't have to become an expert, but you should try to learn enough to conduct a basic conversation. A lot of Spaniards can speak English and once neighbours discover that you are able to speak some Spanish, friendly greetings occur. Try to build relationships with Spanish people as well as with other foreigners. In the first instance some Spaniards can appear quite reserved and reluctant to talk. Perseverance is necessary.

Become accustomed to the authorities and the way they work. Even the simplest task can sometimes become very complicated and difficult for no obvious reasons. Why does the washing machine engineer need four visits? Why is it necessary to keep visiting the bank? Why are five forms required when one would do? Some things take a long time to accomplish, but they usually do get done. Learning to accept this is an important part of settling into life in Spain.

CLIMATE

The principal reason why people go to Spain is the climate. The country sells itself on its sunshine. Sunshine has a beneficial psychological effect and has a big influence on lifestyle. More time is spent outdoors, meaning life is more active, sporty and sociable. Breakfast, lunch and dinner can be taken outdoors on a sheltered terrace, even in winter.

Summers in the UK are delightful. Summers in Spain are very hot – too hot really. It is fine for a two week holiday, but for a permanent resident a whole summer in Spain is very tiring. An ironical situation occurs when tourists flock to Spain during July and August and Spain's new resident foreigners go back home to escape the searing heat.

And there is the wind. Wind that blows hard from the sea every summer's afternoon! The Costa del Sol was formerly called the Costa del Viento, (the windy coast) but it was renamed 'the sunny coast' by clever marketing officials. As the old name suggests, the coast can get very windy, although not as windy as the area around Tarifa and the Costa de la Luz. It is so windy there if you don't find adequate shelter on the beaches you end up getting sand-blasted.

Property is not designed for cold weather. Spanish homes are great in the summer and keep out the heat very efficiently, but in the winter they are like fridges. North-facing properties, open plan, marble floors and air bricks results in the need to wear several sweaters. Heating and air conditioning are now seen as necessary aids to year round living.

The climate isn't as good as many visitors think. When the winter weather is warm and dry, then great, but it can be cool and wet for weeks, too. It is possible to see people wearing vests and shorts in a stiff breeze and squally rain, seemingly unwilling to accept it can ever be anything but warm and sunny. It can be odd to see winter tourists on the beach in swimsuits while locals and ex-pats huddle in coats.

RELAXED LIFESTYLE

Although climate is the principal reason for *going* to Spain, a relaxed lifestyle is the principal reason for people *staying*. Spanish people tend to be calm, don't get over-excited about everyday things, do not indulge in road rage, queue patiently and deal tolerantly with officialdom.

The relaxed way of life is an advantage if on holiday or retired, but perhaps a drawback if employed, so it is a mixed blessing. There are a lot of bank holidays in Spain, so people wind down at work in the days prior to the public holidays and take time to wind back up again after them. Is this relaxed, laid back or lazy? With about 20 to 25 public holidays for various saints days and *fiestas* it is perhaps one of the reasons why things take a long time to get done.

FOOD AND DRINK

One of the best things about living in Spain is that it is possible to eat and drink out quite cheaply. 10€ for a *Menu del Dia* which includes a bottle of wine is cheap by any standard. In fact it is possible to eat and drink for less than the price of an average round of drinks in a British pub. Unfortunately popular bars and restaurants are prey to people selling pirated CDs and DVDs, fake designer sunglasses, rugs, toys, etc. Why restaurant owners allow this is a mystery. It gets tiresome having to say 'No' all the time to the constant stream of persistant vendors.

COSTA DEL SOL

Although the provincial government of Malaga is keen to encourage tourists and new residents, it is also anxious to stem criminality so that, in the long term, this once beautiful area does not lose its appeal as a genuine holiday destination. But it is difficult to get away from the facts.

Dotting the coastline used to be ancient stone towers and fortresses, which served as lookout posts during the Arab occupation of this part of Spain. These days the police are more likely to be watching for drugs smugglers and illegal immigrants.

The murder rate in this part of Spain has risen by 70% over the past 15 years. Crime itself is said to have doubled. Drug-related killings between gangsters are virtually a weekly occurrence. Clashes between British, Spanish, eastern European and Russian criminals are commonplace. They run businesses ranging from brothels to live internet sex services, from boat and property companies to satellite-TV installation firms, and then of course there are the obligatory multi-million-pound drug deals.

When Spain tightened up its extradition laws in 1987, the commonly held belief was that all the big-name criminals would find themselves without a bolt hole and be sent home to the UK. Because the change in the law was not retrospective, many British criminals simply based themselves full time on the Costa del Sol and became even more involved in illegal enterprises. Few British criminals on the Costa del Crime are on the run from justice. They are now businessmen, earning fortunes, while the Spanish authorities are either powerless to prosecute or, in some cases, simply turn a blind eye.

INTEGRATION

Don't expect learning the language to be easy. There is a misconception that Spanish is a straightforward language to learn, but it's not all that easy to learn properly. Easy enough for youngsters, but for retirees … ? Want to integrate properly? Then it is necessary to speak the language correctly. After learning the basics, try to use Spanish as often as possible. That means talking to people in shops, bars, restaurants and anyone who is willing to converse.

Spanish people are tolerant, accepting many foreigners into their country, but it is necessary to persevere to integrate with them. They have mixed feelings about foreigners. On the one hand they are grateful for the prosperity brought to their country, but on the other hand it is difficult for them to understand foreigners because so few integrate. Values have changed in the past 20 years too. Foreigners then were much more of a novelty and generally well liked. Now in some towns the number of foreigners exceeds native Spaniards and they think that they have been taken over, which isn't an unreasonable opinion.

They have some strange views about us. For a start, they seem to lump us all together whatever our nationality, and tend to regard all foreigners as northern European tourists who wear shorts, T-shirts and flip-flops, who spend days drinking beer and who lack education, manners and culture. Many Spaniards are also puzzled by the general British refusal to learn the language, which makes us stand out from other foreigners in our unwillingness to integrate and adapt to the Spanish way of life.

Spaniards can be difficult to get to know well. Friendly and welcoming at face value, but quite difficult to break through to becoming close friends. Young Spaniards are generally more open and friendly than older ones. They are more comfortable with foreigners. Those brought up under Franco had a closed, limited education, while younger people are better travelled and know much more about the world outside Spain.

INEFFICENCY

Probably the worst aspect of life in Spain is inefficiency. It often seems to be a battle to get things done, certainly anything involving officialdom, building repairs and taxes. Having a laid-back approach to life is good in some ways, but not so laid-back that nothing ever gets done. It can be a test of mental strength and persistence.

There is a lot of red tape and bureaucracy in Spain, but it's not as bad as people make out – and things are improving with integration into the EU. Try to deal with paperwork yourself. Do straightforward things which may be difficult and frustrating, but regard it as a learning process even if you are told to do different things, at different times, by different people. Alternatively employ a *gestor* – they are in tune with the way things work, the people involved and hence more likely to achieve things quickly.

Not everything is badly run in Spain. Banking is great! Avoid using bankers' drafts or cheques to transfer money from foreign accounts to Spanish accounts. It takes six weeks to access the money. The health service is excellent too!

EMPLOYMENT

It can be difficult for foreigners to find work in Spain if they don't have specific skills or qualifications, or for those who are not self-starters. This situation is not unique to Spain but to all the Mediterranean countries where much of the work available is in the tourist trade – hotels, restaurants, bars, car hire. These are traditionally poorly-paid requiring long, unsocial hours, often seven days a week.

There is little job security, with many people working without employment contracts having no rights to unemployment pay, healthcare, etc. The conundrum is quite simple. The Mediterranean area is a desirable place to live, employers know the supply of labour exceeds the number of jobs except at the height of the tourist season, so they don't pay well or give contracts. Quite a lot of Brits live hand to mouth, pottering between jobs. Language and qualifications are really necessary to work successfully in Spain.

If you are British, become a plumber, electrician, gardener, bar owner, cleaner or an estate agent and obtain work by sticking to your own nationality. It is thought that some 80% of foreign workers are not registered, which is, of course, totally against the law. Remember, sticking completely to the same communities, only ever working for, or becoming friends with other Brits is the isolationist behaviour the Spanish object to.

Class structure comes into it too. People who live in large villas look down on fellow Brits attempting to make a living running a bar near the

Mediterranean. They think Benidorm or Torremolinos resembles Brighton in a heat wave, polluted by burger joints, British pubs selling draught beer, tacky souvenir shops and all the rest of the clichéd picture. Perhaps they are correct.

BEHAVIOUR

Machismo

You might think that machismo would only be found in older, more traditional Spaniards. You would be wrong. Some of the younger generations are much the same because they are brought up to it. You might think Spaniards on the Costas would be more accustomed to dealing with foreign women and would have softened their attitude. You would be wrong again. The position of women in Spain is sometimes still subservient. Spain is a very macho society, with some very old-fashioned attitudes towards women. It can be seen in everyday life. If you employ a workman to do a task they find it hard to take instructions from a woman, and they don't like their work being checked by a woman either.

And there are definitely some men in their late thirties and early forties who are looking for well preserved ladies of fifty-plus who are well off because they have been widowed or received a good divorce settlement.

On the beach

One noticeable difference is Spanish people's different sense of personal space on the beach. On large exposed beaches they will huddle around the entrance, whereas Brits will spread out. If there is a line of sun beds and parasols to choose from, British people will tend to leave as much space as they can between themselves and the nearest occupants. The Spanish are the complete opposite.

Poor driving

A big minus about living in Spain is poor driving. There is an unwillingness to anticipate problems, use indicators or stick to lanes at roundabouts. Spaniards drive at crazy speeds close to the boot of the car in front, and they park anywhere. All this is accomplished leaving no room for error, while lighting a cigarette, changing a radio station, using the mobile phone and checking appearance in the mirror.

Lack of status

Coming to Spain permanently means leaving all the trappings of status back home. Leave and forget the degree, the company car, the status job and all the other bits and pieces of class distinction. In Spain it is 'who you are' and not 'what you were'. It may take quite a long time to shake off this sense of the old country.

Breaking the rules

Many people come to live in Spain for three or four years. Short-term foreigners can be divided into two groups: those who are legally registered and those who are not. The latter group drives cars from their home country, pay no local car taxes and often have invalid insurance because the law requires a change to Spanish plates and registration after a certain length of time. They often get by doing odd jobs, all cash in hand and do not pay income tax. Such people are looked down on by the Spanish and by the permanent Brits too. Resident Brits rarely get involved with people who they think are only short-term visitors. It is not worth investing energy and emotion in getting to know people who will quite likely disappear overnight within a few months. Animosity is not felt towards these people so much as indifference.

Builders

Anyone undertaking major building work will realise it is stressful, will take longer and cost more than planned. Renovation is best done by Spanish workmen. It is recommended that major work is undertaken by a Spaniard, particularly specialist work such as tiling, plumbing, carpentry and electrical. Spanish craftsmen are well trained in these trades and can access materials quickly.

Pets

There is absolutely no reason why a pet cannot be taken to Spain, or for that matter travel through an intermediate country such as France. The United Kingdom relaxed quarantine regulations a few years ago, bringing their approach more in line with other European countries. It may be necessary to travel to and from Spain frequently or unexpectedly, in which case any pet should have the necessary chips, vaccinations, health checks and accompanying paperwork readily to hand.

Spain has the normal catteries, kennels and many fully-qualified veterinary surgeons to choose from. Urbanisations, towns and cities have codes of behaviour for dogs which results in them being banned from beaches and other public places.

There is another side to keeping a pet in Spain. It is the heartless attitude of some Spanish people to animals and in particular to dogs, many of which are often tied up all day, or left to roam the streets, or simply abandoned. Keeping a large dog is often seen as a necessity for guarding a home, but the ability to bark is not a guarantee of home security. There are dog refuge organisations in many coastal towns invariably run by resident British or Germans who are witness to many barbaric acts committed upon these defenceless animals.

Birds, too, are in the firing line, shot for sport on a Sunday morning as they fly over on their migration routes. Foxes are offered poisoned meat as they live on birds. Pet dogs romping around the country inadvertently eat the poisoned meat too, dying a slow death. Small patches of barley are grown in the mountains, not for illicit alcohol but to attract partridges which are then shot. The Spanish are not known as a nation of animal lovers.

OLD COUNTRY

Spain's new residents should never cut off ties with their home country. It is tempting, but you might find yourself missing the UK and want to return. Remember Britain is one of the very best places in the world in which to live and you might only realise that after leaving. Some people who move to Spain underestimate how much they will miss family and friends at home. At first lots of visitors arrive, but that soon wears off and life settles down to a routine. Keep an open mind and give Spain a decent try before deciding whether the new life suits or not.

APPENDIX 1

KNOWING YOUR WAY AROUND

Major airports

Alicante	Tel: 966919000	Fax: 966919354
Barcelona	Tel: 932983838	Fax: 932983737
Bilbao	Tel: 944869300	Fax: 944869313
Ibiza	Tel: 971809000	Fax: 971809287
Jerez	Tel: 956150000	Fax: 956150061
Lanzarote	Tel: 9288460 01	Fax: 928846022
Las Palmas	Tel: 928579000	Fax: 928579117
Madrid	Tel: 913058343	Fax: 913936200
Malaga	Tel: 952048844	Fax: 952048777
Palma de Mallorca	Tel: 971789099	Fax: 971789010
Santiago de Compostela	Tel: 981547501	Fax: 9815475 07
Sevilla	Tel: 954449011	Fax: 954449025
Tenerife South	Tel: 922759000	Fax: 922759247
Valencia	Tel: 961598515	Fax: 961598510

Babies

Baby foods and disposable nappies are available in all resorts and are obtainable from supermarkets and chemists.

Banking hours

Most banks open from 08.30 to 14.00 Monday to Friday and 08.30 to 13.00 on Saturdays (except in the summer).

Church services

Information on the location of churches and timetables of religious services should be sought locally.

Consular assistance

British Consulates in Spain will assist holidaymakers in emergencies. They can provide a list of local lawyers, interpreters and doctors. They can also give guidance in tracing missing persons.

Credit cards

Most hotels, garages and department stores accept major credit cards, but this should be checked before each transaction. Some additional identification may be required.

Currency

The euro (€) is the currency of Spain. There are seven denominations of notes – 5, 10, 20, 50, and 500€, and eight different coins – 1 and 2€ and 1, 2, 5, 10, 20 and 50 cents. 1€ equals 166 old pesetas. The import or export of cash, notes and bearer-cheques, in any currency, including euros, is subject to declaration where the amount exceeds 6,000€ per person per journey.

Duty free

Allowances on imports from EU countries no longer exist, but are still applicable to goods purchased outside the European Union. Limits on imports of duty-paid goods bought in the EU into the UK are generous, provided they are for personal consumption. For full details contact Customs & Excise on 020 7202 4227 or www.hmce.gov.uk.

Electricity

Voltage 220 or 225 AC. Plugs are standard European two pin.

Entry requirements

A full British passport, valid for the duration of the visit, is required to enter mainland Spain, the Balearic and Canary Islands. EU citizens do not require visas for visits of up to 90 days. For stays over 180 days a residence permit is required.

Health service

British tourists visiting Spain, covered by the National Insurance scheme, will enjoy free medical assistance under the Spanish Health Service during their stay. Please contact the local Health Authority Office for further assistance. EHIC cards are available via the internet or post office branches. Long-term residents, over normal retiring age, are entitled to join the Spanish Health system. Form E121 from the Social Security Services in Newcastle is required.

Insurance

Holidaymakers are advised to take out adequate holiday insurance. This is available from most tour operators, travel agents and general and specialist insurance companies.

Mail

Post correspondence from Spain with Spanish post office stamps in official post boxes or at hotels displaying the logo '*Correos y Telegrafos*'.

Metal detectors

Metal detecting is a strictly controlled activity in Spain and its practice in public places requires a permit from the relevant local council. Permits are normally granted for investigation purposes only.

Motoring

An EU Driving Licence is accepted for driving in Spain. If your current one does not comply with the EU format, you are advised to obtain an International Driving Licence, available from the AA. EU citizens are advised to obtain the EU format licence from the Driver and Vehicle Licencing Agency. A valid driving licence is required at all times when driving in Spain. The vehicle logbook, registration and adequate insurance are also required. On the spot payment of traffic fines is applicable to non-residents.

Museums

All Spanish State museums offer free admission to groups of students or teachers. Permission for free entry must be sought in advance from Ministerio de Cultura, Museums Department, Plaza del Rey, Madrid. Tel: (0034) 91 701 7267, Fax: 91 523 3687, www.mec.es. Free admission for individual students may also be granted in certain cases to holders of International Student Cards.

Further information is available from the Central Bureau for International Education and Training. Tel: 020 7389 4004, Fax: 020 7389 4426, www.centralbureau.org.uk and the Spanish Cultural Office of the Spanish Embassy.

Pets

An export health certificate issued by an official British Veterinary Inspector is required to import pets into Spain.

Public holidays

1 January	New Year's Day
6 January	Kings' Day
19 March	St Joseph's Day
March/April	Good Friday or Easter Sunday
1 May	Labour Day
25 July	St James' Day
15 August	Assumption of the Virgin
12 October	National Day
1 Nov	All Saints' Day
6 December	Constitution Day
8 December	Immaculate Conception
25 December	Christmas Day

Shopping

Most shops in Spain close at lunchtime normally between 13.00 and 16.00. General stores are to be found in most provincial capital towns. They are open all day from 10.00 to 20.00. Open-air markets are held once or twice a week in most Spanish towns and holiday resorts.

Summer time

From the morning of the last Sunday in March to the last Sunday in October.

Taxis

Taxi fares vary in different areas. There is a basic initial charge, a rate per kilometre and additional surcharges added to the meter fare at night, weekends and public holidays. Taxi drivers should have a list of approved fares for inter-city runs, railway stations and airports, and will be able to supply information prior to boarding the vehicle.

Telephone service

To call direct to the UK from Spain dial 00 44 + local UK code less 0. The international code for Spain is 34. Telephone rates need to be checked locally. Full instructions are shown in all international boxes. Dial 112 for all emergencies.

Television

The Spanish television systems are Norma G for black and white and PAL for colour. British television sets are not suitable for either unless previously adjusted by a technician.

Tipping

It is customary to tip 5–10% of the bill, although related to clients' satisfaction with the services received.

Vaccinations
No vaccinations are needed by EU residents to enter Spain.

APPENDIX 2

COMMUNITIES OF SPAIN AND THEIR PROVINCES

The provinces of Spain are grouped into 17 autonomous Communities. Asturias is a *Principado*, Murcia is a *Region*, Navarra is a *Comunidad Foral* while all the rest are classified as *Comunidades*. Their full name, address, first two digits of the provincial postcode and the provincial letters used on older vehicle number plates are shown below.

Northern Spain

Comunidad Galicia, Palacio de Rojoy, 15705 Santiago de Compostela.

Galicia	15	A Coruna	C
	27	Lugo	LU
	32	Ourense	OR
	36	Pontevedra	PO

Principado de Asturias, Calle Suarez de la Riva, 33071 Oviedo

Asturias	33	Austurias	O

Comunidad Cantabria, Calle Casimiro Sainz 4, 39003 Santander

Cantabria	39	Cantabria	S

Comunidad Pais Vasco, Palacio de Ajuna-Enea, 01007 Vitoria

Basque	01	Alava	VI
	20	Guipuzcoa	SS
	48	Vizcaya	BI

Comunidad Floral de Navarra, 31002 Pamplona

Navarra	31	Navarra	NA

Comunidad La Rioja, Calle General Vara del Rey 3, 26071 Logrono

La Rioja	26	La Rioja	LO

Eastern Spain

Comunidad Cataluna, Plaza de San Jaime, 08002 Barcelona

Catalonia	08	Barcelona	BA
	25	Lleida	L
	17	Girona	GE
	43	Tarragona	T

Comunidad Aragon, Diputacion de Aragon, Paseo Maria Agustin 36, 50071 Zaragoza

Aragon	22	Huesca	HU
	44	Teruel	TE
	50	Zaragoza	Z

Comunidad Valencia, Palau de la Generalitat, 46003 Valencia

Valencia	03	Alicante	A
	46	Valencia	V
	12	Castellon	CS

Region de Murcia, Palacio de San Esteban, Calle Acisco Diaz, 30071 Murcia

Murcia	30	Murcia	MU

Central Spain

Comunidad Madrid, Puerta del Sol 7, 28013 Madrid

Madrid	28	Madrid	M

Comunidad Castilla La Mancha, Palacio de Fuensalida, Plaza de Conde 2, 45002 Toledo

Castilla la Mancha	02	Albacete	AB
	13	Ciudad Real	CR
	16	Cuenca	CE
	19	Guadalajara	GU
	45	Toledo	TO

Comunidad Extremadura, Calle Jose Fernandez Lopez 18, 06800 Merida

Extremadura	06	Badajoz	BA
	10	Caceres	CC

Comunidad Castilla y Leon, Plaza de Castilla y Leon, 47006 Valladolid

Castilla y Leon	05	Avila	AV
	09	Burgos	BU
	24	Leon	LE
	34	Palencia	P

37	Salamanca	SA
40	Segovia	SG
42	Soria	SO
47	Valladolid	VA
49	Zamora	ZA

Southern Spain

Comunidad Andalusia, Palacio de San Telmo, Avda, de Roma,
41071 Seville

Andalusia	04	Almeria	AL
	11	Cadiz	CA
	14	Cordoba	CO
	18	Granada	GR
	21	Huelva	H
	23	Jaen	J
	29	Malaga	MA
	41	Sevilla	SE

Islands

Comunidad las Islas Balaeres, Calle Marina 3, Consulado del Mar, 07012
Palma de Mallorca

Balearic Islands	07	Baleares	PM

Comunidad las Islas Canarias, Plaza 25 de Julio 1,
35004 Las Palmas de Gran Canaria

Canary Islands	35	Las Palmas	GC
	37	Tenerife	TF

APPENDIX 3

USEFUL WEBSITES

Accommodation

Asociacion de Termales	www.balnearios.org
Cuevas Perdo Antonio de Alarcon	www.travel-in-spain.com
Paradores	www.paradores.es

News and information

BBC World Service	www.bbc.uk/worldservice
Stanford's (maps, guides and travel books)	www.stanfords.co.uk

Employment

British Council	www.britishcouncil.es
British Executive Service Overseas	www.beso.org
Educational Visits and Exchanges	www.britishcouncil.org
Graduate jobs	www.prospects.ac.uk

Furniture removal

Britannia International Removals	www.britannia-movers.co.uk
Bishops Move	www.bishops-move.co.uk

Holiday home rental, exchange and timeshare

Property search site   www.europropertysearch.com

Intervac Home Exchange   www.intervac.co.uk

Timeshare Consumers Assocation   www.timeshare.org.uk

Interpreting

Susan Bultitude, 03700 Javea   www.susanbultitude.com

Pets

Department of Environment
(export of dogs and cats)   www.defra.gov.uk/animalh/quarantine

Property Sales

Atlas International   www.atlas-international.com

Masa International UK Ltd   www.masainter.com

Propertunities Ltd   www.propertunities.co.uk

Taylor Woodrow   www.taywoodspain.co.uk

Idealista   www.idealista.com

Retirement

Age Concern   www.ageconcern.org.uk

Occupational Pensions Registry   www.opra.co.uk

Pre Retirement Association   www.pra.uk.com

UK State pensions   www.dss.gov.uk

Taxation

Inland Revenue (former UK tax payers now living abroad)
Fitzroy House, PO Box 46, Nottingham, NG2 1BD
www.inlandrevenue.gov.uk

APPENDIX 4

FURTHER READING

Spanish history
Don Quixote, Miguel Cervantes (Penguin). A classic.
Modern Spain, Raymond Carr (Opus). Says it all.
The New Spaniards, John Hooper (Penguin). An excellent work.
The Spanish Civil War, Antony Beevor (Castell). The civil war in perspective.

Culture
Culture Shock, Marie Louise Graff (Kuperard). A guide to Spanish customs and etiquettes.
Death in the Afternoon, Ernest Hemingway (Grafton). His famous look at bullfighting.
The Sun also Rises, Hemmingway (Grafton). Fiestas.
The Spanish Temper, Pritchett (Hogarth). Interesting.

Going to Spain
Best Places to Buy a Home in Spain, Joanna Styles (Survival). All the facts.
Buy to Let in Spain, Harry King (How to Books). For fun and profit too.
Buying a Home in Spain, Harry King (How to Books). An easy to read guide.
Knowing the Law in Spain, Harry King (How to Books). Everything you possibly need to know.

Travel

Eyewitness Spain, (Dorling and Kindersley). The best travel guide.

Special Places to Stay, Alastair Sawday (ASP). A roof off the beaten track.

Sunflower Landscapes, (Sunflower Books). Four walking guides for Spain.

Which Guide to Spain, Consumers Association. A well thought out book.

Learning the language

AA Essential Spanish Phrase Book, (AA). Common sense phrases.

Oxford Spanish Starter Dictionary, (Oxford University Press).

Suenos World Spanish, (BBC). Multi media course for beginners' Spanish.

Viva Espana, (BBC). Beginners' language course.

Humour

An Englishman Abroad, Phil Ball (Embury Press). Beckham is everywhere.

Nord Riley's Spain, Nord Riley, (Santana). The life of a humorous wanderer.

Spanish Lessons, Derek Lambert (Embury). Beginning a new life in Spain.

Driving Over Lemons, Stewart (Sort of Book). A humourous optimist in Andalusia.

Retirement

Active retirement, (Which Guide). Highly recommended.

Allied Dunbar Retirement Planning Handbook, David Bertram (Financial Times).

Good non-Retirement Guide, Rosemary Brown (Kogan Page). Updated annually.

Retire Abroad, Roger Jones (How to Books). A guide to a happy retirement abroad.

Employment

Doing Business in Spain, (Price Waterhouse). A business guide.

Getting a Job Abroad, Roger Jones (How to Books). Now in its 5th edition.

Teaching English Abroad, Griffith (Vacation Work). Getting a teaching job.

Teaching Abroad, (AGCAS). More about teaching.

Food and drink

Cooking in Spain, Janet Mendel (Santana). The essential cooking book for Spain.

Tapas and more great dishes from Spain, Janet Mendel (Santana). Spain's bar food.

The New Spain, John Radford (Mitchell Beazley). A well-illustrated wine guide.

World food Spain, (Lonely Planet). Buying fun food.

Health

Fact sheets from the *Ayuntamiento*, in English, on Spanish procedures.

Health and Illness in Retirement, Anne Roberts (Ace Books). Recommended.

Tell the Doctor, Calle El Moreral 3, 03792 Parcent, Alicante.

We are in Hospital, Alicante University/Cam Bank. One for the bookshelf.

Newspapers

Costa Blanca News. Weekly English newspaper with a host of advertisements.

Sur in English. As above for the Costa del Sol.

The Guardian Weekly, Guardian Publications. Sent to your home.

The Weekly Telegraph, Telegraph Publications. Also by post.

Index